THE POLITICAL ECONOMY OF URBAN SCHOOLS

*A publication of the Joint Center for Urban Studies of the
Massachusetts Institute of Technology and Harvard University*

THE POLITICAL ECONOMY OF URBAN SCHOOLS

Martin T. Katzman

Harvard University Press, Cambridge, Massachusetts, 1971

PREFACE

The ideas in this volume first took shape as a doctoral dissertation, "Distribution and Production in a Big City School System" (Yale University, 1966). As has happened in so many areas of inquiry, the economics of educational systems has been subjected to simultaneous scrutiny by many, ranging from the research team which produced the Coleman Report to the more modest but important efforts of Charles Benson and Jesse Burkhead. One purpose of this work is to synthesize the knowledge gained from these studies, which are strikingly similar despite their manifest differences. A second purpose is to extend the analysis of the impact of schooling on children (production) to the evaluation of school quality, efficiency, and equality. Third, the quantitative analysis of production and distribution in schooling is related to policy questions of institutional restructuring.

While much of what follows is highly technical, the method and findings can be and *should* be summarized in lay language because of the exigency of rationalizing debate in the arena of educational policy. On the other hand, methodological issues cannot be ignored or glossed over. Because research results depend critically upon techniques of measurement and of statistical manipulation, the validity of these operations determines the validity of one's findings and, hence, of their interpretation. To preserve continuity, most of the methodological material is relegated to appendixes.

I owe a vote of thanks to Richard Ruggles, Neil Chamberlain, Merton J. Peck, and John MacGowan, all gurus at Yale, and to Mrs. Dorothy W. Bisbee, John Kain, Frank S. Levy, Walter

B. Miller, Lawrence W. O'Connell, and Charles Tilly for invaluable advice in the formulation of the original work. Parts of this volume were carefully and constructively criticized by Samuel Bowles, Joseph Cronin, Laurence Iannaccone, David Kirp, Frank S. Levy, Roger L. Miller, Elliott Morss, and, especially, by Stephan Michelson and Christopher Jencks. In addition, I have benefited from the statistical advice of Richard J. Light.

My institutional debts for support go to the Department of Economics at Yale University, and, most of all, to the Joint Center for Urban Studies of the Massachusetts Institute of Technology and Harvard University, which sponsored both my original dissertation and the present extension.

An earlier incarnation of Chapters 3 and 5 appeared in *Yale Economic Essays* and, of Chapter 6, in *Urban Education*. Chapter 4 evolved from a presentation at a Conference on Urban Public Expenditures, held September 1966 in Washington, D.C., sponsored by Resources for the Future, while ideas in Chapter 6 were refined when I participated in the Project on Pricing Urban Public Services of the Urban Institute with Stanley Paul.

The earlier version of the chapters that appeared in the *Yale Economic Essays* contained errors in regression coefficients resulting from my relative inexperience in using computer programs. Fortunately, these were errors in magnitude rather than in substance, as subsequent reanalysis confirmed. Special apologies are due those who have cited my erroneous calculations, nevertheless.

I want to thank my father, Ira Katzman, for drawing the included graphs; my wife, Arlene, for help in editing the many drafts; and Judy Stevens, Jessica Rukin, and Cindy Wohlleb for extraordinary stenographic service.

One of the main findings of educational research is the importance of family background in explaining the performance of children. In this context, I feel it most appropriate to dedicate this book to my parents.

M.T.K.

Cambridge, Massachusetts
May 1969

CONTENTS

CHAPTER 1. INTRODUCTION   1

Technological and Institutional Failures

Political Conflicts

An Outline of the Present Analysis

CHAPTER 2. EVALUATING EDUCATIONAL QUALITY   19

Traditional Modes of Evaluation

The Production Model of School Systems
Characteristics of Human Development. Characteristics of the Production Function

Measuring the Objectives of Schooling
What is Learned in School? Indicators of Educational Objectives. Problems of Multiple Objectives

Studies of Educational Production: A Review

Conclusion

CHAPTER 3. PRODUCTION IN BOSTON'S ELEMENTARY SCHOOLS   45

Operationalizing the Production Model
Measuring Performance. School Resources. Social Characteristics

Some Working Hypotheses

Best Linear Production Functions
Comparisons with Other Studies. Racial Segregation and Performance. Evaluating School Quality

Contribution of School Resources to Performance
School Factors and Level of Performance. Elasticity of Performance to Input Changes. Contribution of School Factors to Variance in Performance. Production Possibilities

Conclusion

CHAPTER 4. EFFICIENCY AND THE COSTS OF EDUCATIONAL QUALITY   77

Educational Efficiency in Practice
Middle-class Orientation. Working-class Orientation

The Costs of Educational Quality
Input Costs. Economies of Scale. Linear Approximation to Input Costs. Derivation of the Supply Curve. Some Illustrations. Production Possibilities under Budget Constraints. The Supply Price versus Actual Expenditure. Compensatory Education

Conclusion

CHAPTER 5. THE DISTRIBUTION OF EDUCATIONAL OPPORTUNITY   105

Defining Objects of Distribution
Absence of Racial Segregation. Equal Control over Resources. Equal Resources. Equal Effective Resources. Equal Academic Performance. Equal Opportunity for Maximum Development. Objects of Distribution as Social Indicators. Equality for Whom?

Patterns of Distribution
Inequalities. Factors Contributing to Bias. Degree of Bias

Distribution within Big Cities
Some Hypotheses: The Process of Distribution in Boston. Some Hypotheses: The Beneficiaries of Bias. Distribution of Resources in Boston. Distribution in Other Big Cities

Conclusion

CHAPTER 6. RESTRUCTURING BIG CITY SCHOOL SYSTEMS   140

Current Organization of Big City Schools
Consumpton Efficiency. Equality. Integration. Distribution Consequences

Patching the Current System
Altering Placement Policies. Complete Integration. Federal and State Financial Aid

Decentralization
Technological Efficiency. Participation. Integration

Metropolitanism

Tuition Vouchers
Nature of the Market. Technological Efficiency. Integration

Conclusion

CHAPTER 7. THE BURDENS ON BIG CITY SCHOOLS   169

Summary

The Burdens
Effectiveness and Technological Efficiency. Responsiveness. Equality

The Promise

Conclusion

APPENDIX A. MISCELLANEOUS DATA PROBLEMS   185

Methods of Calculating School Variables

Methods of Calculating Socioeconomic Variables

APPENDIX B. THE USE OF MENTAL TEST SCORES IN
REGRESSION ANALYSIS   189

APPENDIX C. SPECIFYING AN EDUCATIONAL PRODUCTION
FUNCTION   194

Functional Forms

Statistical Techniques

Error Terms

Behavioral Assumptions

NOTES   204

INDEX   227

TABLES AND FIGURES

TABLES

2.1   Comparisons of major studies of educational production . . 42
3.1   Dispersion of performance indicators 48
3.2   Correlations among performance indicators 49
3.3   Dispersion of school resource indicators 51
3.4   Correlations among school resources 52
3.5   Correlations among social class and racial variables 53
3.6   Working hypothesis: Performance as a function of school
      expenditures 54
3.7   Working hypothesis: Performance as a function of physical
      resources 56
3.8   Best linear model: Regression coefficients (standard errors
      of coefficients) 58
3.9   Best multiplicative model: Regression coefficients (standard
      errors of coefficients 59
3.10 Racial composition of school and performance, residuals of
      production functions 63
3.11 Correlations among quality measures 66
3.12 Contribution of school resources to average level of perform-
      ance 68
3.13 Resource elasticity of performance: Linear models at mean
      input values versus multiplicative models 69
3.14 Sample analyses of variance: Reading gains 71
3.15 Percentage contribution of social class and school resources
      to variations in performance 71
3.16 Production possibilities frontier 73
4.1   Current expenditures per student, Boston elementary and
      intermediate districts, calendar year 1964 86
4.2   Average expenditures per student as a function of enrollment,
      nonteaching items of expenditure: Regression coefficients
      (standard errors) 87
4.3   Marginal costs per student of school resources: Regression
      coefficients (standard errors) 91
4.4   Output and cost coefficients of school resources 94
4.5   Output/cost ratios 94
4.6   Some vertexes of the production possibilities frontier: Ex-
      penditure of $80 above minimum 97
4.7   Comparisons between Boston's average and most deprived
      district: Socioeconomic status, expenditures per student, and
      performance 101
4.8   Minimum costs of compensatory policies for deprived district 101
5.1   Coefficients of variation in school resources: Between and
      within states 120
5.2   Influences on participation in School Committee elections
      and public school utilization: Regression coefficients (stand-
      ard errors) 128

5.3   Dispersion of social factors influencing the distribution of resources 130

5.4   Correlations among social factors influencing distribution .. 130

5.5   Distribution of resources as a function of social factors: Regression coefficients (standard errors) 131

5.6   Changes in expenditures per pupil as a function of changes in total expenditures and changes in enrollment, 1960-1964 133

5.7   Distribution of school quality as a function of social factors: Regression coefficients (standard errors) 134

5.8   Inequality of school resources in three big cities: Coefficients of variation 136

6.1   Comparisons of school resources among Boston school districts and Massachusetts towns matched for income and size of public elementary school enrollment, 1964 145

6.2   Rankings of educational organizations: Attainment of policy goals and preferences of interest groups 166

7.1   Socioeconomic characteristics of metropolitan Boston, central city versus suburbs, 1960 176

A.1   Comparisons of costs and master's degrees among various categories of school districts 186

B.1   Percentage of sixth-grade mental ability attained by specified grade 192

C.1   Linear residuals of linear and multiplicative models 196

C.2   Several production functions: Beta coefficients, alternative methods 198

C.3   Residuals from best linear models: Intercorrelations, factor loadings associated with largest latent root 200

FIGURES

3.1   Racial Composition of Boston School Districts 65

4.1   Supply Curves, Input Constraints Only 95

4.2   Reading Gains Supply Curves 96

4.3   Some Production Possibilities Curves 99

5.1   Allocation of Community Income between Schooling and Other Goods 115

5.2   Income-Expenditure Curve for Schooling 116

5.3   Distribution in a Big City School System 116

6.1   Preferred Resource Allocations: Communities with Different Preferences 143

6.2   School Budgets: Communities with Different Incomes 147

6.3   Preferred Resource Allocations: Peer Effects 148

THE POLITICAL ECONOMY OF URBAN SCHOOLS

Chapter 1. INTRODUCTION

*Mental hospitals provide a useful comparison to the police
. . . Like the police they are routinely and repeatedly condemned
for failures and inadequacies . . . The appalling conditions
found in hospital wards . . . have been described, and all the
accounts are no doubt in large measure correct. Repeated
efforts at reform have been made. Budgets have been
increased, hospitals have been reorganized, better-qualified
personnel have been sought, staff services have been
increased, and volumes of research have been published. And
yet each decade sees essentially the same lamentable
conditions exposed and the same indignation unleashed. With
the failure of successive reform efforts, the prescriptions have
become more radical. At first the need was thought to be for
"better men" and "more money." Then the attack shifted to the
professional staff itself . . . The problem is not one of
ideology, but one of technology.[1]*
—*James Q. Wilson*

The formulation of public policy toward social problems is in a
state of crisis. Although the public has extremely high expectations about the solvability of social problems, either swiftly by
government intervention or slowly but steadily through the "invisible hand" (depending upon one's ideology), most problems
seem annoyingly resistant to any "final solution," and they per-
sist or recur contrary to our best intentions.

Although this nation spends more per capita and more
proportionately than any other nation on medical care, for example, indicators of health place us fairly low among indus-

trialized societies, and the life expectancy for those in middle age has hardly increased in decades. Efforts in the area of mental health have been essentially Sisyphean because there is little evidence that any form of psychotherapy, whether under private or public auspices, can "cure" mental illness.[2]

"Crime in the streets" has become a perennial election issue, yet no methods of crime deterrence seem clearly effective. Neither "cracking down" on offenders by aggressive patrol and by "throwing the book" at them, nor preventive group therapy by social workers, seems to have any lasting effect on the incidence of violence in our society.[3]

There is little evidence that society has been able to improve educational attainment any more than it has been able to improve health or decrease crime. Despite the doubling of expenditures on "disadvantaged pupils," compensatory education has borne little fruit.[4]

As Edward Banfield has so perceptively noted, when confronted with a persistent social problem the American cultural ideal, most fully exemplified by the upper and upper middle classes, presumes that these problems are fully tractable through determined collective action. The guiding principle of social policy is: "Don't just sit there. Do something."[5] Doing something generally takes one or more of the following forms: devoting more resources to solving the problem; using given resources "more efficiently," or at least in new ways; or reorganizing the institutions that consume, transform, and distribute the resources.

The strategy of devoting more resources to the solution of social problems presumes that current policy is qualitatively correct but that it has not been pursued vigorously enough. For example, if doubling expenditures per pupil is ineffective in improving academic achievement, the failure is only one of quantity. Tripling or quadrupling expenditures and cutting the size of classes to ten or even five students will do the job! While such a strategy is not prima facie maladaptive, it shows no indication of intelligent muddling through to the solution of a problem.[6]

The strategy of reallocating resources is generally operationalized as combining resources in new ways. If, for example, cutting the size of classes in half is ineffective, then introduce new curricula, with team teaching, and modular class scheduling. While pleading for efficiency is certainly laudatory, there are rarely alternative strategies of *known* effectiveness from which to choose. Second, continual reallocation may be maladaptive if the consequences of policy are long term in nature and hence not determinate in the short run. Although the reallocative strategy is certainly cheaper than spending more money (by definition), it is not necessarily more effective.

The reorganizational approach suggests that misallocation and maldistribution are inherent consequences of the institutions for financing and administering social services. For example, current big city school systems are allegedly responsible for providing irrelevant curricula and bigoted teachers to black children, which stunt their intellectual growth. By a long chain of reasoning it is presumed by some that decentralization and community control will allow parents to select more relevant curricula and more amiable teachers, which will improve the academic performance of the children. The fact that existing institutions do not work, however, does not guarantee that alternative institutions will work any better, and there is little evidence that either parental participation or student achievement are higher in smaller districts.

To advocate any policy intelligently requires a solid understanding of the nature of the problem at hand. In this book I am concerned with social policy in general and educational policy in particular from a positive rather than a prescriptive point of view. My focus is on several analytic issues of policy relevance. Why are schools unable to solve persistent educational problems? To what extent are the failures of schools traceable to lack of technology, to institutional failure, or to political conflict? To what extent are educational problems amenable to purely technical solutions? To what extent do solutions require redistributions of power? What are the causes of inequalities and biases in the distribution of educational opportunity?

TECHNOLOGICAL AND INSTITUTIONAL FAILURES

There is a frightful ignorance of "social technologies," or, in other words, the controllable factors that contribute to the existence of a social problem and, thereby, to its potential solution. Unlike the industrial sector of the economy, the social service sector generally lacks a "How to Do It" manual which specifies well-known ways of achieving particular ends, such as curing mental illness or reducing crime. Without such information, effective, much less efficient, policies are only arrived at by chance.

Social technologies are underdeveloped for both narrow scientific and broader ideological reasons. The inherent complexity of the laws of human social behavior are a profound obstacle to the speedy development of a social science that can be applied to the solution of current problems.[7] Although one may be reluctant to posit a "natural procession" of scientific advance, it seems unlikely that many social technologies could have been evaluated before the advent of computers and the development of econometrics. Whether or not derivable from social science, social technology may elude definitive evaluation for three major scientific reasons.

First, because social phenomena are often so poorly defined or poorly measured, it is difficult to determine whether a problem is getting better or worse. It is not easy to determine whether, for example, schools are becoming more or less "relevant" or are producing better or worse "educated" individuals. Consequently, public policies have had to pursue either poorly defined goals or to operationalize goals of lower order and possibly of lesser importance, as, for example, the increasing of reading scores.[8] Whether the achievement of such goals is consistent with achieving the less measurable goals of creativity, empathy, or conformity is obscure.

The second reason is that social problems are generally subject to multiple influences, most of which are beyond the control of the policy maker. For example, in the area of health, René Dubos argues that the modern American suffers from the delusion that health is purchasable: "He is encouraged to believe that money can create drugs for the cure of heart disease, cancer, and mental disease, but he makes no worth-while effort to recognize, let alone correct, the mismanagements of his everyday life that contribute to the high incidence of these conditions." In other words, the health of a patient is influenced by his diet, his genetic constitution, and his habits, as well as by the skill of his doctor. In the absence of quasi-experimental control, it is difficult to tell whether a health policy has had any effect at all, good, bad, or indifferent. Conceivably, even if a policy were effective, a problem could get worse because of deteriorating exogenous factors. Increased air pollution, for example, may offset improvements in coronary surgery as an influence on the rate of heart disease.[9]

The last consideration involves the recognition that the most valid outcomes of social policy are generally long term and not immediately measurable. For example, schools are supposed to prepare children for adult roles of citizen, worker, consumer, and parent. It is not clear that proximate indicators of success in school, such as reading scores, are highly related to measures of ultimate concern, such as occupational achievement and psychic well-being. Unless this proximate-ultimate relationship is known, evaluating an enterprise on the basis of current consequences may be invalid.

Institutions for financing, administering, and distributing social services are generally run bureaucratically or, in other words, without internal or external pricing signals. Unlike profit-making firms, social service enterprises have weak incentives to produce the right mix of outputs in the right manner for the right consumers even if the technology were known.

The delivery of social services — education, police protection, psychotherapy, and others — is largely in the hands of monopolies or oligopolies administered by those who perceive themselves as professionals. Although they presumably apply rationality to their domain of competence, professionals are rarely concerned with technical efficiency in the strict sense: reaching a specified output objective at lowest cost or obtaining the greatest output for a specified expenditure. Ideally, professional "standards" — usually input- rather than performance-oriented — are not sacrificed at any price. Professionals tend to reject such economizing as profit seeking, which they deem incompatible with "public service."[10] Those operating within nonprofit-making enterprises can indulge this desire with impunity because their budget depends not on profitability but on "need."[11]

Whether or not a social service enterprise is operated on a nonprofit basis, its clientele tends to be captive. For example, public schooling is offered on a largely take-it-or-leave-it basis by the neighborhood school "monopoly," with the option of purchasing private schooling or moving to another district. Even if the clientele were able to compare and choose, they would be relatively unable to distinguish whether the low costs result from efficiency or from shoddiness. This is because the effects of the service are long term and are subject to multiple influences. Consequently, inefficient as well as efficient social service enterprises survive. In fact the private rewards of the social entrepreneur may be incompatible with efficiency. If professional prestige depends upon the size of one's empire (budget and personnel), imperial growth may depend upon proving that problems are getting worse because current resource levels are too low.[12] Alternatively, high resource use may be perceived by the clientele as an indicator of quality, hence good administration.

There are even more important ideological reasons for the retarded development of social technologies. More so than in the natural sciences, discoveries in the social sciences tend to redistribute power within and among three major constituencies: the intellectuals, the professionals, and the public.

Leading thinkers in the social sciences have not, until recently, been particularly interested in the research and devolopment of social technologies. Rather, they have tended to deduce technologies from their broader theoretical concerns. The evaluation of these technologies was often done in an action context by lesser men, with consequently little feedback between application and theory.[13] Such feedback may be quite unwelcome should it conflict with theoretical presuppositions.[14]

Professional practitioners or users of social technology tend to believe in their own efficacy. For example, although physicians credit the historical decrease in infant mortality in the West to their own efforts, Dubos argues that improvements in sanitation, housing, nutrition, and clothing were more influential.[15] The practitioners' attitudes toward "action research" is worse than ambivalent. They tend to generate data in the course of their operations that either serve no evaluative function or vindicate their efficacy.[16] When sponsoring research, they often claim "we know we are doing good, and want you to prove it." For adaptive rather than sinister reasons, professionals may shift their style of operations in the face of perceived success or failure so that the policy being reviewed has protean characteristics.[17]

Even if a social technology were properly evaluated by scientific standards, there is no guarantee that the public would utilize the findings. Few people can be indifferent to any finding that challenges basic conceptions about the nature of man and his social relations. By a logical leap of faith, social scientific facts or theories are invariably interpreted as support or refutation of some ideology.[18] Americans, for example, tend to view the state of the school as a legitimate public responsibility, but they regard the state of the family as being beyond the legitimate concern of society (unless such problems as incest and child beating are involved). In the light of this ethical conception, which is ascientific or metaphysical, a finding that shows the close correlation between family background and academic performance would be interpreted by a large segment of the community as an indictment of the family and the absolution of society. While scientific logic does not lead to such a conclusion, ideo-logic does.[19] In general, by the time any social scientific finding, whether valid or not, filters down to the public, it is heavily laden with emotional valence.

In contrast to the nonprofit-making social service sector, evaluation in the goods producing market sector of the economy is relatively easy.* For example, the modern farmer has a

---

*In large, profit-making industrial enterprises there are analogous evaluation problems in determining the levels of research and development, marketing, and "good will" expenditures. See Anthony Downs, *Inside Bureaucracy* (Boston: Little, Brown, 1967), 29–30.

well-defined notion of crop quality and quantity. He can distinguish a good ear of corn from a bad ear of corn and can distinguish corn from potatoes (alternative outcomes). From the findings of controlled agronomical experiments (menu of technology), he can select the best combination of seed, fertilizer, land, and other factors that most efficiently produce a given crop. Finally, from a market analysis of factor and output prices, he can determine the crop mixture likely to produce the greatest profit (the pricing of alternative policies). Policy failures result either from bad luck, such as drought, or from unwillingness to use information provided by agronomists and agricultural economists.[20]

The contrast between social and agricultural technologies does not imply that we should wait for more definitive research before rushing into social programs. Inaction in the face of uncertainty is as much a policy decision as the determined pursuit of a program. While research can often be helpful in improving decisions, social policies research is usually inconclusive or on a level of abstraction that defies application.[21]

Agricultural scientists can, nevertheless, be emulated by the social policy "dudes" on three levels: social accounting, systems analysis, and cost-benefit analysis. First, social accounts may provide indicators of the state of society, which may also serve as signals for guiding social policy.[22] Second, systems analysis of "natural experiments" in social policy may help in the specification of social technologies.[23] Presumably such analysis would identify those variables which significantly affect the direction of the social indicator. Third, cost-benefit analysis simulates a market evaluation of alternative policy outcomes.[24] The ability of technology to solve social problems, however, is highly constrained by political considerations.

POLITICAL CONFLICTS

Because social service enterprises are charged with solving problems of collective interest, they are political as well as "neutral" service-providing institutions. To the degree that there is dissensus on goals, purely technical solutions to social problems are difficult to achieve.

Even if social service enterprises were technologically effective, efficient, and responsive, the fact that they are subject to collective control makes them an arena of conflict among groups with incompatible notions of public interest and of self-interest. These conflicts, which are keenest in heterogeneous big cities, reflect two sets of issues: the norms governing the *modus operandi* of a social service enterprise and the allocation of resources to and the distribution of benefits from these enterprises.

The normative conflicts reflect differences in subculture, a concept that has, unfortunately, received little attention in the theory of public finance. By subculture we mean: "sets of responses that have developed out of people's attempts to cope with the opportunities, incentives, and rewards, as well as the deprivations, prohibitions, and pressures, which the natural environment and society offer them."[25] In terms most familiar to economists, subcultures can be represented as *patterned* propensities to behave or as preference structures.

Subcultures are more closely related to educational-occupational status (both as a cause and an effect) and ethnic affiliation than to income. Income distributions for different class subcultures overlap widely, and there is no reason to assert ethnocentrically that all individuals or social groups would behave identically if their incomes or opportunities were identical.*

*For white males, age twenty-five to thirty-four, the zero order correlation between income and occupational status, measured as a *continuous* variable of only .39, overestimates the closeness of fit between income and subculture. Besides the fact that occupation is only a surrogate for subculture, the index of occupational status is itself a function of mean income, and subcultures are best represented as discrete clusters of occupations. See Otis Dudley Duncan, "Ability and Achievement," *Eugenics Quarterly*, 15 (Mar. 1968), 1–11; and Otis Dudley Duncan and Peter Blau, *The American Occupational Structure* (New York: John Wiley and Sons, 1967). Cf. the classic study of W. Lloyd Warner, *Yankee City* (abridged ed., New Haven, Conn.: Yale University Press, 1963), pt. 1.

While we do not stereotype *all* members of a given ethnic-class group as unanimously adhering to a particular subcultural pattern, considerable anthropological, survey, and electoral evidence suggests that subcultures differ in child rearing practices, kinship patterns, age and sex role differentiation, and civic attitudes.[26]

Of special interest here are the conflicting norms regarding the behavior of public enterprises, particularly schools. At issue are the following norms: What should be the function of schools (educating children, or providing jobs and recognition for adults)? What should be the educational goals of schools (teaching the basic three R's, or maximum individual intellectual development)? What children should the system devote preferential attention to (the elite, the average, the "problem" students)? Who should the clientele of the educator be (his peers, "enlightened" parents, the majority of voters, the children)? What is the relative importance of expertise (formal qualifications) versus experience in selecting administrators, teachers, and consultants? What is the role of the school in socializing children (reinforcing parental norms, reinforcing "superior" norms)? Into what class subculture should the schools socialize children (upper middle, lower middle, working class)? What is the proper policy role of educational administrators (setting goals, determining means, neither)? How effective are school resources (are small classes and new buildings "frills")?

Abstracting from income, there are striking differences in modal attitudes toward these issues among social classes and among ethnoreligious groups. The working class tends to be relatively unconcerned with events that occur in school. Having relatively little faith in the efficacy of schooling on individual development, it expects the schools to keep its children out of "trouble," to teach them how to behave (in accord with working-class norms), and to teach them the "basic" subjects. It generally respects the competence of school administrators with similar cultural outlooks and trusts them to make the right decisions regarding both the ends and means of schooling. It resents the "interference" of upper-middle-class parents and outside "experts" in schools affairs, especially when these parties pressure the administration to devote attention to the academically talented students. In one middle-income suburb, William Dobriner observed that the working class "stands for [the] traditional and conservative approach to education. It opposes what it terms 'frills' in the public school system. It stands for larger classes rather than increased building. Generally it opposes the employment of additional staff and advocates the reduction of special services such as guidance counselors and psychologists. It hews to a basic 'three R' view of education and its primary concern seems to be economy in order to hold the tax rate in check."[27]

The upper middle class tends to place considerable faith in the efficacy of schooling and is generally interested in participating in matters of school policy. It views the schools as an agency for promoting the maximum intellectual development of its children, culminating in admission to a "name" university. Not only does it presume this goal for its own children; it also expects the schoool to provide this for children in other subcultures. The upper middle class respects formal training and qualifications more than experience, and because it is often better educated than school administrators it feels competent to voice its opinion on matters of both goals and means. It favors aggressive building programs, small classes, and the adoption of the latest educational technologies, such as the "new math."[28]

The lower-middle-class normative patterns are an uneasy compromise between working-class and upper-middle-class norms. If the establishment of these norms is a collective decision, as in a heterogeneous big city, the norms of each subcultural group cannot be implemented simultaneously. Since demography tends to give greater power to the working and lower middle classes in the big cities, upper-middle-class norms are generally implemented only in exclusive suburban and private schools. Consequently, the upper middle class tends to abhor events in big city school systems. Being articulate, this class produces individuals who write and read sensational exposés of the failures of big city school systems, which may be interpreted as covert attacks on working- and lower-middle-class subcultures.[29]

Contrasting upper-middle- and working-class orientations are also reflected in fiscal issues. On local referenda, where the incidence of costs and benefits of any proposal are generally apparent to the voter, the two subcultures vote as if they were guided by different principles of welfare. The upper middle class tends to favor high spending on social services which benefit the "public" even though they personally may not benefit, and they undoubtedly pay a disproportion of the costs. The working class, on the other hand, votes generally for those proposals from which they personally benefit. The more "public-regarding" orientation of the upper middle class cannot be explained in terms of lower marginal utility of income relative to the working class. Public-regarding people vote for expenditures from which they cannot possibly benefit, as, for example, hospitals for indigents, and they are less likely to favor expenditures benefitting "special interests," besides their own, than those benefitting the "public interest."[30]

In addition to subcultural differences along class dimensions, there are differences along ethnic dimensions. On patterns of life style, Herbert Gans distinguishes between "restrictive" and "expansive" subcultures, which differ in attitudes toward discipline versus permissiveness, respect for authority versus autonomy, and, hence, toward styles of socialization in schools.[31] Although all social classes and ethnic groups comprise individuals of both subcultures, a disproportion of Irish Catholics and rural Protestants are restrictive in orientation, while a disproportion of Italian Catholics, Jews, and other Protestants are expansive.

On matters of fiscal policy, Banfield and Wilson distinguish those ethnic groups, within social classes, that are relatively public-regarding (Jews and Protestants) from those that are relatively private-regarding (Irish, Italians, and Poles).[32] Within the Catholic subculture, the Irish vote as if they were more public-regarding than Poles, *ceteris paribus*.

The implication of these normative conflicts is that issues of the "optimal" allocation of resources to schooling or the style of administering those resources require political rather than technical solutions. Normative positions being basically irreconcilable, it seems difficult to find a way of making all participants better off.

Normative conflicts aside, a large number of educational problems are basically distributive and, therefore, fundamentally political rather than technical in nature. These include the issues of equality of educational opportunity, of racial integration, and of allocation of resources to schooling.

Equality of educational opportunity is a distributive issue by definition. Racial integration is also basically distributive. Although upper-middle-class suburbanites generally applaud racial integration in the big cities, they do little to invite any significant integration in their own communities. Presuming that racial integration improves the education of Negroes and soothes the consciences of the suburbanites, the lower- and working-class whites who are directly affected tend to view integration as a gratuitous burden. Meaningful integration becomes politically unfeasible because compensation mechanisms have not been developed that will spread the costs of integration to the broader community rather than to a geo graphically and economically circumscribed group. Nor is it obvious that the rest of the community favors integration so much that they are willing to undertake any costs whatsoever for its implementation, especially if the big city working class can be forced to bear the major brunt.

Even the allocation of resources to education is distributive because of the fiscal system by which education is financed. Big city property taxation is generally disproportional to educational benefits received, and upper-income groups and Catholics who use parochial schools tend to subsidize the rest of the community. State funds for education are drawn from sales and income taxes that are generally even more redistributive from upper- to lower-income groups. Consequently, allocation decisions embody distributive decisions, as the lack of unanimity of school bond referenda suggests.

The introduction of compensation mechanisms in allocative decisions will not necessarily benefit everybody. Evidence re viewed below suggests that public school expenditures are higher when the electorate can "exploit," through taxation, business enterprises and Catholic school parents who receive no direct benefit from public schooling. If, for example, Catholic school parents were exempted from public school taxes, the burdens on the rest of the community would increase, and public school expenditures would drop.

AN OUTLINE OF THE PRESENT ANALYSIS

Schools have been popularly characterized as many things, among them, "the great equalizer of the conditions of man" and "the destroyer of the hearts and minds of young children." Whether romanticized or reviled, schools are presumed to have considerable influence on their charges. Psychologists, for example, view the schools as an environment in which learning is expedited; sociologists see the schools as situations in which adult roles are learned; economists have generally regarded the school as a "black box," for, although they do not know what goes on inside, they do know that passing through it increases one's earning power. In contrast, schools in this study are viewed as economic enterprises of intrinsic interest; they consume resources, transform resources into outputs, and distribute these outputs to consumers.

Nonprofit enterprises, like schools, are important not only for their social responsibilities but also for their increasing economic role. Such enterprises are now providing one-half of the nation's job growth.* While there is a considerable literature, both theoretical and descriptive, as to how profit-making enterprises *do* and *ought to* behave, there is little systematic knowledge about the production and distribution decisions of nonprofit enterprises.[33] As the nonprofit enterprise replaces the agricultural or manufacturing enterprise as the representative

---

*Eli Ginzberg, Dale L. Hiestand, and Beatrice G. Rubens, *The Pluralistic Economy* (New York: McGraw-Hill, 1965), include in the nonprofit sector both governmental (ranging from cost-plus defense contractors to public schools) and private nonprofit activities (such as hospitals and fraternal associations).

firm, microeconomics as a behavioral theory must come to grips with this emerging sector or fade to irrelevance. Without understanding why social service enterprises behave as they do, it is quixotic to prescribe how they should act.

The traditional theory of the firm hypothesizes several necessary conditions for efficient production of the outputs consumers want. Some of the more obvious conditions are: producers have knowledge of the production relationships; producers are profit maximizers; consumers have knowledge of their preferences; both producers and consumers have knowledge of market prices; these prices are uncontrolled by any of the numerous buyers or sellers; entry of firms and consumers into markets is relatively free; production factors are mobile; and no externalities exist.

In the nonprofit, social service sector, few of these conditions hold: producers are fairly ignorant of production relationships; producers are not profit maximizers or even profit seekers; consumers and often producers cannot evaluate the worth of alternative products; goods are distributed freely within geographic boundaries rather than by user charges; major cost elements are controlled politically (salary schedules, capital budgets); producer markets are monopolistic or oligopolistic; and production factors are not highly mobile (tenure restrictions, high intraurban transportation costs).

This work is intended as a contribution to three frontier specialties in economics: the theory of the nonprofit firm, local public finance, and human resources. It will, I hope, interest not only academic economists but also those engaged in the planning and administration of social policy in areas besides education.

Chapters 2 through 4 explore the production process of elementary schools. Chapter 2 begins as a dicussion of approaches to evaluating school systems. Although schools have been traditionally evaluated on the basis of resource inputs or of student performance, I argue that the validity of any such evaluation depends upon prior knowledge of the resource-performance relationship, or the educational production function. A section of the chapter is devoted to a discussion of this key technological concept: defining the terms of this function, operationalizing the definitions, empirically estimating the function. This analysis is followed by a review of the literature of major studies of educational production.

Chapter 3 is a case study of production in the Boston elementary schools. In that chapter I explore the technology of a school system and identify the extent to which interschool variation in academic performance is uniquely attributed to differences in school resources, the impact of changes in educational resources on such performance, the production possibilities of the school system, and the quality of different schools in the system.

While in Chapter 3 the major concern is technology, the focus of Chapter 4 is the behavior of school systems with respect to technological efficiency. First, I consider the normative view of efficiency held by various segments of the community, which are substantially different from that of the orthodox economist. Second, I estimate the cost of improving educational achievement, using existing schools most efficiently, that is, supply curves of educational quality. Then, I compare the actual level of productivity of the Boston school system to that indicated by the supply curve. Finally, I use the supply curve to estimate the costs of bringing the academic performance in a "culturally deprived" school district up to city standards.

The process of distribution for nonprofit enterprises is the focus of Chapter 5. In the market sector of the economy, goods and services are generally distributed on the basis of ability and willingness to pay for them. Educational services, at least at the public elementary level, are not entirely distributed on such a basis. Generally access to elementary schooling is circumscribed by residential location, which may be related to the ability to pay for housing. A small town, for example, tends to have a few neighborhood elementary schools and a single secondary school to which all residents have equal access, but from which nonresidents are excluded. Towns of different income or taste are likely to allocate unequal sums for educational expenditures. Consequently, there tend to be inequalities in access to education among towns, but equality within.

The process of distribution in a multiplant, big city educational system must be seen as quite different. As in the suburbs, particular neighborhoods do not generally share educational services with other neighborhoods. Unlike small towns, however, neighborhoods are not permitted to tax themselves to support their own schools to the exclusion of others. Decision making on educational resources is made on a city-wide basis. Although there are theories of distribution by government agencies, they predict little about school inequalities in big cities. Are services distributed equally? If not, is the distribution of services biased in favor of residents with such definable characteristics as income, ethnicity, political party? If such a bias exists, what factors — a conspiracy of the "Establishment," the "invisible hand" guiding the decentralized decisions of individuals — account for it?

In Chapter 5 several notions of equality are operationalized and compared in terms of their reliability, validity, and controllability. The degree of educational inequality among states, cities, and big city neighborhoods are contrasted. Finally, those institutions which produce inequality and bias in school resources within big cities are identified.

While Chapters 3 through 5 discuss production and distribution within the *existing institutional structure*, Chapter 6 considers the impact of structural reorganization. Three alternatives to the current system of administering and financing big city schools are discussed: decentralization, metropolitanism, and "privatization" through tuition vouchers. These alternatives are compared with respect to their effects on four educational goals: technological efficiency, consumer efficiency or responsiveness to consumer demands, equality of resources or homogeneity of curricula, and integration or heterogeneity of students. In addition, the impact of various structural changes on several interest groups are considered.

The concluding chapter is a review of the major points of this study. They are incorporated into a general discussion of why big city school systems are in trouble, in terms of failure of technology, failure of incentive, and class-ethnic conflict.

A positive analysis of the political economy of schools is

essential for any effective school reform. Production and distribution processes must be understood before the goal of increasing quality or equality can be achieved rationally. One by-product of this analysis is to identify technical as opposed to political solutions; hence, the potentialities and limitations of normative welfare economics as a tool for "improving" public decisions.

Chapter 2.   EVALUATING EDUCATIONAL QUALITY

How does one know whether a school is effective? Any
teacher can tell by just walking through the halls. He
sees whether the students are wearing coats and ties, whether
they are orderly in the corridors, whether they are respectful
of authority.
—A Boston school administrator

During the Boston School Committee election campaign of
1965, I canvassed several working-class districts for a "civic-
minded" slate whose major issue was "quality" education.
After attacking the policies of the incumbent majority, I was
challenged by one of their supporters: "There is nothing wrong
with our schools. What is so desirable about new buildings,
small classes, and better-trained teachers? The parochial
schools do very well without these frills."

I was stunned and speechless. Wearing ideological blinders,
it had never occurred to me that a large segment of the electorate, indeed a majority in Boston, had contrary beliefs about
educational reality and different evaluative criteria. The issues
that my challenger raised are fundamental: How does one determine whether or not a particular school, or any other social
service enterprise, is performing satisfactorily and whether one
school is better than another?

TRADITIONAL MODES OF EVALUATION

There have generally been two sorts of answers to these questions. One is that the quality of schools is ineffable or, at most, describable in terms of the charismatic qualities of "dedicated teachers" who "develop the minds" of their students. With this view, the characteristics of a good school are certainly irreducible to numbers, and no more rigorous a formula for quality can be applied than obtaining "good" personnel. A corollary to this view, often explicit, is that only professional educators are qualified to render authoritative judgments on the subject. Evaluation then becomes the existentialist operation of Verstehen.[1]

There is a modicum of validity to the notion of relying on the subjective judgment of experts for evaluating school quality. Surely the educational process is so complex that a layman or a naïve systems analyst would have great difficulty in determining whether a school is doing a good job. Abstracting this process into a few numbers clearly omits much of its essence, and, furthermore, student performance does indeed seem to be positively related to teacher expectation, an intangible, and teaching ability, as rated by experts.[2] (The relationship between teacher expectation and ability, on the one hand, and student performance, on the other, is probably reciprocal: a good student makes a teacher look successful and creates high expectations.)

Reliance on professional evaluation is a two-edged sword, however. Professionals may be able to protect the unwitting client from making decisions on the basis of "extraneous" criteria, but, although the professional's expertise may give him greater competence to make purely technical decisions for his client, in practice it often legitimizes his claim to determine the client's "needs." Indeed, professional standards or the evaluated needs can be so high as to either force the client to overconsume his services or to price them out of the market.[3]

In the case of education, it is doubtful whether the judgment of professional educators is inherently superior to that of the clients. Expert evaluations of school quality rest lightly on professional arcana; ratings of schools by superintendents tend to correlate highly with rather pedestrian indicators, as, for example, the ratio of pupils to teachers, teacher experience, teacher training, salary schedules, and *student performance,* which depends upon factors other than schooling.[4] This lack of technical expertise is recognized by the public. Laymen sit on school boards and control standards of accreditation, leaving educators with less control over their *modus operandi* and entry to their profession than barbers and plumbers.[5]

When educators do not share a common subculture with their clientele, the problems are magnified for it is not clear that the needs, much less the abilities, of the charges are recognized.[6] Although their own perceptions may not be any more accurate,[7] the "culturally deprived" minorities, in the context of current politics, view professional claims to expertise with less than awe.[8]

What then is the utility of professional Verstehen in the evaluation of school quality? As an informed participant in the educational process, the educator is certainly in a position to raise hypotheses, which can then be operationalized and tested. The value of these judgments, however, is quite limited in formulating policy. Even if we were to believe that intangibles such as teacher expectation and dedication as determined by educators formed the essence of school quality, such a belief provides no information on how to improve poor schools. Charisma is a scarce resource, and there may be no choice but to accept the existing quality of teachers as fixed in the short run. Second, professional judgment is an inextricable mixture of value and fact. While teachers generally advocate higher salaries and smaller classes, the pedagogical consequences of these policies are obscure. In other words, it is not clear that educators want what children need.

An overreaction to the existentialist view is seemingly mindless quantification. Rather than relying on subjective judgments, some educators point to "objective" measures of school resources and curriculum or to student performance on standardized tests. Although quantitative measures are manifest to the public, some can be seriously misleading and quite invalid.[9]

The most commonly used measure of resource quality is expenditure per student. Although they are appealing for their simplicity, expenditure measures do not distinguish between high costs owing to inefficiency and those needed to maintain quality. For example, high expenditures may result from the high cost of maintaining and repairing an outmoded plant or from operating on a wasteful scale. If there were economies of scale in education, by definition less could be spent in producing a given output in larger schools. A more serious deficiency of expenditure as an indicator of school quality is its uselessness as a policy guide. It does not suggest how money should be spent to improve student performance. Equal amounts may be expended to decrease class size or to hire more experienced teachers, but the consequences of the two policies on what is learned may be quite different.

The most serious objection is that there seems to be no relationship between school expenditures per pupil and long-term student achievement when social background and years of schooling are held constant.[10] This finding suggests either that expenditures do not translate into school quality or that school quality has no relation to eventual success. In any case, simply spending money on schooling (at least within the observed range of expenditures) is apparently not effective.

A more meaningful approach to evaluation is the measurement of "physically" defined inputs. Schools can be ranked on the basis of pupil-teacher ratios, guidance counselors per thousand students, library books, and other measures of facilities and curriculum.[11] Only if schools had an equal rank on every input measure would there be an unambiguous, unique ranking for all schools. In most systems such is not the case, and this method does not permit us to compare two schools whose ranks differ on various inputs. It is not clear, for example, whether a school with more experienced teachers but larger classes is better or worse than a school with less experienced teachers and smaller classes.

Unique quality ranks can be derived by averaging the ranks on the several input scales for each school. Averaging ranks requires a prior assumption about the effects of each input on student performance. It requires assuming, for example, that teacher experience and class size have *some* educational consequences, which is not at all obvious. Even if these input dimensions had educational consequences, the relative importance of each input dimension is unclear. A simple arithmetic average, for example, assumes all inputs are *equally* important.[12]

The most serious disadvantage of evaluating schools by input ranks is the amount of information the procedure throws away. Take three schools where 20, 30, and 50 percent, respectively, of the faculty members have master's degrees. Merely ranking schools on this basis makes no use of the information that the difference between the first and second schools (ten points) is less than half as much as the difference between the second and third schools (twenty points) and the best school has 250 percent more highly trained teachers than the worst school.[13]

Such information is useful if we only want to know by *how much* quality increases as expenditures increase. We also need to know whether a particular school contributes nothing, or even negatively, to student success, however, and these concepts cannot be expressed by rank indexes. It is commonly assumed, for example, that the longer the school day, the better. Including the rank of a school on this measure in an average index would invalidate the index if, in fact, the length of school day had little effect on performance or if such an effect were deleterious.

Another "objective" method is to evaluate schools on the basis of student performance on standardized tests. Even if we concede the validity of such tests as measures of what children know, they do not by themselves measure the effectiveness of schooling. High levels of student achievement may reflect motivation and skills imparted by the home as well as by the school.[14]

Rather than blindly counting school resources, one can most usefully evaluate schools in terms of their consequences on children. This orientation leads us on a search for an "educational production function" that shows the relationship between school resources and student performance.

THE PRODUCTION MODEL OF SCHOOL SYSTEMS

Education may be viewed as a production process in which school resources, the family, and the peer group influence the development of a child's cognitive skills and emotional and social behavior. Changes in the kind of teachers a child is exposed to, in the economic status of his parents, and in the values of the children he associates with — all have some effect on cognitive, emotional, and social development.

A production function can be described as the precise relationship between changes in these school and social variables, or inputs, and aspects of child development, or outputs. An educational production function might posit the following relationship: an X percent increase in teacher's verbal ability, or a Y percent increase in father's income, or a Z percent increase in the social class of his peers all produce a ten-point gain in reading scores in the second grade. The production function, then, describes not only the numerical impact of particular input changes; it also allows comparison of the relative impact of alternative input changes: changing teacher verbal ability as opposed to changing peer group.

Because both inputs and outputs can be analyzed on many levels of detail, there is a conceptual hierarchy of production functions describing any process. In principle, the educational process may be described at any of the following conceptual levels: biochemical — changes in the chemical structure of desoxyribonucleic acid (DNA);[15] physiological — changes in the functioning of neuromuscular tissue as a result of patterned electro-stimulation;[16] behavioral — changes in patterns of behavior resulting from patterned rewards and punishments;[17] institutional — changes in representative aspects of behavior as a result of exposure to school resources and social situations, abstracted from the patterns of reward and punishment; societal — changes in adult status, such as income or occupation, due to educational attainment, abstracted from the behavior of educational institutions.

In epistemological terms all such levels of analysis have equal validity, but differ essentially in the kinds of questions they attempt to answer. An outstanding behaviorist, B. F. Skinner, argues that reduction to physiological or biochemical levels is unnecessary in order to gain enough understanding of the learning process to assert powerful control over behavior.[18] The assumption of institutional studies is analogous: that descriptions of the behavioral patterns within schools is unnecessary in order to gain enough understanding of the effects of school resources to make rational economic choices.

Characteristics of Human Development

The last assumption does not imply that psychological insights are useless in the institutional analysis of schools, only that they may be unnecessary. Just as it is helpful for an agricultural economist to know the gestation period of a cow, the educational economist might profit from some knowledge of child development and learning processes; these fields suggest some plausible characteristics of the educational production functions.

Importance of Early Experience. Psychologists have known for a long time that the behavior of individuals is highly influenced by early childhood experience. The characteristics of early environments have an especially great influence on intelligence or "problem solving capacity based on . . . information processing strategies . . ."[19] The early environment can have such great impact on "learning how to learn" that early deficits cannot always be compensated for by later stimulation.

The consequences of this proposition for institutional analysis are enormous. First, much of the cognitive ability of children is developed prior to schooling. Although schooling itself may provide a rich environment for stimulating the development of intelligence, its leverage is limited. Second, since earlier events tend to have greater impact on ultimate development than later events, there are probably diminishing returns to school resources on cognitive abilities, with respect to age.

While general intelligence develops relatively early in life, specific kinds of intelligence may develop at different rates. Benjamin Bloom estimates that an individual develops roughly 50 percent of his adult general intelligence and 20 percent of his adult numerical ability by kindergarten.[20] If such estimates are valid, then the leverage of schooling is potentially greater on numerical ability than on general intelligence.

Stages of Development. There appear to be well defined and uniquely ordered stages in cognitive, emotional, and social development. Instead of developing continuously and incrementally, manifest human abilities advance in spurts. What may be taken for the lack of effect of school experiences on intelligence and achievement may actually be latent development prior to an overt spurt. Related to the phenomenon of stages is the concept of a "critical period" during which readiness to learn certain skills is optimal. In linguistic development, for example, children seem most responsive to instruction in reading around the age of five.[21]

There are several economic implications in the notion of developmental stages and learning readiness: First, discontinuities in the developmental process may imply discontinuities in the educational production function; second, the effect of resources applied at an inappropriate stage might be either negligible or latent; and, the effects of school resources may be maximal at some critical period of development. Consequently, monotonic and continuously differentiable production functions, so commonly used in economics, may be inappropriate in describing education.

There may be further discontinuities in the effects of resource changes at given moments in time. For example, within the range of two to fifteen students, classes may assume the characteristics of a seminar and changes in enrollment may have no effect on the amount each student learns. At enrollment levels having above sixteen to twenty students, the class may abruptly change its character from seminar to lecture, with a hypothetically swift decline in learning. Once a class has the character of a lecture, increases in enrollment to, say, fifty students may make little difference in how much each student learns.

Learning Theory. Developed through laboratory studies of animals, learning theories specify the conditions under which behavior is most efficiently shaped. The major principles of effective teaching derived in this way are the shaping of behavior by *successive approximation,* or incremental changes, brought about by reinforcing responses compatible with the desired behavior and by extinguishing incompatible responses by nonreward.

Learning theory suggests that the most crucial attribute of schooling is the "program" by which responses are primed or elicited, by which they are rewarded, and by which undesired behavior is extinguished. This concept of program goes beyond the traditional concept of curriculum, which simply lists objectives and instructional materials. Controlled experiments with children suggest that rates of progress for those taking properly programmed instruction are strikingly greater than rates for those involved in traditional curricula.[22]

Concepts from learning theory suggest that the detailed way in which students and teachers interact is more important in influencing achievement than any gross measures of school resources. Although it is difficult to characterize such interaction, we can try to approximate it by a proxy for intensity of student-teacher interaction (class size) and by a proxy for the teacher's "programming ability" (accreditation, training, experience, verbal facility).

Characteristics of the Production Function

A general educational production function[23] can be formally described in the following terms:

The academic performance of an individual at any time depends upon his history of school and peer experiences and his family characteristics, the form of this relationship being subject to measurement error:

1) O_{it} — function of (S_{it}, F_{it}, P_{it}, e_t), where
   O_{it} = vector of academic performance measures for the *ith* individual at time *t*.
   S_{it} = vector of school resources applied to *ith* individual over time path *n* to *i*, where *n* is age of entry to school;
   F_{it} = vector of family characteristics of *ith* individual during his lifetime, including genetic endowments;
   P_{it} = vector of peer group characteristics of *ith* individual over his lifetime;

e_t = error in measuring variables and in specifying equation.*

Generally, earlier experiences have greater impact on learning ability than later experiences:

2) $\dfrac{\partial O_t}{\partial S_t} < \dfrac{\partial O_{t-1}}{\partial S_{t-1}}$ where $S_t = S_{t-1}$

For specific intellectual abilities, there may be critical periods of learning readiness:

3) $\dfrac{\partial O_{t-1}}{\partial S_{t-1}} < \dfrac{\partial O_t}{\partial S_t} > \dfrac{\partial O_{t+1}}{\partial S_{t+1}}$ where $S_t = S_{t\pm1}$

There are stages in development during which external influences have no effect or have latent effects observable at some later period:

4) $\dfrac{\partial O_t}{\partial S_t} = 0$ but $\dfrac{\partial O_{t+j}}{\partial S_t} \neq 0$ for some elements of O at some times t and $t+j$

Three other characteristics of generalized production functions that do not necessarily follow from the nature of human development and learning are the properties of interaction, of diminishing returns, and of discontinuities.

The impact of school characteristics on performance depends upon, or interacts with, the particular characteristics of peers and family. In other words, the effect of changing class size on reading ability may be greater for poor children than for wealthy children.

5) $\dfrac{\partial O_t}{\partial S_t} = f\,(F_t,\,P_t)$, etc.

*To obtain unbiased parameter estimates by regression analysis, the error terms must have an expected value of zero and must be uncorrelated with any of the independent variables. Neither condition is likely in reality. Biases and errors in reporting have been well described by Oskar Morgenstern, *On the Accuracy of Economic Observations* (Princeton, N.J.: Princeton University Press, 1965). The facts that biased reports are more likely from lower-class individuals and that errors are probably correlated with unmeasured aspects of social class and school resources both tend to attenuate the measured effect of independent variables on performance, that is, bias the parameter estimates downward.

In general, the gain in performance to each succeeding small increment in resources becomes less and less:

6) $\dfrac{\partial^2 O_t}{\partial S^2{}_t} < 0$

There may be large "quantum jumps" in performance for some small changes in resources:

7) $\dfrac{\partial O_t}{\partial S_t}$ undefined for some S

MEASURING THE OBJECTIVES OF SCHOOLING

Like most social service enterprises, schools are multiproduct firms attempting to achieve a large number of subgoals — reading, writing, and arithmetic — which are components of "education." Unlike profit-making enterprises, schools encounter two major problems in characterizing their objectives: measuring the multitude of subgoals and reducing the large number of subgoals to a more comprehensible set of indicators or, ideally, to a single indicator.

What Is Learned in School?

Schools are presumably agents of "socialization" and transmitters of cognitive skills. Socialization is the process by which children acquire the psychological capacity to cope with the demands of other institutions of society such as the economy and the political order. Schools are only one agent among many (family, peer group, mass media) in transmitting values such as independence and need for achievement. In addition, schools may be uniquely able to transmit some norms that other agencies are unable or unwilling to transmit. For example, school children are exposed to peers of similar age and observe that different rewards are distributed primarily on the basis of achievement. Within the family, however, rewards are not distributed on the basis of achievement, but on the basis of need or of age or sex.[24]

In the course of affecting the students' abilities to cope with

29

bureaucratic institutions, schooling may cause personality changes that can ultimately shape these very institutions. For example, schooling on the college level tends to reduce the degree of authoritarianism and to increase the degree of tolerance, liberalism, and receptiveness to ideas in individuals. Similarly, schooling can affect consumption tastes by the degree to which it develops aesthetic ideals.[25]

In addition to imparting specific skills and bits of knowledge, school environments may increase the student's intelligence or capacity to process information, and, thereby, his ability to learn, to solve problems, and to create.

Indicators of Educational Objectives

What kinds of measurements are obtainable for these objectives? Ideally, educational indicators should possess a high degree of quantifiability, reliability, and validity.

Quantifiability refers to the mathematical properties of the scale by which an educational objective is measured. Most cognitive abilities can be measured on a scale that at least has *ordinal* properties; that is, we can tell whether one student is more or less literate, better or worse at arithmetic, and possibly more or less creative than another. Some cognitive scales have *interval* properties, which indicate *by how much* one student surpasses another. For example, if three students (A, B, and C) obtain 70, 80, and 90 percent correct answers on an arithmetic test, we can not only rank these students C-B-A, but we may infer that the difference in achievement between C and B is the same as the difference between B and A. Finally, a few cognitive scales have ratio properties, which presumes both a measure of equal intervals and an absolute zero point. For example, reading speed (words/minute) has both a unit interval (a word) and an absolute zero point (zero words/minute).

It is considerably more difficult to quantify the dimensions of socialization although several psychologists have attempted to construct scales of authoritarianism, empathy, and liberalism.[26] Such scales generally can be given at most an ordinal interpretation. For example, if students A, B, and C scored 10, 15, and 20 points on an ascending scale of authoritarianism, we would probably agree that C was more authoritarian than B, but not necessarily that the differences in authoritarianism between C and B were equivalent to that between B and A.

It would be most desirable to scale all measures of cognitive development and socialization on ratio scales. Such scales not only permit percentage comparisons of scores, but they also permit complex mathematical transformations like geometric mean and coefficients of variation. The difficulty with obtaining ratio scales from interval scales is the inability to locate an absolute zero point, as, for example, "zero intelligence."

If ratio scales are unobtainable, the next in order of preference are interval scales, which permit mathematical operations such as calculation of a mean, standard deviation, correlation, and regression coefficient. The difficulty with such scales is in obtaining an intuitively meaningful unit interval (see Appendix B). Consequently, most educational objectives are not quantifiable on a scale with more than ordinal properties, which permits only the lowest level of statistical manipulations: calculation of the median and rank order correlations.

Obtaining *reliable* measures of educational objectives is another problem in operationalizing goals. One source of unreliability is the variety of conceptual instruments used to measure a particular objective. Because a concept like "intelligence" is so imprecise, there is no universally accepted test for measuring "true" intelligence. If tests A and B do not define this ability by the same criteria, then scores of the same set of individuals on the two tests will be imperfectly correlated.

Even if there were consensus on the operational definition of all educational goals, the reliability of measurement would be affected by imprecision inherent in the testing instruments. If "intelligence" were subjectively rated by experts, the likelihood of perfect interobserver agreement is low. If intelligence were "objectively" tested by a pencil and paper test, a given individual would not obtain identical scores at two different time periods; nor would his scores on different parts of the test be perfectly correlated. In general, the less palpable and more complex an objective, the less reliable is its measurement.

The validity of an educational objective is its relationship to a

phenomenon of ultimate concern. A "talmudic" view of education suggests that scholarly success is of inherent value and
needs no further justification. Adherence to this orientation implies that the validity of a particular educational indicator depends on how well it fits the concept it attempts to measure. For
example, if "knowing how to play the violin" is an objective,
then actual performance of a concerto is a more valid indicator
of this knowledge than the ability to write about the violin.

Education, however, is viewed as more than an end in itself;
it is also a means to occupational and income status. From this
vocational orientation, the validity of an educational objective
has two dimensions. *Criterion validity* is the degree to which
success on a proximate educational indicator influences success on an indicator of ultimate concern. The well-known relationship between years of schooling and *expected* or average
income suggests that educational success has criterion validity, that is, the regression coefficients relating income to educational factors are statistically significant.[27] Because so many
other factors affect income, the *predictive validity* of these educational factors for ultimate income is not very high, the zero-
order correlation between income and mental ability being
only .41.[28]

To the extent that improvements on educational indicators
generate increases in labor productivity, or in health, or in zest
for life, individual welfare gains can be aggregated to the social
level. To the degree that schools serve a primarily selective
rather than educative function, individual welfare gains may be
cancelled by the losses of others.

Schools may be plausibly viewed in any of the following
ways: schools develop marketable skills, and academic success
is a valid indicator of these skills; families develop the marketable skills of their children, but academic success is a valid
indicator of these skills; or schools do not develop marketable
skills and academic success is an invalid indicator of those
skills, but employers discriminate in favor of educated people.

The well-known relationships between school years completed and income or unemployment are consistent with all
three models. Regardless of which hypothesis is true, an indi-

vidual is better off if he has more education; however, that is true of society as a whole only under the first hypothesis. If the second or third hypotheses were true and everyone obtained more education, there would simply be higher educational "standards" for all jobs, with no gain in social productivity. The marginal social costs of additional education would, consequently, result in zero social benefits.

While most human resource economists assume that schooling increases the supply of marketable skills, in line with the first hypothesis, there is some evidence that school achievement also performs a purely selective function. In studies of manufacturing industries in countries with widely differing educational levels, Manuel Zymelman and Mordecai Kreinen found little relationship between labor productivity and absolute educational attainment, holding capital stock constant. In other words, while relative education determines who gets the most productive jobs, absolute education has little effect on the productivity of a particular job.[29]

A more serious problem in interpreting indicators of educational performance is that schools change the tastes of their students. Economic theory currently has no conceptual tools for determining whether one set of tastes is preferable to another set, that is, whether an individual is better off learning to dislike the music of Lawrence Welk and to appreciate Stravinsky. Such a change of tastes seems little different from learning to want a new car each year. But, in the sense that we cannot link changes that occur in school to ultimate individual and social welfare, the normative implications of educational indicators are profoundly ambiguous.

Problems of Multiple Objectives

How can the multiplicity of goals be reduced to a more comprehensible set? The multiple products of a manufacturing firm can be aggregated to a single measure of value of output because every output of the firm can be measured and prices can be placed on every output. Consequently, a manufacturing, or indeed any profit-making, firm can literally add incommensurable apples and oranges by weighting each according to its price. For example, a hundred oranges priced at ten cents each plus two hundred apples priced at five cents each come to a total value of two hundred dollars.

Neither of these two conditions hold in multiproduct social service enterprises because the services performed are so complex and diffuse that a complete listing, much less quantification, is unfeasible. Nor are there any intuitively meaningful prices to equate learning Shakespeare with learning algebra.

One strategy of accounting for the multiple outcomes is by *representation* or fractional measurement. A single outcome, which is deemed representative of all other outcomes, is selected as a unique indicator of "education." The achievement of this representative subgoal is, presumably, compatible with the achievement of all others. There are dangers in such fractional measurement, however, for there are probably trade-offs between the attainment of the representative subgoal and other goals; the representative subgoal itself might well be chosen because it is easily measurable, rather than for its importance.

Perhaps the safest method of dealing with the multiplicity of educational goals is through multiple representative indicators. As many subgoals as possible should be measured and correlated. Sets of subgoals which are highly intercorrelated, such as "reading speed" and "reading comprehension," can be represented by a single indicator. Sets of subgoals which are not highly intercorrelated should be represented separately. For example, if all the indicators of "reading ability" are poorly correlated with all the measures of "artistic ability," then at least two distinct indicators are needed to represent these subgoals.

Generally, one is not free to measure as many subgoals as he would prefer. Because only the most quantifiable objectives are measured, any evaluation based on fractional measurement should be recognized as incomplete and possibly biased.

STUDIES OF EDUCATIONAL PRODUCTION: A REVIEW

Ideally, we like to specify the parameters of an educational production function by performing a controlled experiment. First, we would design a sample of schools comprising all interesting resource combinations. For example, if the only resources of interest were class size and teacher experience, the sample space would include at least the following four categories: 1) big classes, experienced teachers; 2) big classes, inexperienced teachers; 3) small classes, experienced teachers; and 4) small classes, inexperienced teachers. Next, we would randomly assign students each year to each of the four situations. Finally, we would compare the performance of students with similar family characteristics but different schooling histories. Thus, we might find that students who had always had experienced teachers performed X percent better on a particular test than students who had always had inexperienced teachers; that the effect of teacher experience was more pronounced for lower-class than for middle-class students; and that the impact of teacher experience was independent of class size.

Needless to say, such experiments have not been performed. At best we can study "natural experiments" by comparing the performance of children in existing schools. The data generated by existing schools are usually inadequate from the viewpoint of experimental design because schools do not strikingly differ from each other, at least not as much as children differ among themselves; school characteristics tend to be highly correlated, so there are few schools with big classes and experienced teachers, or with small classes and inexperienced teachers; and school characteristics are highly correlated with student characteristics, so most lower-class children obtain what are generally recognized as worse resources. Consequently, it is difficult to distinguish the effects of school resources from those of family and peers, much less to extricate the independent effects of different school resources on student performance.

Given that natural experiments are the only source of data likely to be available in the near future, should we use their results as guides to policy making? Although the complexity of the production model outstrips by far the type of data required for proper estimation, careful statistical analysis of natural experiments can in some cases provide useful results. For example, it can help us reject as implausible the hypothesis that a particular resource has a major effect on performance if used in a particular way. We might find, perhaps, that, when other factors are held constant, there is no relation between mathematics achievement and variations in pupil-teacher ratio in the ranges of 20:1 to 30:1. Such knowledge would be useful if a school board were contemplating spending 50 percent more per pupil by reducing class size from thirty to twenty. Because we expect discontinuities in the production function, it would be injudicious to extrapolate the "no size effect" to classes above and below this range. In other words, the analysis of natural experiments tells us little about the consequences of novel and radical modes of school organization and resource use. With these caveats in mind, the major studies of educational production are interpreted as suggestive of plausible hypotheses about schools as they currently operate.

Many investigations purporting to identify school characteristics that influence academic performance are rather inconclusive. For example, in a massive longitudinal study of 7000 high school students from Project TALENT, Marion Shaycoft was unable to identify "any readily apparent relation of school characteristics . . . to the very substantial school differences in performance."[30] Although this study measures social characteristics and academic performance rather carefully, the measurement of school resources is fairly unreliable, in terms of curriculum instead of in terms of physical resources.

From the TALENT sample, J. Allen Thomas selected 206 high schools serving towns ranging in population from 2,500 to 25,000.[31] Holding community characteristics constant, there appear to be significant relationships between cognitive gains from the tenth to the twelfth grade, on the one hand, and several school characteristics, on the other. Achievement gains varied directly with starting teacher salary (a surrogate for quality), teacher experience, and school size, indicative of economies of scale within the range of observed enrollments. Performance also varied inversely with class size. Finally, performance varied directly with expenditures per pupil, when the above characteristics were held constant, suggesting that unspecified expenses beyond teacher salaries were effective.

Thomas found no significant relationship between age of school building and performance.

In one of the earliest studies, Mollenkopf and Melville regressed a set of achievement scores of ninth and twelfth graders in one hundred randomly selected high schools against a list of school, community, and parental characteristics.[32] While production functions differ by test score and by grade, achievement tends to be directly related to specialized staff per pupil and instructional expenditures per pupil, and inversely related to class size, social factors being held constant.

A similar study of fourth-, seventh-, and tenth-grade students in 103 school systems, was undertaken by Samuel Goodman in New York State.[33] When student background is held constant, a composite achievement score is positively correlated with teacher experience, expenditure per pupil, specialized staff per thousand pupils, and "classroom atmosphere." It is not clear from the data whether these correlations control for all other independent variables, or, in other words, whether these correlations reflect independent effects on performance.

In one of the most interesting studies, Charles Benson attempted to explain variations in median fifth-grade reading scores among the largest school systems in California, which enrolled 70 percent of the state's elementary school pupils.[34] The most significant results emerge when the systems are stratified on the basis of enrollment (less than 2000, 2000-4500, and above 4500 average daily attendance [ADA]). As enrollments increase to 2000, average student performance improves. Between 2000 and 4500, increases in enrollment worsen performance. Increases in enrollment above 4500 have no apparent effect on performance.

In the smaller districts there is a significant inverse relationship between teachers per administrator and performance, but in larger systems this relationship is direct. This suggests that bureaucratization is inherently harmful in large-scale school systems, but presumably beneficial in smaller systems.

In middle-sized and smaller systems, there are direct relationships between instructional expenditures per student, mean administrator salary, and mean teacher salary, on the one hand,

and student performance, on the other. These findings are difficult to interpret because it is not clear on what items money is
expended and because salaries may reflect the level of salary
schedules as well as teacher experience and training. In larger
systems, which include the big cities, these relationships are
inverse. Perhaps the inversions reflect the salary incentives
needed to induce teachers to work in undersirable ghetto
schools.

Herbert Kiesling considered the effects of expenditures per
student and level of enrollment on student achievement in 102
New York State high schools, which were stratified by size and
location and whose students were stratified by parental occupation.[35] The relationship between performance and expenditures
is highly sensitive to these other factors. For example, the effect
of expenditures varies significantly with social class, the lowest
class being especially insensitive to expenditures. Also, the effect of expenditures (elasticity) on performance, as well as the
precision of the regressions (coefficient of determination), is
greater at the lower grades. It is not clear whether this finding
demonstrates diminishing returns with respect to age or reflects the greater degree of error in relating current resources to
achievement levels at higher grades. Performance is directly related to expenditures only in the larger districts (above 2000
ADA), a finding contrary to Benson's. Finally, Kiesling observes
that there are scale economies in the smaller districts and slight
diseconomies in the larger, as does Benson.

Because Kiesling measures school resources by expenditures
per pupil, his study does not serve as a useful policy guide. As
mentioned earlier, expenditures per student can be increased in
many ways: by reducing class size, by raising the salary schedule and attracting better teachers, by hiring teachers with more
experience and training. Benson suggests that the first option is
fairly ineffective, but Kiesling provides us with no insight as to
the effective and *a fortiori* the efficient alternative.

Jesse Burkhead and his collaborators make several useful
contributions to the study of educational production.[36] First,
they focus on production in separate high schools in two big
cities, Atlanta and Chicago, thereby providing controls for sal-

ary schedules and intangibles such as "administrative response." Second, they view school systems as multiproduct enterprises which may make trade-offs in outputs as well as inputs. Third, functions are derived for both levels of achievement and achievement gains.

Burkhead's study suggests that it is no more reasonable to conceptualize *the* educational production function than *the* agricultural production function, abstracted from crop or geography. Not only are the regression coefficients variable with respect to output; they also vary among schools in Atlanta and Chicago and across two hundred small-town high schools. In general, Burkhead finds that school resources in high school have a rather minor effect on level of achievement and on gains. The weakness of all resource effects on gains measures is consistent with the notion of diminishing returns with age since he is dealing with high school students. While no input affects all measures of output in all groups of regressions, a few outputs have a significant effect in some cases: newness of building, teacher turnover, teacher experience, and teacher salary (which may be a proxy for either average teacher experience or the proportion of teachers with advanced degrees). Expenditures per student have minor effects on output, and class size has no effect on output, within the unstated range of the data.

The Equality of Educational Opportunity (EEO) Survey, widely known as the Coleman Report, after its principal author, provides information on a wide range of student, teacher, administrator, and school resource characteristics for nearly 600,000 students in grades three, six, nine, and twelve.[37] The detail with which school resources are described at a point of time exceeds that of all other studies of education. An analysis of variance is used to explain differences in ability, achievement, and attitudes for students who are stratified by region and ethnicity. The rationale for classifying students by ethnicity (white, Negro, Mexican-American, Puerto Rican, American Indian) was the concern for elevating the achievement levels of minority groups, but it could also have been justified on the basis of well-known subcultural differences in patterns of mental development.[38] Unfortunately, the study did not stratify by social class, which is correlated with ethnicity. What are interpreted as ethnic differences may really be class differences.*

All of the findings and conclusions of the EEO Survey cannot be reviewed here. The conclusion most relevant to this study is that school resources have little or no effect on student achievement. At least two devastating critiques of the report argue that the data show nothing of the kind and that the survey data can be manipulated to controvert that "finding."

Reanalysis of the survey data using regression techniques demonstrates that school resources, especially teacher characteristics, do indeed make a difference. Samuel Bowles and Henry Levin demonstrated that teacher verbal test score or salaries are directly related to reading achievement among twelfth-grade northern Negroes. In a study of sixth-grade reading and mathematics scores of whites and Negroes, Eric Hanushek found that teacher verbal score, experience, and color had a great impact on both measures of achievement. Because of high intercorrelations among input variables, neither Bowles and Levin nor Hanushek was able to identify the effect of other school resources considered in previous studies (class size, teacher degree, enrollment).[39]

The Plowden Report from the United Kingdom is similar in scope to the Coleman Report.[40] The two studies share the emphasis on teacher quality as the most important school characteristic. Stratified by sex and age, students read better when they are instructed by teachers with more experience and more training. In addition, subjective ratings of teacher quality seem to be positively correlated with the reading ability of students. When other educationally relevant factors are held constant, there is apparently no effect of class size on learning, a finding sup-

---

*The precedent for making ethnic comparisons without controlling for social class is well established in academic circles as well as in public debate. Often invidious ethnic comparisons are interpreted by liberals as proof of discrimination and by conservatives as proof of cultural failures in the underachieving group. See the fascinating papers in Lee Rainwater and William Yancey, *The Moynihan Report and the Politics of Controversy* (Cambridge, Mass: MIT Press, 1966).

ported by reanalysis of the EEO survey.

In a series of studies of college undergraduates, Alexander Astin and his co-workers found almost no relationship between gains in cognitive achievement (value added) and continuation-attrition, on the one hand, and gross measures of college resources (expenditures per student, faculty-student ratio, faculty training, library facilities) and "objective" peer characteristics, on the other.[41] These measures of performance are related, however, to the more intangible characteristics of peer and administrative environment ("independence," "flexibility of curriculum," "severity of policy against cheating"). Consistent with the notion of output trade-offs, those environmental factors that increase cognitive achievement tend to decrease the degree of continuation.[42]

By comparing input and output growth rates, Woodhall and Blaug attempted to calculate recent *trends* in productivity in secondary schools in Britain.[43] Output indexes were calculated with the number of graduates being weighted by three alternative methods (by earnings, by number of years completed, by certificate received), while several physical inputs were measured: books, age of building, pupil time, staff time, and staff numbers. From 1950 to 1963 the growth rate of inputs was substantially greater than the growth rate of any of the output indexes, suggesting that productivity is tending to drop in British secondary schools. Such analysis provides little light on why productivity dropped (worse students?, worse teachers?), nor does it identify effective or efficient resource policies. Both issues are best handled in a regression framework in which the quality of students and teachers are held constant, with the productivity trend being represented by a "time" variable. While productivity trends are interesting, they provide little guide to policy unless the details of the technologies are described.

CONCLUSION

The evaluation of social service enterprises presupposes both valid measurements of their objectives and knowledge of the

Table 2.1. Comparisons of major studies of educational production.

	Grades	Method[a]	Performance measure	Sample	Stratification	Effective school resources
Plowden	kindergarten, elementary	S	cognitive	UK individual	sex grade	teacher "ability," experience, training
Coleman	3, 6, 9, 12	V	cognitive attitudes	US individual	ethnicity region grade	almost none[b]
Goodman	4, 7, 10	V	cognitive	NYS schools	—	expenditures/student, teacher experience, specialists/student
Benson	5	V	cognitive	Calif. schools	ability social class district size	teacher and administrator salaries, enrollment, "bureaucracy"
Hanushek	6	R	cognitive	northeast urban individuals	race	teacher experience, verbal score
Kiesling	4–11	R	cognitive	NYS individuals	urban-rural school size social class	expenditures/student, enrollment

Burkhead	high school	S	cognitive dropout	Atlanta, Chicago, 200 towns	city	teacher salary, turnover, experience; age of building
Mollenkopf-Melville	9, 12	S	cognitive	100 schools individuals	—	expenditures/student, specialist/student, class size
Shaycoft	high school	V	cognitive	national individuals	—	none
Bowles-Levin	12	R	cognitive	national individuals	race	teacher experience *or* verbal score
Astin	college	V	cognitive dropout	national individuals	—	"administrative environment"
Thomas	high school	S	cognitive	206 schools	—	enrollment, class size, teacher salary schedule, teacher experience, expenditures/student

[a]V = correlational, analysis of variance; S = standardized regression; R = raw regression (coefficients given).
[b]This "finding" is challenged by Hanushek and Bowles-Levin.

relationship between the behavior of these enterprises and their success in obtaining these objectives. As our discussion of school systems indicates, both of these steps are extremely difficult to take. Even if we could obtain reliable and valid measures of educational outcome, identifying the impact of school policies on these measures is nearly impossible in the absence of controlled experimentation. Because of the high intercorrelations among school resources and social class of students, no studies reviewed here were able to identify more than two or three effective resources (see Table 2.1). To that extent these studies remain inconclusive.

Although they provide no definitive parameters for evaluating school systems, such studies are useful in conveying the impressive complexity of the educational process. First, the effect of a particular resource may depend upon the sex, grade level, ability, social class, or ethnicity of the student. Second, an increase in resources which improves one dimension of performance may have no effect or may even worsen another dimension of performance. Third, the number of resources which may have significant effects on student achievement is substantial: physical facilities; teacher experience, training, accreditation, turnover, and verbal ability; salary schedules; class size; the number of auxiliary instructional and administrative personnel; the enrollment levels of a school; and possibly expenditures on supplies. Finally, because no two studies produced the same results, it is plausible that none of these studies are reliable or that the production characteristics of each school system are unique.

Chapter 3   PRODUCTION IN BOSTON'S
ELEMENTARY SCHOOLS

*Social science is at its weakest . . . when it offers theories of
individual or collective behavior which raise the possibility, by
controlling certain inputs, of bringing about mass behavioral
change. No such knowledge now exists. Evidence is fragmented,
contradictory, incomplete.*[1]
—Daniel P. Moynihan

The specification of educational production functions is the
sine qua non of evaluating school quality, determining whether
school resources are equally distributed, and identifying effective and efficient educational policies. In this chapter I estimate
some production functions for the Boston elementary school
system. Although each school system is unique, a case study
is useful not only in spelling out the major methodological
issues but also in testing the generality of cross-system findings.

OPERATIONALIZING THE PRODUCTION MODEL

There are several classes of methodological problems inherent
in any attempt to specify educational production functions:
measuring the relevant variables (educational objectives,
school resources, social background of students); choosing the
proper mathematical form of the production function; and
arriving at a nonexperimental statistical design for estimating
the parameters of the functions.

While most of the methodological discussion of primary interest to econometricians is relegated to the appendixes, the
variables linked by the production equations are described in
some detail.

To summarize the approach, measurements of *average* student performance, school characteristics, and family background were obtained for each of Boston's elementary school districts. Six linear or additive production relationships, of the following form, are estimated by the multiple regression technique of ordinary least squares:

$$O_i = a_i + b_{i1}X_1 + b_{i2}X_2 \ldots + b_{ik}X_k + e$$

where O_i is a measure of student performance; $X_1 \ldots X_k$ are measures of school characteristics and social class; and e is an error term.

These functions have the properties of: independence and additivity of resource effects, and constant returns to resource changes. Independence implies that a unit change in X_1 has an effect of the magnitude b_{i1} on O_i, regardless of the magnitude of other resources. Additivity implies that the effect of increasing X_1 and X_2 simultaneously by one unit is simply the sum of b_{i1} and b_{i2}. Constant returns implies that the value of b_{i1} — that is, the effect of changes of X_1 on O_i — is independent of the magnitude of X_1 and fixed.

Measuring Performance

For students in Boston's elementary schools, only six indicators of performance were available to measure the myriad consequences of schooling. Although the socialization function of the schools is relatively important to administrators and to many parents in the city, no meaningful indicators of success in performing this function were obtainable.

Two measures of the attractiveness or the "holding power" of schools are the rate of average daily attendance and the rate of continuation of elementary school graduates through high school. Presumably, the more attractive schools draw greater daily attendance from the student membership.[2] Because early school experiences affect attitudes toward learning, the attractiveness of elementary schooling might generalize to secondary schooling, and students who attended more attractive elementary schools may be less likely to drop out of high school.[3]

Cognitive development is measured by the standard battery

of tests administered annually to the entire school population in Boston.[4] While, ideally, one would measure the gains of a given group of students, no such longitudinal data were available. One proxy for cognitive gains is the *difference* in median reading scores between a district's second and sixth graders, the largest range of grades available by district. A second measure is the median level of mathematical competence among fifth graders, the only group for which such scores are available.[5] Both reading and mathematics scores are measured in normative grade units divided into hundredths, for example, reading competence at 4.35 grade level.

In addition to indicators of holding power and cognitive development, there are two measures of academic achievement. In Boston, the best sixth graders are selected for admission to the elite Boys' or Girls' Latin High Schools on the basis of a competitive examination.[6] These high schools are so attractive that many students who receive elementary schooling under private secular or parochial auspices take the examination, which is the sole admissions criterion. The Latin High Schools, about 95 percent of whose alumni subsequently attend college, are by far the most important funnel through which the city's public school pupils enter institutions of higher learning. Of the fifteen remaining high schools in the city, only two consistently send more than 10 percent of their graduates to college.

One measure of academic aspiration is the percentage of sixth graders in a district who take the Latin School examination. Since there are no restrictions on who may take the test, the rate of application is a good indication of those who hope to attend college. The percentage of sixth graders passing the Latin School examination indicates the degree of academic achievement relative to other districts, the city-wide number who pass being fixed.

These six measures of performance vary rather widely among the city's fifty-six school districts (see Table 3.1). The mean level of the two measures of cognitive development deserves some comment. The average reading gains from the second to the sixth grade is only 2.3 grades, although nationally the normal gain by definition is 4.0 grades. Similarly, the level of math-

Table 3.1. Dispersion of performance indicators.

Indicator	Mean	Standard deviation	Minimum	Maximum
O_1 Attendance (percent)	91.9	2.5	87.8	96.0
O_2 Continuation (percent)	93.5	4.2	74.5	98.5
O_3 Reading gain	2.35	0.46	1.45	3.30
O_4 Math level	4.18	0.57	3.13	5.30
O_5 Latin apply (percent)	21.9	12.6	2.9	45.5
O_6 Latin pass (percent)	8.5	8.5	0.0	32.1

ematics achievement is about one grade below normal. The underachievement of Boston's children cannot be gliby explained on the basis of "cultural deprivation," for the second-grade reading level was 2.35, and the sixth-grade intelligence scores were 104, both above the national norm. These data suggest a failure of schooling.

That all six indicators of performance do not reflect some unique factor of "success in school" is obvious from their inter-correlations (see Table 3.2).* The two measures of holding power are not highly correlated with each other or with the remaining indicators of performance. These latter measures, however, are fairly well correlated with each other.

Changes in indicators of performance are unlikely to have equal impact on all students in a school district. For example, students of higher socioeconomic background and ability are highly likely to complete high school regardless of the quality of their elementary schooling. Thus, any increase in the holding power of a school has its greatest effect on the less able, or lower-class student. On the other hand, changes in the school's success in preparing students for the Latin School examination

*A principal components analysis of these correlations reveals that the first, first two, and first three "factors" or latent roots explain only 51, 68, and 81 percent of the variance in the performance indicators, respectively. This suggests that at least two or three independent dimensions of success in school are inherent in these six indicators. See D.N. Lawley and A.E. Maxwell, *Factor Analysis as a Statistical Method* (London: Butterworth, 1963).

Table 3.2. Correlations among performance indicators.

	O_1	O_2	O_3	O_4	O_5	O_6
O_1 Attendance	1.00					
O_2 Continuation	.15	1.00				
O_3 Reading	.21	.25	1.00			
O_4 Math level	.33	.37	.59[a]	1.00		
O_5 Latin apply	.06	.54[a]	.49[a]	.49[a]	1.00	
O_6 Latin pass	.31	.36	.61[a]	.56[a]	.66[a]	1.00

[a]Significant .05 (one-tail). See Allen L. Edwards, *Experimental Design in Psychological Research* (New York: Holt, Rinehart and Winston, 1968), Table Xa; $t_{.05} = 3.42$ (55 d.f., 6 variables).

will have little effect on the poor student, who is too far down the achievement scale. Perhaps only median reading and mathematics scores reflect the effects of schooling on all students. Whether schools tend to be good on all measures of achievement is tested below.

School Resources

The most easily measured and commonly used indicators of school resources are expenditures (total, current, or instructional) per student. Because of the pitfalls of expenditure measures discussed in Chapter Two, resources are better expressed in "physical" dimensions.

Teacher resources can be characterized in terms of their level of accreditation, duration of previous experience, and level of formal training. Organizational characteristics can be described by enrollments, class size distributions, and teacher turnover. For each district in Boston, we have the following resource data:

S_1 (percentage of teachers accredited): The effect of accreditation on student performance must be interpreted with care. A teacher acquires permanent status or accreditation by passing an examination designed and administered by the Boston School Committee. Although the test may be an invalid indicator of teaching skill, the perquisites of nonpermanent status are so paltry (no contract, eighteen dollars per day, no paid holidays or sick leave) that only the least qualified of the "reserve army" of teachers are likely to accept such positions. Consequently, accreditation becomes a self-fulfilling measure of quality.

S_2 (percentage of teachers with a master's degree or beyond): It is assumed that more training imparts skills, or reveals greater motivation to teach, or produces a self-image conducive to better teaching.

S_3 (percentage of permanent teachers with over ten years of experience): It is assumed that experience improves teaching ability. The only data available on experience indicated the percentage of teachers with 0–5, 5–10, and over 10 years of experience, the last category being the best predictor of student success.[7]

S_4 (percentage of students in uncrowded classrooms): Most classrooms in Boston have thirty-five seats, so that rooms with more students require using makeshift desks or doubling up on seating. At any rate, a crowding measure provides additional information on the distribution of class sizes.

S_5 (pupil to teacher ratio): This ratio includes in the denominator the specialized school staff, who are especially important in the seventh-and eighth-grade curricula. This serves, furthermore, as a proxy for class size.*

S_6 (annual rate of teacher turnover): Defined as the percentage of new teachers hired in relation to all teachers, turnover may be a symptom of an undesirable teaching environment from two points of view. When vacancies occur in desirable districts, teachers from other schools transfer. Only the least desirable schools have to hire from outside the system. Annual turnover is also a proxy for turnover within the school year, which is assumed to be educationally disruptive.[8]

S_7 (number of students per district): This variable permits us to test for economies or diseconomies of scale.[9]

*Data on median class size are available but ignored because: 1) pupil-teacher ratio is a good proxy for class size ($r = .55$);2) pupil-teacher ratio is more highly correlated with performance than is class size, *ceteris paribus*; and 3) both variables appearing in the same production function leads to severe multicollinearity. Comparisons of the best regressions with either pupil-teacher ratio or median class size entered show little difference, and in no case is median class size (in the range of 22 to 36) inversely and significantly related to performance.

Characterizing the quality of school buildings and equipment is problematical. Ideally, one would like to relate student performance to a wide range of building characteristics. In the absence of such data, one would like to know the present value of school facilities in order to compare the marginal productivities of capital versus current expenditures. Unfortunately, neither type of data is available. This statistical gap has a political analogue: the School Committee in recent years has been so reluctant to engage in construction activity that capital spending does not seem to be an important policy option. The school buildings in Boston are so old and in such a common state of disrepair that there are probably no educationally significant differences among the vast majority of pre-World War II plants. In fact, in 1962 "experts" from the city's redevelopment authority recommended that 75 percent of the school plants be abandoned by the end of the decade.[10] Although it is not clear that any of the building standards used by the experts in evaluation have validity (educational impact), the age of school plants (S_8) may be a surrogate for obsolescence and general safety.[11]

Most of the school inputs vary widely enough among the Boston districts to test their impact on performance (see Table 3.3). For most of the inputs, the maximum value is more than twice the minimum.

In order to identify the effects of particular school inputs, the set of inputs used should be relatively uncorrelated. Because

Table 3.3. Dispersion of school resource indicators.

Resource	Mean	Standard deviation	Minimum	Maximum
Current expenditure/ADM	$364	59	275	580
Instructional expenditure/ADM	$307	46	234	463
Teachers, permanent (percent)	76.3	9.9	54.6	00.0
Teachers, masters + (percent)	47.9	11.1	23.6	73.7
Permanent, > ten years experience (percent)	50.5	12.2	30.9	80.3
Pupils uncrowded (percent)	85.3	14.2	44.7	100.0
Pupil:teacher	23.3	4.1	13.8	30.2
Teacher turnover (percent)	14.6	9.6	0.0	55.3
District enrollment	1199	382	519	2284
Age of plant (years)	53.5	17.3	22.0	96.0

the multiple correlations between each input and all the others in our sample are fairly high (see diagonal, Table 3.4), we cannot expect to identify the effects of each resource on performance.

Social Characteristics

The Coleman Report distinguishes the effects of family on student performance from that of the peer group. Data from the present study, aggregated by school district, do not permit us to distinguish these effects. Such distinction is not essential if we are merely concerned with holding social characteristics constant in order to focus on school resource effects.

Ideally, the social environment should be described in terms of subculture or ethos. While the Coleman and Plowden surveys come closest to this ideal in measuring parental attitudes and material goods at home, most other studies reviewed in the previous chapter measure social background by one or more status variables, such as father's occupation or income. This last tradition is followed here.

It is not clear which and how many social status characteristics best describe culture. Among my data are the traditional measures of social class (income, education, occupation, rent)

Table 3.4. Correlations among school resources.[a]

	S_1	S_2	S_3	S_4	S_5	S_6	S_7	S_8
S_1 Permanent	.57[c]							
S_2 Masters	−.22	.32						
S_3 Experience	.09	−.40	.45[c]					
S_4 Uncrowded	.08	.18	−.05	.39[c]				
S_5 Pupil:teacher	.59[b]	−.28	.11	−.40	.64[c]			
S_6 Turnover	.01	−.06	−.34	−.14	.16	.31		
S_7 Enrollment	.31	−.29	−.07	−.39	.51	.08	.41[c]	
S_8 Age of building	.18	−.09	−.29	.20	−.14	.22	−.18	.32

[a]Diagonal elements (in italics) are coefficients of determination of particular input by other inputs and a social-class variable used in regressions below.

[b]Significant .10 (two-tail, 55 d.f., 8 variables), after Edwards, *Experimental Design*, Table Xa.

[c]Significant .05 (one-tail, 49 d.f., 8 tests).

as well as measures of preschool preparation (intelligence scores and first-grade reading readiness). Because these variables are so highly intercorrelated (see Table 3.5), I choose to represent cultural background by that single variable that contributes most to explaining the variance in performance, holding school resources constant. By this standard, percentage of males in white collar occupations is best. The addition of measures of reading readiness and intelligence as control variables left the coefficients of school resources virtually unchanged, so they were excluded from further consideration. While measures of racial composition left the equations similarly unchanged, the effects of race on performance are considered in more detail below.

SOME WORKING HYPOTHESES

In this section a large number of linear production functions are explored in order to produce the "best" description of the relationship between school resources and student performance.

Table 3.5. Correlations among social class and racial variables.

	C_1	C_2	C_3	C_4	C_5	R_1	R_2
C_1 Median family income	1.00						
C_2 White collar workers (percent)	.78[a]	1.00					
C_3 Adult median school year	.81[a]	.88[a]	1.00				
C_4 Adults completing high school (percent)	.80[a]	.91[a]	.97[a]	1.00			
C_5 Median contract rent	.74[a]	.88[a]	.89[a]	.91[a]	1.00		
R_1 Students white (percent)	.59[a]	.44[a]	.34	.31	.13	1.00	
R_2 Population white (percent)	.53[a]	.48[a]	.36	.34	.16	.92[a]	1.00

[a]Significant .05 (one-tail, 55 d.f., 7 variables), after Edwards, *Experimental Design*, Table Xa.

As a first approximation, measures of student performance are regressed against expenditures per student and social class (see Table 3.6). In none of the six regressions is the expenditure coefficient significant, but in five they are positive (sign test insignificant at .10 level). These findings hold whether total current or instructional expenditures are considered. On the

Table 3.6. Working hypothesis: Performance as a function of school expenditures.

Independent variable	Attendance (percent)		Continuation (percent)	
	b	t	b	t
Constant	88.2		86.9	
Instructional expenditure/ADM	0.01	1.34	0.002	0.0
White collar (percent)	0.02	0.8	0.20	4.88[a]
R^2 (corrected)	.00		.37[a]	

Independent variable	Reading		Mathematics	
	b	t	b	t
Constant	148.1		245.6	
Instructional expenditure/ADM	0.06	0.6	−0.08	−0.7
White collar (percent)	2.24	5.17[a]	3.25	6.82[a]
R^2 (corrected)	.37[a]		.45[a]	

Independent variable	Latin application (percent)		Latin pass (percent)	
	b	t	b	t
Constant	−6.9		−13.1	
Instructional expenditure/ADM	0.02	0.9	0.03	1.56
White collar (percent)	0.74	7.08[a]	0.39	7.44[a]
R^2 (corrected)	.46[a]		.26[a]	

[a]Significant .05 (one-tail, six tests).

other hand, in all the regressions there is a positive relationship between social class and student performance, and in five regressions these coefficients are highly significant. This evidence suggests that *either* expenditures are a poor surrogate for "true" school resources *or* that resources have little or no impact on performance.

As a second approximation, student performance is regressed against all physical measures of school resources and social class. The coefficients of determination for these regressions are consistently higher than for the corresponding expenditure regressions (see Table 3.7). These equations show that resources, when properly measured, do indeed influence performance. Not all eight school inputs, however, affect all performance measures, and at most two resource coefficients are significant in the expected direction in any equation.

The existence of multicollinearity among the independent variables hinders the specification of these working models. Multicollinearity is the existence or near existence of linear dependence among independent variables, such that the determinant of the X'X matrix approaches zero. In common-sense terms, multicollinearity means high multiple correlations among these variables as shown in Table 3.4. While there is no clear-cut criterion for determining whether these correlations are too high, the existence of multicollinearity is suggested by the high zero order and multiple correlations among these variables, and the small determinant of the correlation matrix (.066). Two symptoms of multicollinearity are the paucity of significant regression coefficients and the several cases in which coefficients have the "wrong" or unexpected sign.[12]

Despite the existence of multicollinearity, three suggestive hypotheses emerge. First, the several production functions are quite different from each other in the amount of variance explained and in the pattern of regression coefficients. Second, no resource variable has a consistently significant coefficient in every regression. Third, in every regression teacher turnover has a negative effect on performance, and, in all but one, increasing enrollment has a positive although insignificant

Table 3.7. Working hypothesis: Performance as a function of physical resources.[a]

Independent variables	Attendance (percent)		Continuation (percent)		Reading	
	b	t	b	t	b	t
Accredited (percent)	.092	1.86	.072	1.06	−.438	−0.62
Masters (percent)	.028	.80	−.053	−1.08	−.017	−0.03
Experienced (percent)	−.003	−.08	.044	.90	1.355	2.65[b]
Uncrowded (percent)	−.014	−.48	.009	.22	.665	1.60
Pupil:teacher	−.090	−.70	−.293	−1.64	1.149	0.62
Teacher turnover (percent)	−.015	−2.59[b]	−.077	−1.38	−1.144	−1.97
Enrollment	.000	.01	.003	2.15	.014	0.91
Age of building	.010	−.43	−.025	−0.79	.372	1.15
White collar (percent)	−.034	−.92	.161	3.20[b]	1.373	2.63[b]
Constant	86		133		144	
R² (corrected)	.08		.38[b]		.43[b]	

Independent variables	Mathematics		Latin application (percent)		Latin pass (percent)	
	b	t	b	t	b	t
Accredited (percent)	1.306	1.93	.355	1.90	.079	.56
Masters (percent)	−1.007	−2.08	.178	1.32	.046	.45
Experienced (percent)	.746	1.53	−.059	.43	.084	.83
Uncrowded (percent)	−.152	−.38	−.016	−.14	.152	1.84
Pupil:teacher	1.087	.61	−.131	−.27	−.121	−.33
Teacher turnover (percent)	1.869	−3.36[b]	−.205	−1.33	−.246	−2.12
Enrollment	−.012	−.79	.004	.85	.004	1.36
Age of building	−.861	−2.78[b]	−.009	−.11	−.003	−.05
White collar (percent)	1.675	3.35[b]	.601	4.33[b]	.227	2.18
Constant	335		−35.5		−22.9	
R² (corrected)	.66[b]		.47[b]		.34[b]	

[a]$|X'X = .066$.
[b]Significant, .05 (one-tail, six tests).

effect on performance. No other resource variable has coefficients whose pattern of signs is unexpected by chance.

BEST LINEAR PRODUCTION FUNCTIONS

The "best" regression equations were obtained by selecting that subset of school inputs which best predicts performance, as indicated by the standard error of estimate. The search for this subset was facilitated by a stepwise regression algorithm that enters only those independent variables whose coefficients have a t-value of at least 1.00 and removes those already entered whose t-value falls below 1.00. A t-value of 1.00 means that both the probability of accepting a variable which truly has no effect (error of commission) and the probability of rejecting a variable whose effect was estimated correctly (error of omission) are both equal to .17. In an exploratory study such as this, I feel that lowering the probability of an error of commission is not worth the cost of increasing the probability of an error of omission.

The regression equations that produce the smallest errors of estimate include relatively few inputs whose identity varies from equation to equation. In other words, a change in a particular school resource will not necessarily affect all aspects of performance. Social class appears in every equation (see Table 3.8). Of the several school inputs, teacher turnover appears in all six equations, but no other input has such universal impact.

Five of the six measures of performance are significantly related to a subset of independent variables representing social class and school resources. The best linear models are discussed in detail below, while the findings for multiplicative models are presented in Table 3.9.

Performance is highly related to other teacher characteristics besides turnover. As suggested by previous studies, both accreditation and experience in teachers tend to have positive effects on performance. On the other hand, the findings do not support the hypothesis that more teacher training has a significantly positive effect on student performance.

Table 3.8. Best linear model: Regression coefficients (standard errors of coefficients).

Performance measure	Teachers				Organizational				Social class
	Accredited (percent)	Experienced (percent)	Masters (percent)	Turnover (percent)	Uncrowding (percent)	Pupil: Teacher	Enrollment	Age of building	White collar (percent)
Attendance $R^{2a} = .13$	.064 (.032)		.029 (.028)	-.108[b] (.035)					-.030 (.029)
Continuation $R^2 = .40$[b]	.059		-.068 (.042)	-.074 (.053)		-.310 (.135)	.004[b] (.001)		.155[b] (.044)
Reading $R^2 = .45$[b]		1.360[b] (.430)		-1.110 (.550)	.523[b] (.35)		.015 (.014)	.291 (.291)	1.19[b] (.49)
Mathematics $R^2 = .67$[b]	1.410 (.473)	.891 (.458)	-1.079[c] (.450)	-1.776[b] (.512)				-.898[b] (.285)	1.582[b] (.466)
Latin application $R^2 = .51$[b]	.309[b] (.125)		.155 (.114)	-.200 (.140)			.004 (.004)		.582[b] (.118)
Latin pass $R^2 = .38$[b]		.102 (.084)		-.241[b] (.108)	.180[b] (.069)		.004 (.003)		.231[b] (.097)

[a] R^2 corrected throughout table for degrees of freedom.
[b] Significant .05 (one tail, six tests).
[c] Significant, with "wrong" sign.

Table 3.9. Best multiplicative model: Regression coefficients (standard errors of coefficients).

Performance measure	Teachers				Organizational				Social class
	Accredited (percent)	Experienced (percent)	Masters (percent)	Turn-over (percent)	Uncrowding (percent)	Pupil: Teacher	Enroll-ment	Age of building	White collar (percent)
Attendance $R^2 = .14$	.054 (.025)			-.012[a] (.004)	.003 (.002)				.065[a] (.014)
Continuation $R^2 = .38$[a]	.068 (.048)		-.045 (.023)			-.096[a] (.037)	.035 (.020)		.176[a] (.060)
Reading $R^2 = .36$[a]		.184[a] (.071)		-.049 (.031)					.176[a] (.060)
Mathematics $R^2 = .62$[a]	.288[a] (.093)	.055 (.043)	-.060 (.056)	-.029 (.013)				-.076[a] (.031)	.174[a] (.034)
Latin application $R^2 = .46$[a]	1.479[a] (.649)			-.129 (.124)					1.279[a] (.228)
Latin pass $R^2 = .54$[a]				.591[a] (.176)	.310[a] (.098)		1.010[a] (.330)		1.483[a] (.332)

[a]Significant .05 (one-tail, six tests).

Performance is not significantly related to the pupil-teacher ratio within the range of the data (14:1 to 31:1). Extremely crowded classes, with more than thirty-five students, however, have negative effects on reading gains and success in passing the Latin examination. Whether the number 35 has "magical" properties or simply indicates the capacity of classrooms cannot be determined in the absence of external evidence.

There appear to be economies of scale within the range of enrollments (500–2300) observed in our sample. Whether economies diminish and diseconomies appear at some higher enrollment levels is discussed in the next chapter.

Older buildings significantly impair performance in only one function. Perhaps the weakness of this effect is due to the invalidity of considering age as synonymous with plant quality.

Comparisons with Other Studies

Continuation. Burkhead found that gross measures of school resources (building age, faculty salaries, library expenditures) influenced the high school dropout rate in two big cities, but not in the two hundred small communities studied. I find that elementary school resources also have an impact on continuation through high school. Clearly, there are trade-offs between earlier and later expenditure of resources, but the Burkhead data do not permit estimation of either the marginal costs or marginal effects of high school policies.

College Attendance. Burkhead found that high school resources had no significant effect on aspirations toward, or the likelihood of, college attendance. While I do not measure college attendance directly, I find that elementary school resources have an impact on applying for and gaining admissions to the Latin High Schools, which is tantamount to college entrance. The contrast between our findings presumably reflects the diminishing returns of school resources with respect to student age.

Reading Scores. The present analysis lends additional support to the hypothesis that teacher quality influences reading achievement. The comparable study of Hanushek shows that teacher experience and verbal ability exert positive effects on sixth-grade reading scores of both whites and Negroes. Similarly, Burkhead found a positive effect of experience on eleventh-grade reading gains and twelfth-grade reading levels. In addition, he found that teacher turnover had a negative effect on tenth-grade reading scores.

Mathematics Scores. Hanushek found that sixth-grade mathematics and reading score production functions were quite similar. In the present analysis, teacher experience exerts a positive effect in both functions, but the other arguments of the functions differ.

Racial Segregation and Performance

Racial segregation can be held harmful on two different grounds: if school resources are biased in favor of white schools, then Negroes in segregated schools would perform worse than in integrated schools; and segregation may be educationally harmful per se, even with equal resources. This latter hypothesis is testable only with utmost difficulty because, in most cases observed, segregated and integrated schools differ not only in resources but in socioeconomic composition. The production analysis above permits us to hold both school resources and social class constant in order to test the effects of racial composition on performance.

My production functions were derived on the assumption that the same coefficients for resources and social class described behavior for whites and Negroes. To test the effects of race, school districts are divided into four classes: forty white districts (50–100 percent Caucasian), eight integrated districts (25–50 percent Caucasian), seven Negro districts (less than 25 percent Caucasian), and one predominantly Chinese district. Most of the white districts have over 90 percent Caucasians and most of the Negro districts less than 20 percent Caucasians. The "less than 50 percent Caucasian" categories are particularly interesting because the Commonwealth of Massachusetts has articulated a policy of eliminating "imbalanced" schools defined as containing less than 50 percent white students.

An analysis of variance is performed to determine whether the residuals of the production regressions are related to racial categories. In addition, pairwise comparisons of mean residuals are performed by the protected t-test (see Table 3.10).*

The analysis reveals that the racial composition of the school districts is not significantly related to performance, *ceteris paribus*. In Boston, the average student in a Caucasian school does not perform better than the average student in a Negro school when social class and school resources are equal. Similarly the average student in an integrated school does not perform differently from the average student in mostly Caucasian or mostly Negro schools. In other words, there do not seem to be clear gains to both white and black by integration per se when social class and school resource factors are held constant, at least for the aspects of performance measured here.

There are three exceptions to the above generalizations. Students in integrated schools perform worse, *ceteris paribus*, in mathematics than students in white schools. Whether the loss from integration hits the whites, the blacks, or both in the integrated school is not clear. The second and third exceptions reflect the overachievement of the Chinese students with respect to taking and passing the Latin School examination. This may be interpreted as a reflection of the value of scholarship in the Chinese subculture rather than as a result of racial segregation.

These findings are not too different from those of Hanushek, who studied the effect of racial composition on the performance of individual whites and Negroes in the Northeast and Midwest.[13] For whites, only when the Negro concentration exceeded 75 percent in the classroom did the percentage of Negroes have any harmful effect on achievement. For Negroes, only when their concentration exceeds 45 percent (nearly equal to the "imbalance point" under Massachusetts law) in a school

---

*The more paired comparisons one makes, the more likely it becomes that some statistically significant differences will emerge by chance. To protect against the rejection of a true null hypothesis of no difference, one can insist upon higher t values in his tests. See Allen L. Edwards, *Experimental Design in Psychological Research* (New York: Holt, Rinehart and Winston, 1968), 134–138, Tables Xa-Xe.

Table 3.10. Racial composition of school and performance, residuals of production functions.

Attendance	Mean	Standard deviation	n	Significant analysis of variance
White	.245	2.407	40	none
Integrated	−0.471	1.040	8	
Negro	−0.950	1.003	7	
Chinese	1.600	—	1	
TOTAL	−0.000	2.135	56	
Continuation				
White	−.270	2.980	same	none
Integrated	1.000	1.890		
Negro	.275	4.247		
Chinese	1.500	—		
TOTAL	−.002	3.035		
Reading				
White	−1.087	31.219	same	none
Integrated	−14.971	31.615		
Negro	12.287	29.697		
Chinese	50.300	—		
TOTAL	0.005	31.775		
Mathematics				
White	6.317	30.199	same	WxIxN : $F = 3.70$[b]
Integrated	−24.314	18.367		WxI : $F = 6.69$[a]
Negro	−12.300	39.906		
Chinese	15.600	—		
TOTAL	0.005	31.888		
Latin application				
White	−1.355	7.842	same	WxC : $F = 8.72$[a]
Integrated	0.486	7.733		IxC : $F = 8.25$[a]
Negro	3.512	6.229		
Chinese	23.100	—		
TOTAL	0.007	8.242		
Latin pass				
White	−0.265	6.033	same	WxC : $F = 9.79$[a]
Integrated	−1.586	4.611		IxC : $F = 13.24$[a]
Negro	0.150	4.447		NxC : $F = 10.22$[a]
Chinese	21.100	—		
TOTAL	0.011	6.254		

[a] $p < .05$, Edwards, *Experimental Design*, Table Xa.
[b] $p < .10$, ibid., Table Xb.

does this percentage have any effect on achievement. The racial composition effects, however, are extremely small. Mean educational performance of Negroes in a classroom with 75 percent Negroes is, *ceteris paribus*, .95 of that when the class-room has less than 45 percent Negro. Such estimates of the racial effect are biased upward because social class of peers is uncontrolled and race and social class are highly correlated.

The present conclusions and those of Hanushek conflict with those from a study of segregation in California.[14] When con-trolled for individual social class and race, aspirations and achievement are greater in either white or middle-class schools than in black or lower-class schools. This study does not, how-ever, control for school quality, which is probably correlated with racial and class composition of the student body. In fact, no study including this one has yet properly controlled for school resources, and both race and social-class characteris-tics of peers.[15]

Boston's Negro population is not especially deprived eco-nomically in comparison with the non-Negro population, for only about 30 percent of the variance in the socioeconomic sta-tus of the city's districts is associated with racial composition. The finding that school performance and racial composition are unrelated, *ceteris paribus,* suggests that the city's Negro students are not "culturally deprived" relative to the Caucasian (mostly Irish and Italian) public school population. In other words, Negro achievement in Boston can be explained by social class and school resources without any recourse to notions of the inferiority of "black subculture" or genes. If anything, both Negroes and Caucasians are culturally deprived relative to the Chinese students.

Evaluating School Quality

The production functions enable us to evaluate school quality in a relatively valid manner. Each regression coefficient repre-sents the effect of an input on performance. The sum of inputs weighted by their appropriate coefficients indicates the impact

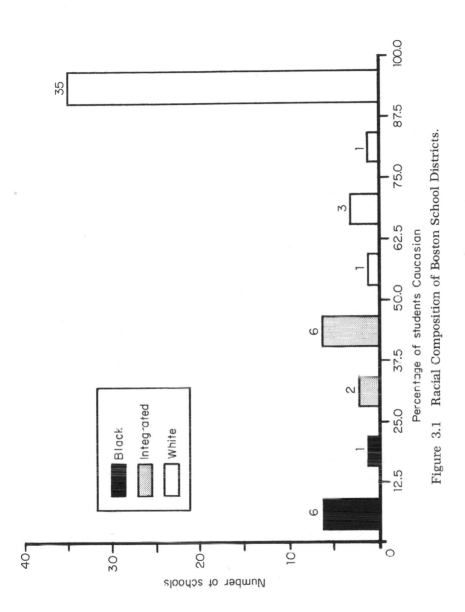

Figure 3.1   Racial Composition of Boston School Districts.

65

of the school on performance, which is the output of the school. For example:

Reading output (in hundredths of a grade) =
    .58 × % uncrowding + 1.30 × % experienced
    − 1.06 × % teaching turnover + .01 × enrollment

For each measure of performance there is a corresponding production function, set of regression coefficients, and quality measure. Schools effective on one output measure are not necessarily effective on all measures. While the correlation among output measures are generally positive, they are far from unity even among related holding power or cognitive outputs (see Table 3.11). The implication of this finding is that there is no unique, technically deducible system of evaluating schools. Only after the political decision is made as to the relative importance of various outputs can an evaluation be made. Since different outputs affect different segments of the population, there is likely to be great dissensus on the "proper" output prices. Given a set of prices (P_i), the quality equals:

$$Q = P_1Q_1 + P_2Q_2 \ldots P_nQ_n = \sum_i P_i \sum_j b_{ij}X_j$$

CONTRIBUTION OF SCHOOL RESOURCES TO PERFORMANCE

There has been considerable controversy in recent years over the question "Do schools make a difference?" Much of the controversy emerges from the divergent approaches to expressing

Table 3.11. Correlations among quality measures.

	Q_1	Q_2	Q_3	Q_4	Q_5	Q_6
Q_1 Attendance	1.00					
Q_2 Continuation	.30	1.00				
Q_3 Reading	.74	.18	1.00			
Q_4 Mathematics	.76	.25	.56	1.00		
Q_5 L. application	.82	.40	.59	.59	1.00	
Q_6 L. pass	.79	.36	.86	.62	.61	1.00

the relationship between school resources and performance. Here three of these approaches are explored: contribution of school resources to *level* of performance; the *elasticity* or responsiveness of performance to school resource changes; and the effect of inequalities and bias in the distribution of school resources on *variations* in performance.

School Factors and Level of Performance

The linear production model states that the magnitude of performance is determined by the sum of school influences, home influences, and a constant term. The constant term represents the unallocatable effects of the most deprived home and/or of the most meager school.[16] By focusing on the average levels of performance, school resources, and social class, the relative contribution of school resources to performance levels can be estimated.

There are two plausible measures of the contribution of schooling to performance. On the one hand, under the assumption that the constant term reflects home influences, the relative contribution of schooling is the ratio of the weighted sum of school resources to performance. On the other hand, under the assumption that the constant term reflects school influence, the relative contribution of schooling is increased by the ratio of the constant to performance. Comparing measures under the former assumption, it is observed that the relative contribution of schooling is high for reading gains and low for continuation rates (see Table 3.12). Even if only a small fraction of the constant term can be allocated to school influences, then the effects of school inputs are by no means inconsequential.

Elasticity of Performance to Input Changes

A second way to answer the question "Do schools make a difference?" is to focus on the responsiveness of performance to changes in inputs. One measure of this responsiveness is the elasticity: $(dO/O)/(dS/S)$. Comparing the constant elasticities (coefficients) from the best multiplicative models to elasticities at the mean from the best linear models (consider-

Table 3.12. Contribution of school resources to average level of performance.

Performance measure	Average level of perform-ance	Con-stant	School	Home	Contribution of school resources (percent)	
					Mini-mum[a]	Maxi-mum[b]
Attendance	91.9	88.1	4.7	–0.9	5.1	101.0
Continuation	93.4	91.7	–3.0	4.7	–3.2	95.0
Reading	2.35	0.71	1.29	0.35	54.8	85.2
Mathematics	4.18	2.49	1.23	0.46	29.4	89.0
Latin application	21.9	–27.4	32.1	17.2	21.4	147.0
Latin pass	8.5	–21.6	22.8	7.3	14.2	268.0

[a]Minimum $= \dfrac{\text{school}}{\text{performance}}$ x 100.00

[b]Maximum $= \dfrac{\text{school} + \text{constant}}{\text{performance}}$ x 100.00

ing coefficients significant at $p = .05$), one finds that although the same resource variables are not always included in the best equations of both forms, the elasticities are generally similar (see Table 3.13).

The elasticities indicate that improving the quality of all resources by 10 percent leads to rather high increases in the Latin School outputs (10-23 percent); moderate increases in the cognitive outputs (1-5 percent); and low increases in holding power (less than 1 percent). The elasticities from the cognitive equations are consistent with those computed by Hanushek. The magnitude of elasticities suggest that the performance of the advanced students is more responsive to changes in school resources than performance of poor students, a finding consistent with that of Benson and that of Kiesling.

Contribution of School Factors to Variance in Performance

Regression analysis identifies the effect of changes in school resources on changes in performance. While the identification of regression coefficients is facilitated when resources vary

Table 3.13 Resource elasticity of performance: Linear models at mean input values versus multiplicative models.[c]

Performance measure	Model	Accredited (percent)	Experienced (percent)	Masters[b] (percent)	Turnover (percent)	Uncrowding (percent)	Pupil: Teacher	Enrollment[a]	TOTAL
Attendance	L				-.02				.02
	M				-.01				.01
Continuation	L							.04	.04
	M			-.05			-.10		.10
Reading	L		.33			.21			.54
	M		.18						.18
Mathematics	L	.26		-.12	-.06				.32
	M	.26	.06	-.06	-.03				.35
Latin application	L	1.08							1.08
	M	1.48							1.48
Latin pass	L				-.52	1.80			2.32
	M				-.59	.31		1.01	1.91

[a]Assume increase better.
[b]Masters omitted from totals because of perverse signs.
[c]L = linear model at mean; M = multiplicative model; blank stands for zero elasticity.

69

over a wide range in a relatively uncorrelated manner, the amount of variation in input and output variables in the sample observed is of only secondary interest. In contrast, analysis of variance treats variations in the observed data as a matter of primary concern. This latter form of analysis focuses on explaining the historically observed variation in performance rather than in predicting the effects of policy changes.

When independent variables are highly correlated, not only is it difficult to specify the regression coefficient with great accuracy, it is also difficult to identify the variance in output explained by variance in input. The variation in the output depends upon the variation in inputs, the correlation among inputs, and the regression coefficients for these inputs:

$$\sigma_o^2 = b_s^2\sigma_s^2 + b_c^2\sigma_c^2 + 2r_{sc}b_sb_c\sigma_s\sigma_c + \text{error variance}$$

where s = school resources and c = social class.

When there is a high positive correlation between school resources and social class, the contribution of either factor to the explained variance depends upon the order in which it is introduced into the analysis. Because social-class factors were introduced into the analysis prior to school factors in the Coleman Report, the relative contribution of school factors to performance variance was found to be trival. A reversal of this order shows that the contribution of school factors is far from trivial.[17]

The *total variance explained* is independent of the order in which the explanatory variables are introduced into the analysis. The unique contribution of either factor ($b_i^2\sigma_i^2$) is the marginal contribution to explained variance when such a factor is introduced last. The explained variance minus the sum of unique variances is the joint contribution ($2r_{sc}b_sb_c\sigma_s\sigma_c$), which is conceptually as well as mathematically unallocatable between school and home factors (see Table 3.14).

The relative contributions of school resources, social class, and both factors jointly varies among production functions (Table 3.15). The unique contribution of social class to the variance in performance is 5 percent on the average, which is much less than the joint contribution of class and school re-

Table 3.14. Sample analyses of variance: Reading gains.

Source of variation	Sum of squares	Degrees of freedom	Mean square	△R²
Social class	37,933	1	37,933	.33
add School	20,619	4	5,155	.18
all input	58,552	5		.51
residual	55,711	50	1,114	
TOTAL	104,263	56		
School	44,092	4	11,023	.42
add Social class	6,560	1	6,560	.09
all input	58,552	5		.51
residual	55,711	50	1,114	
TOTAL	104,263	56		

Table 3.15. Percentage contribution of social class and school resources to variations in performance.

Performance measure	Unique social class	Unique school resources	Joint class/ resource	Total ex- plained	Un- explained
Attendance	0	13	0	13	87
Continuation	13	17	18	48	52
Reading	9	18	24	51	49
Mathematics	0	30	37	67	33
Latin application	4	6	41	51	49
Latin pass	2	8	30	40	60
AVERAGE	5	15	25	45	55

sources to the explained variance. In no case is the unique contribution of social class greater than that of school resources. In all but one case, the joint contribution is greater than either unique contribution.

The analysis of variance indicates the effects of eliminating biases and inequalities in the distribution of school resources. Even if inequalities in the distribution of resources remained fixed, the elimination of bias in resource distribution reduces interdistrict variation in performance. This is because eliminating bias is defined as reducing the joint variation (or correlation) between school resources and social class to zero. For example, the elimination of bias in resource distribution reduces interdistrict variation in continuation rates 18 percent and in reading gains 24 percent.

The elimination of resource inequalities means reducing the variance in school resources to zero. The effect of resource equalization is the reduction of interdistrict variations in continuation rates by an additional 17 percent and in reading gains by an additional 18 percent of the original variance.

Unless school systems undertake compensatory policies, which distribute resources in inverse magnitudes to social class (negative correlation), the irreducible minimum interdistrict variation in performance equals the variation due to social class and the unexplained variation. For example, the elimination of resource inequalities reduces interdistrict variation in reading gains to 58 percent of its former magnitude.

Production Possibilities

A concise description of the effectiveness of schooling is the production possibilities hyperspace. The frontier of this hyperspace describes the maximum feasible combinations of all outputs. The production possibilities frontier for Boston is obtained by inserting extreme input values into the production functions, holding social class constant. Some extreme values are logically determined — the percentage of teachers accredited can only range from zero to 100 percent. The pupil-teacher ratio ranges within the extreme values of the sample, 14 to 30, because there are probably discontinuities in the production functions beyond these limits. Enrollment ranges up to 1650 students, at which point scale economies begin to vanish, as shown in the next chapter. Turnover is ignored because it is relatively uncontrollable on a district level.

Although we assume a model of joint production, the production possibility frontier does not reduce to a single point. This is because maximizing the percentage of master's degrees raises two outputs but decreases two others. The frontier then is a convex combination of two vertexes in six-dimensional space.

Actual production in Boston is considerably inside the frontier, so defined (see Table 3.16). Whether this is due to a budget constraint or to inefficient use of a given budget is discussed in the next chapter.

CONCLUSIONS

Any cross-sectional statistical analysis of education should be interpreted with a tremendous degree of caution. Even longitudinal studies of "natural experiments" in education are no substitute for carefully controlled laboratory experiments in which wide variations in resources are applied to students. Second, no generalizations about the educational process should be made on the basis of findings about a few performance criteria or a few school characteristics. Surely, we would want to know about the effect of more intangible resources, such as "classroom atmosphere," on the elusive aspects of cognitive development (problem solving, creativity) and upon socialization (emotional maturity, citizenship).

In the face of these caveats, the current evidence suggests several hypotheses about the relationship between schooling and student performance. First, there is no evidence that simply spending more money per student improves performance unless the money is spent in rather specific ways. Spending more money by decreasing class size does not seem to be educationally effective, at least within the range of sixteen to thirty-

Table 3.16. Production possibilities frontier.[a]

	Attendance	Continuation	Reading	Mathematics	Latin school Application	Pass
Vertex 1	94.5	99.6	2.54	4.79	9.9	13.0
Vertex 2	97.4	92.8	2.54	3.71	25.4	13.0
Actual	92.8	88.7	2.00	3.72	4.7	1.2

[a]Including constant terms of production functions.

five students. On the other hand, spending money to reduce crowding, whereby classes with more than thirty-five students can be eliminated, has some effect, at least in Boston. Spending more money to hire more accredited and more experienced teachers is generally effective, while spending more money to hire teachers with more formal training is ineffective. Other studies suggest that increasing the salary scales of teachers and administrators tends to attract more educationally effective personnel. Because of scale economies, expenditures can be reduced and performance improved as enrollments increase to about two thousand students. Finally, in the area of plant and equipment, there seems to be a weak positive relationship between performance and the newness of school buildings.

The policy implications of these findings is that schooling makes a difference. Indeed, changes in school resources within the very narrow range observed in nature can make a substantial impact on student performance. A change of 10 percent in the level of resources can translate into performance changes of from 1 to 20 percent. The elimination of resource inequalities among Boston's schools can reduce interdistrict variation from 22 to 57 percent.

A second set of findings concerns the relationship between race and performance when school resources and social class are held constant. In Boston, where race and class are not highly correlated, the racial composition of a district seems to have little effect on six performance measures. These findings do not suggest that racial integration is an ineffective policy. It may be quite effective in improving the performance of Negro children if Negro schools get worse resources than white schools or if racial integration means social-class integration.[18]

Racial integration is probably not politically feasible in most big cities at the present time, even if it were pedagogically desirable, because of pressures from both whites and blacks. This political impasse suggests that alternatives to racial integration for upgrading performance of Negro youngsters must be developed. The production functions developed here suggest that effective alternatives do exist. "Compensatory education" is probably more palatable politically and is possibly more effective educationally than racial integration. By compensatory education I do not necessarily mean remedial curricula, but rather more and better resources for Negro and lower-class schools in accord with the realities of educational production functions.

The regression coefficients specified in the several production functions provide powerful tools for evaluating school quality. Since these coefficients reflect the effectiveness of inputs, they provide an intuitively meaningful set of weights for summarizing school inputs. For example, one measure of school quality is the contribution of resources to mathematics achievement. This contribution is estimated by the sum of inputs, weighted by the regression coefficients from the mathematics production function. Such a quality index permits us to rank schools, to measure the absolute impact of schools, and to calculate the percentage differences in quality between schools.

An index of quality can be calculated from the regression coefficients of any production function. Because these coefficients are different in each function, the indexes are neither identical nor even perfectly correlated. The implication of this finding is that there is no technically deducible method for providing a unique evaluation of school systems. A political choice as to the relative importance of the various outcomes of schooling must first be specified.

Are the Boston schools doing a good job in educating children? In order to reply to this query, one must also ask "In comparison to what?" Compared to national norms, reading gains in Boston from the second to the sixth grade are only 2.3, despite the fact that both second-grade reading scores and sixth-grade intelligence quotients are above the national norms. The underachievement of Boston's elementary school children cannot be interpreted unequivocally as a failure of the system A sympathetic interpretation is that the system uses what educational resources it has efficiently, but simply lacks sufficient resources. An alternative interpretation, suggested in the next chapter, is that the system has sufficient funds, but they are not expended efficiently in terms of pedagogical goals because such goals are not of prime importance to its administrators.

Finally, let us consider these findings and those reviewed in Chapter 2 on the effectiveness of educational resources in light of subcultural perceptions. The upper-middle-class presupposition that differences in school resources are important appears to be borne out; the particular beliefs as to which resources are effective are only partially substantiated by the evidence, however. The views that high teacher salaries result in better education and that teacher turnover is harmful are substantially correct. The working-class assumptions that new buildings, small classes, and "qualified" teachers are frills and that experience is more important than formal training as a determinant of teaching quality are generally supported by the data. Neither subculture has any clear ideological position on the optimal size of schools, which is an extremely important variable. Consequently, it is doubtful that the upper-middle-class perceptions provide more effective operating principles than those of the working class.

Chapter 4   EFFICIENCY AND THE COSTS OF EDUCATIONAL QUALITY

*The government of American cities has for a century been
almost entirely in the hands of the working class. This class,
moreover, has had as its conception of a desirable political
system, one in which people are "taken care of" with jobs,
favors, and protection, and in which class and ethnic attributes
get "recognition." The idea that there are values, such as
efficiency, which pertain to a community as a whole and
to which private interests of individuals ought to be
subordinated has never impressed the working-class voter.[1]*
—*Edward C. Banfield*

An enterprise is technologically efficient if, by reallocating its
resources, it cannot produce more of one output without producing less of some other. According to traditional microeco-
nomic theory, market-oriented firms in the aggregate will in the
long run behave efficiently, *whether or not individual entrepreneurs have any intention of doing so.*[2] That technological efficiency is desirable is beyond question in normative welfare
economics.

Given the assumptions of the theory of the firm, it is easy to
understand the remarkable theoretical convergence of the
ideal and the actual behavior of profit-making enterprises. The
producers know the relationships by which well-defined inputs are transformed into well-defined outputs. Aware of the

prices of both inputs and outputs, the producer maximizes profit by selecting those inputs that transform into a given set of outputs most cheaply and selects those outputs that yield the greatest returns. Consumers, on their part, know what goods they want and purchase them from the cheapest source. Consequently, inefficient producers must either emulate their efficient competitors or perish.

Because social service enterprises do not sell their ineffable services, their outputs cannot be unquestionably identified with their stated purposes or manifest functions. In other words, while schools are "supposed to" produce educational outputs, no mechanism links their survival to the successful, much less efficient, attainment of this objective.

Specifically, schools are controlled by a diverse constituency. One segment of this constituency, particularly parents of private school children, reaps few direct benefits from the output of urban public schools, but pays considerable taxes. A second segment, namely teachers and custodians, views schools as a source of employment. A third segment, mainly parents of public school children, are interested in varying degrees both in how much their children learn and in how much they pay in taxes. Given that school administrators have only the vaguest knowledge of educational production functions, it would be astounding if the resolution of these conflicting forces were technologically efficient.

EDUCATIONAL EFFICIENCY IN PRACTICE

Educators have tended to divide into two camps with respect to the pursuit of educational efficiency, depending upon the nature of their constituency. Educators responsive to the middle class or to the business community have tended to be actively concerned with educational efficiency narrowly defined: obtaining the most education at a given cost, meeting given educational standards at the lowest cost. A corollary to this orientation is the norm that schools should be run professionally and divorced from politics. Many scholars of educational administration who, like economists, share the norms of the middle class, assume that school systems do, or at least ought to, conform to the ideal of seeking efficiency.[3]

On the other hand, educators responsive to a working-class constituency have not been so actively concerned with efficiency narrowly defined. Rather than considering only the pedagogical consequences of their policies, such educators are deeply involved in politics, and they control the jobs, protection, and recognition that are its currency.

Middle-class Orientation

In a fascinating study of the "Cult of Efficiency" in education, Raymond Callahan reviews the attempts of some educators in the first three decades of this century to emulate business practices. The dicta of the "efficiency experts" in education are strikingly similar to those of latter-day systems analysts: "The advocate of pure water or clean streets shows by how much the death rate will be altered by each proposed addition to his share of the budget . . . Only the teacher is without such figures. Why . . . spend money on schools instead of subways, parks, and playgrounds?"[4] They related the purposes and objectives of "Scientific Management" to schools as follows:

1. to "increase the efficiency of the laborer, i.e., the pupil";
2. to "increase the quality of the product, i.e., the pupil"; and, thereby,
3. to "increase the amount of output."[5]

The Scientific Management, or Taylorism, which they espoused was in vogue in the powerful and prestigious business sector of society, and the stimulus for it was political rather than professional or intellectual. During the period 1900-1920 the educator was faced with rapid urbanization, record rates of immigration, and growing demands for free secondary schooling, all of which placed enormous burdens on available resources. As is true today, the educators were blamed for the perceived deterioration of the quality of the schools, especially the learning failures of the immigrants. In order to legitimize both his request for larger budgets and his own position as an effective executive, the educator had to provide the illusion of following the best business practices of the era. Unlike the businessman or independent professional, however, the educator was extremely vulnerable, dependent upon the public purse for solvency, dependent upon its goodwill for his job. The price of his survival under these circumstances was responsiveness to the public not only for the goals of his enterprise, which is consistent with democracy, but for the "correct" technology, which generally reflects the arbitrary fads of the day.[6] While this latter dimension of responsiveness is not inherently inconsistent with pedagogical efficiency, it is not necessarily a sound basis for technical rationality.

Although Scientific Management in the business sector depended upon relatively creative and detailed experiments, *"educational administrators . . . showed no real interest in, or ability to carry out, such painstaking research, . . ."*[7] even though many experiments were suggested by the efficiency experts. The lack of true interest in Scientific Management as an optimizing tool is due more to the ideological functions of the Cult of Efficiency rather than to the inherent difficulties of educational research. Verbalization of this cult was sufficient for survival; implementation of the cult, however, could be dangerous. As was discussed in Chapter 1, whenever research is undertaken in an action context, the administrator looks for vindication of his efficacy and efficiency; an opposite finding makes his position virtually untenable. Discovering better ways to run schools does not benefit him directly in the same way that inventions benefit the profit-seeking industrialist.

The more creative superintendents went beyond lip service in supporting the Cult of Efficiency. Some sought measures of output by which school quality could be gauged: attendance rates, aspirations for further education, and time to complete a given curriculum, measures similar to those used in Chapter 3. Most educators, however, soon recognized fundamental distinctions between educational and business enterprises: the relative fixity of student background, multiple and exogenous influences on academic performance, and long-term consequences not immediately measurable. An occasional educator attempted to relate student performance to school resources although improper controls for student background made most findings spurious.[8]

In practice, the efficiency orientation was operationalized as cost cutting rather than economizing, and as a vocational rather than a classical goal orientation. While outcomes of educational policy were not easily measurable, costs were, and the more sophisticated efficiency experts calculated the costs per hour of Latin versus mathematics, big schools versus small schools, and large classes versus small classes. In the absence of definitive notions of output, lowest-cost solutions tended to find favor in the eyes of the business dominated municipalities of the era.

In retrospect, the lowest-cost solutions might not have been unwise for an enterprise undergoing enormous growth in enrollment. Current research supports the notions of economies of scale and of equal effectiveness of large and small classes (within limits). Double sessions and year-round use of school plants are not imprudent in the face of pressures on space. Indeed the round-the-clock "community school" and the eleven-month year are becoming increasingly popular. With respect to the choice between classical versus practical education, the decision to cut costs may have also been correct, given the pedagogical assumptions of the time. Classical subjects (Latin, art) were not justified solely in terms of their inherent good, but as vehicles for developing the general faculties of the mind. In terms of the contemporary doctrines of "transfer of training,"[9] the mind could be developed by learning almost anything. Since there was no way to tell whether classical or practical subjects developed the mind more effectively, the cheapest course, invariably the practical one, was favored, with its vocational spillovers. This vocational view of education is currently reincarnated in much of the literature on "human capital."[10]

Efficiency experts in education never developed a body of knowledge that was scientific in any sense. Instead, educators developed the public image of the "professional school executive," who had the authority to take bold action and who would be professionally concerned with educational rather than accounting matters. The signs of the new profession were adherence to standards in accreditation, teacher loads, class size, buildings, and curriculum; publication of businesslike annual reports and surveys; and hiring of expert consultants. Such an image of "expertise" lessened the educators' vulnerability to public pressure.[11] Paradoxically, the adherence of educators to professional standards reduces the feasibility of developing a body of knowledge by studying natural experiments because variations among schools are thereby minimized.

Working-class Orientation

The middle class, especially the businessman, views the schools as a primarily educational enterprise comparable to a factory; it produces some output, albeit more varied, less measurable, and with considerably less efficiency. In the past the working class viewed all local government agencies, including the schools, as an employer as well as a purveyor of services.

Selig Perlman has characterized the working class as conditioned by history to a mentality of scarcity, especially of jobs, rather than one of opportunity.[12] Although the American working class has proven some exception to that generalization, in some cities, like Boston, local economic stagnation and the experience of the depression made the working classes relatively dependent upon local government as a source of secure, white-collar jobs. Local government, a highly labor-intensive set of activities, has had considerable power of employment in exchange for political support.

In a perceptive study of the Boston schools, Lawrence W. O'Connell sketches an ideal-type working-class school system: an electorate not particularly impressed with the mystique of education, a relatively stagnant economy, at least for semi-skilled labor; and a political ethos in which personalities rather than principle or program are of prime importance.[13] Since the turn of the century, municipal jobs have been the currency of the city's public affairs, and a school system which employs four thousand teachers and three thousand administrators, secretaries, and custodians is no mean prize.

Not only does the working-class electorate feel that the school's functions as an employer are legitimate (most have a friend or cousin who has or is seeking a job), but the teacher and custodial associations are recognized as significant political forces in the city.[14] Under such a regime, salary schedules, class size, and school consolidation become issues of more than pedagogical importance.

The employee orientation of the School Committee has considerable impact on the allocation of educational resources and, hence, on the technological efficiency of the schools. Relative to pedagogical affairs, the School Committee invests an enormous amount of time and effort in matters of personnel, both collective (salary schedules), and particular (waiving sick leave or retirement regulations for a favored custodian).[15]

This employee orientation is strikingly exemplified in three policy areas. Since 1930 enrollments in the city have declined from 135,000 to a low of 86,000 students in 1960, with a slight increase since then.[16] One result of this decline is excess seating capacity and high fixed costs per student for administrative, secretarial, and custodial personnel. Rather than consolidating schools to reduce overhead and to benefit from scale economies, the School Committee tended to reduce class size, thereby preserving jobs. It is unlikely that the committee reduced class sizes on purely pedagogical grounds, since the electorate believes that small classes are ineffective frills.

Second,during the Depression school positions became available only to residents of the city, and, presumably, to registered voters, a restriction that still has legitimacy today. Promotions to high administrative posts are, moreover, invariably given to insiders, a practice that rewards loyalty, but not necessarily productivity.

Third, by the 1950's the teachers won a single salary schedule, which compensates them solely on the basis of experience, training, and accreditation. The single salary schedule creates greater pressures for across-the-board salary increases than a schedule based on market forces where individuals who can earn relatively higher incomes outside of teaching need relatively higher salaries to be attracted to teaching. One need only compare the job options of physics and English majors. Similarly, higher salaries are needed to attract teachers of all types into relatively undesirable schools. Under the single salary schedule there are potentially greater shortages of physics teachers than of English teachers, and potentially greater shortages of all teachers in less desirable schools. Consequently, in order to avoid shortages of particular specialists in particular schools, salaries of *all* teachers in all schools must be high enough to attract the scarcest specialist to the least desirable school. That this policy has had the effect of overpaying most teachers is suggested by the allegation that appointments to the school system could be arranged for some side payment.[17]

Boston's educational administration can be best described as employee serving and wage bill maximizing rather than student serving and learning maximizing. This orientation has not gone unchallenged. Early in the century, the Commonwealth, which was relatively responsive to middle-class suburban and business interests, created a Finance Commission to scrutinize the municipal budgets. The city's business community supports a municipal research bureau for the same purpose. The major concern of these agencies, however, is cost-cutting rather than economizing, as strictly defined. None of the reform groups whose major concern is improving education have had any lasting impact on educational policy in the city.[18]

Although Boston may provide an extreme example of a working-class, employee-oriented school system, it may portend for the future. Although the spread of affluence, middle-class values, and homeownership among the working class have killed the patronage styles of the older big city machines, other factors may, paradoxically, have created a new machine of organized municipal employees. The rise of teachers' unions may force "professional" educators, in the middle-class suburbs as well as in the working-class cities, to devote more attention to their labor relations than to maximizing the learning of their students.[19]

THE COSTS OF EDUCATIONAL QUALITY

Switching from a behavioral to a normative perspective, I would now like to consider the policies that a school board might pursue if it were interested in technological efficiency narrowly conceived. Such a board would be interested in the following relationships: the minimum costs of attaining different levels of a particular output, and the alternative output bundles attainable at a given expenditure level. The first relationship is known as a supply curve; the second, a production possibilities frontier. Here, new ground is broken by estimating these relationships for the Boston school system.

It is commonly supposed that there is a direct relationship between increased expenditures and increased educational quality. While there may be some truth in this supposition, it is not necessarily a useful guide to improving the quality of schools. First, it is not clear on which items — smaller classes, better paid teachers, new plant — the marginal costs should be expended to be effective, much less *efficient*. Furthermore, because school administrators have rather vague notions of effectiveness of inputs, it is highly unlikely that they economize. Consequently, it may be possible to increase output by the more efficient use of a given budget. In this section we hope to probe beneath the expenditure-output relationship and specify a true cost function for educational quality.

Input Costs

There are two types of cost curves of interest in economics. The first relates costs (total, average, or marginal) to input quantity. The second, the supply curve, relates costs to output quantity. If and only if both the production function and the input cost function are known, can the supply curve be derived.

Direct instructional items absorb, by far, the major share (85 percent) of all current schooling expenditures. Supporting items — plant operation, attendance, and health — nearly exhaust the rest. The average expenditure per student on each item varies substantially among the 56 school districts in Boston (see Table 4.1). The relative (coefficient of) variation is greatest on plant and clerical costs and least on teachers.

The total (TC_t) and average (ATC_t) costs of teaching, the major item of expenditure, are derivable from an explicit salary schedule.[20] The accounting identities are:

TC_t = no. teachers [3000 + % permanent (2000 + 460
  × % masters + 240 × experience)]
ATC_t = TC_t/no. students

The accounting identities for the other expenditure items are not derivable from the published input data. Quite plausibly administrative and clerical costs also depend upon experience and training of the personnel; maintenance costs upon the condition of the building and tenure of the custodian. In addition, these costs may be based on some administrative rule of thumb tied to enrollment. Conceivably, the short-run function (rule of thumb) may be U-shaped; the long-run function being

Table 4.1. Current expenditures per student, Boston elementary and intermediate districts, calendar year 1964.

Item	$ Mean	Standard deviation	Coefficient of variation	Mini- mum	Maxi- mum
Instructional	296	48	.16	222	493
teachers	231	38	.17	171	374
administrators	47	12	.24	25	89
clerks	4	1	.39	1	10
supplies	13	3	.25	7	26
Plant	39	14	.36	20	90
Health, attendance	12	3	.25	7	23
Misc.	4	—	—	—	—
TOTAL	351[a]	62	.18	261	580

Source: *Annual report of the Business Manager to the School Committee of the City of Boston*, School document No. 4–1965, Table 2, Elementary day school districts; Table 3, Junior high schools.
[a]Plus $42 per student for costs of central administration (unallocatable among districts).

an envelope of these curves. The simplest formula for this family of curves is:[21]

$$AC_i = \text{constant} + a_1 \,(\text{enrollment}) + a_2 \,(\text{enrollment})^2 + a_3 \,(\text{capacity}) + a_4 \,(\text{capacity})^2 + a_5 \,(\text{capacity} \times \text{enrollment})$$

Regressing cost elements on independent variables in this form across seventy-two elementary and intermediate school districts,* we find that generally only the coefficients a_1 and a_1 are significantly different from zero (see Table 4.2). The remaining coefficients are zero because capacity presumably has no impact on *current* operating costs, only on *capital* costs for which we have no estimates.

Table 4.2. Average expenditures per student as a function of enrollment, nonteaching items of expenditure: Regression coefficients (standard errors).

Item	Corrected R^2	Constant	Enrollment	Enrollment^2	Computed minimum
			in thousands		
Administration	.57	102.22 (9.34)	−75.68 (18.0)	20.79 (8.30)	1820
Clerical	.29	11.96 (1.78)	−12.69 (3.42)	4.53 (1.58)	1410
Supplies	.23	26.99 (4.22)	−17.74 (8.20)	5.05[a] (3.73)	1760
Plant[b]	.33	103.63 (13.72)	−97.83 (26.50)	33.17 (12.10)	1460
Health	.36	26.32 (3.03)	−22.32 (5.87)	7.48 (2.69)	1490
Total nonteaching	.53	279.29 (24.66)	−236.74 (47.60)	76.85 (21.90)	1550

SOURCE: *Annual Report of the Superintendent of School Buildings,* (Boston) City Document No. 20, 1963, Appendix 5.

[a]This is the only coefficient that is not significant .025.

[b]The regression coefficient for age of plant (nearly orthogonal to size variable) is insignificant at $p = .10$.

*By pooling data from fifty-six elementary and sixteen intermediate districts, I obtain regression coefficients insignificantly different from those obtained by using the fifty-six elementary school observations; moreover, pooling narrows the confidence intervals.

These equations explain only a moderate percentage of the rather wide variation in expenditures per student on each item. Presumably, interdistrict differences in the seniority and training of the personnel account for the remaining variation. All expenditure curves have a parabolic shape, with computed minima in the range 1400-1800. The curve for total nonteaching expenditures has a minimum of 1550, within a rather wide 95 percent confidence interval of 1400-2100 students.

The expenditures on maintenance are especially interesting in light of the hypothesis that custodians were hired in order to provide jobs rather than to perform an essential educational service. Although expenditures per student on maintenance are related to district size, they are unrelated to age of building, which is presumably a surrogate for difficulty in maintenance. Apparently old and new buildings are staffed with similar complements of custodians.

In summary, average total expenditures are a nonlinear function of teacher characteristics and enrollment. By itself, this equation says nothing about the shape of the *output* cost function or supply curve. For example, the U-shaped function merely describes input expenditure behavior with respect to levels of enrollment, regardless of quality. If input quality tended to vary directly with input costs, the output cost function would be linear with respect to enrollment.

Economies of Scale

There is considerable evidence that output functions are also of parabolic shape with the extreme values (in this case maxima) at the same level of enrollment as the observed input cost functions. In the production analysis of six outputs summarized below, there are economies of scale for four equations and diseconomies in none, as district enrollment varies from 500-2300. Both a study of urban high schools in New York State[22] and a study of unified school systems in California[23] found economies of scale when enrollments were less than 2000 and diseconomies when enrollments were greater. Burkhead, in examining Chicago high schools with an average enrollment of 2000, found no scale effects, which is not surprising if the maximum (minimum) of the production (cost) function is near that average.[24] Finally, in a study of high school expenditures in Wisconsin, John Riew found a minimum cost at 1,675 students.[25]

The magic number 2000 appears to be quite robust across different types of small educational institutions: high school plants (Riew, Burkhead); multiplant elementary districts (Katzman); and multidistrict systems (Kiesling, Benson). Rather than depending upon plant characteristics, scale effects might reflect the characteristics of small organizations: the gains from specialization being offset by problems in span of control. Why the optimum enrollment occurs at 2000 pupils (or approximately 80 teachers, plus supporting personnel) is not at all obvious.

Apparently there are hierarchies of scale economies, each level of which reflects a different set of fixed costs. Although the evidence is based upon studies of expenditures without respect to output, apparently minimum costs per student for central administrative functions are attained somewhere in the range of 20,000 to 50,000 students. Since a case study by definition focuses on a single central administration, the production functions derived for Boston shed no light on these higher order scale effects.[26]

Counterevidence to these generalizations is suggested by a study of extracurricular participation and leadership in sixteen Kansas high schools.[27] As enrollment increases from 35 to 2200, the amount and variety of participation tends to decrease, with a maximum in the range of 100-200 students. Because small schools have only slightly fewer extracurricular activities than big schools, students in the former have greater opportunity for leadership positions. Not only are students in the small school more likely to assume such positions, they express greater satisfaction in extracurricular participation than students in big schools. The long-term effects of participatory experience are not spelled out in the study, but they may have important consequences for the political order.[28]

Linear Approximation of Input Costs

To make marginal costs and productivities of each input readily comparable, we force the true nonlinear cost function into the same linear form as the production functions. The coefficients of two linear approximations are consistent with those of the true cost function, when inputs are held at their mean (see Table 4.3).*

In the first linear approximation we regress instructional costs per student against teacher characteristics and pupil-teacher ratios (column 2, Table 4.3). Although these coefficients are somewhat unreliable, in regard to standard errors, they are not significantly different from the theoretical coefficients. The unreliability of these coefficients is probably due to specification error, that is, the forcing of a nonlinear relationship into linear form.

In the second linear approximation we regress total costs

Average total costs $(ATC) =$
271 $-0.22626 \times$ no. students $+ .0007 \times$ (no. students)^2
$+$ no. teachers $\times$ [3000 $+ \%$ permanent (2000 $+$
460 $\times \%$ masters $+$ 240 $\times$ years experience)] $\div$ no. students

When inputs take mean values:

$$\frac{\partial\ ATC}{\partial\ \text{no. students}} = 0.022626 + 0.00014\ (1198) = 0.0371$$

$$\frac{\partial\ ATC}{\partial\ \%\ \text{permanent}} = \frac{\text{no. teachers} \times 2000}{\text{no. students}} = \frac{2000}{23.3} = 0.86 \times 100$$

$$\frac{\partial\ ATC}{\partial\ \%\ \text{masters}} = \frac{\text{no. teachers} \times \%\ \text{permanent} \times 460}{\text{no. students}} =$$

$$\frac{0.76 \times 460}{23.3} = 0.15 \times 100$$

Let p (% teachers with more than ten years experience) $=$
0.60 $\times$ 100%
Then assume that those with less than ten years experience average five years.

$$\frac{\partial\ ATC}{\partial\ p} = \frac{\text{no. teachers} \times \%\ \text{permanent} \times p \times 2400 = [1 - p] \times 1200)}{\text{no. students} \times p} = .39$$

$$\frac{\partial\ ATC}{\partial\ \text{pupil:teacher}} = \frac{3000 + 0.76\ (2000 + 460 \times 0.48 + 0.60 \times 2400 + .40 \times 1200)}{(23.3)^2} = 11.30$$

Table 4.3. Marginal costs per student of school resources:
Regression coefficients (standard errors).

| | | Linear approximations | |
Resource	True form, mean values	Instructional expenditure/ student	Total current expenditure/ student
Constant	279.0	—	282.0
Enrollment	−.037	—	−0.045
			(0.015)
Accredited (percent)	.86	0.78	2.04
		(0.54)	(0.79)
Masters (percent)	0.15	0.14	0.40
		(0.23)	(0.37)
Ten years of experience (percent)	0.40	0.61	0.75
		(0.29)	(0.46)
Pupil : teacher	−11.30	−6.57	−7.46
		(1.38)	(1.89)
Uncrowded (percent)	—	—	0.98
			(0.44)

per student against the six inputs of the production functions.
The coefficients of this function are insignificantly larger than
those of the true function. Notice that we include "percentage
uncrowded" as an input variable to ensure compatibility with
our production function. Although intuitive arguments could be
suggested for the direction of crowding effects on costs, we
have no theoretical basis for computing the magnitude of these
effects.

Derivation of the Supply Curve

Given an input cost function and a set of production functions, the minimum costs of producing any bundle of outputs
can be solved for. The techniques of linear programming provide an algorithm for cost minimization of the following type:

$$\text{minimize } C = \sum_i a_i X_i - \sum_i \lambda_i (O_i - \sum_i b_{ij} X_i)$$

where a_i = marginal cost of input X_i

b_{ij} = marginal product of input X_i with respect to
output O_j

Because of the joint conditions of production, the solution of the minimization problem requires prior specification of the levels of *all* outputs. The supply curve for any single output Oj is derived by minimizing costs as Oj varies parametrically:

$$\text{minimize } C = \sum_i a_i X_i - \lambda_j(O_j - \sum_i b_{ij} X_i) - \sum_{k \neq j} \lambda_k(\overline{O}_k - \sum_i b_{ik} X_i)$$

where $\overline{O}_k = $ fixed levels of all other outputs.

The cost curves derived here are subject to several important qualifications. First, the inputs considered comprise only those which vary among schools within the city of Boston. The technology, the quality, and the "style" of the administrators are held constant throughout the system. The productivities of these inputs may vary from system to system as these intangibles vary.[29]

Second, the inputs vary only within the constraints observed in practice. Specifically, pupil-teacher ratio is permitted to vary within the range of 14:1 to 30:1, which are the extremes found in Boston. This constraint stems from my unwillingness to extrapolate the production relationship beyond the range of the data whence it was derived because of anticipated discontinuities in the coefficient for this variable. My own conservatism has its counterpart in the aversion Boston's educators have in deviating from past practice. In addition, enrollments are constrained to a maximum of 1500, at which point scale economies apparently vanish.

Third, only current expenditures are considered. This narrow focus is not a matter of choice; it emerges from the unavailability of estimates of the capital value of school plants, much less annual depreciation (flow of services). Fortuitously, this statistical shortcoming has its political analogue. In recent years, the school board in Boston has been reluctant to engage in significant building activity, and less than 10 percent of the school plant has been constructed since World War II. Consequently, the administration makes few choices between capital and current expenditures.

Fourth, only inputs that have explicit costs are considered.

Teachers are not paid on the basis of their productivity or some proxy such as verbal ability, but on the basis of their experience, training, and accreditation. While it may be desirable to reward teachers on the basis of their productivity, few systems do so. Therefore, we consider the marginal costs and productivity of experience, training, and accreditation.

Fifth, only controllable inputs are considered. In Boston, teachers are granted the right of transfer in order of seniority, and a single salary schedule equalizes the out-of-pocket costs of placing a teacher at an undesirable school versus a desirable school. Teacher turnover, therefore, is higher at the undesirable school, with the more experienced and more highly trained teachers, who have better alternatives, drifting away. The implicit costs of placing a teacher include that schedule of bonuses which would make him indifferent to opportunities available at all the schools. Because the system refuses to pay these implicit costs, it sacrifices some of its ability to control teacher composition and turnover among its districts. Consequently, turnover is ignored in deriving supply curves.

Finally, the supply curves represent the *expected* minimum cost of output. A range of uncertainty exists because of stochastic terms in all production and cost equations.

The characteristics of the linear programming problems can be seen more clearly when all coefficients are placed into matrix form (see Table 4.4). First, roughly half of the elements have a zero value; that is, changes in an input do not affect every output. Second, the matrix cannot be partitioned into a block diagonal matrix; that is, cost minimization cannot be performed on any subset of outputs without affecting the level of some other outputs.

A useful transformation of the matrix above is obtained by dividing the marginal productivity coefficients by the respective marginal costs (see Table 4.5). It is clear that the enrollment input dominates all others: as scale increases, so does output, but costs fall. The discussion below always assumes that enrollment is at its constrained maximum. As mentioned in the previous chapter, the coefficients in the master's degree vector are not homogeneous in sign. Consequently, increased expen-

Table 4.4. Output and cost coefficients of school resources.[a]

	Enroll- ment	Uncrowd- ing	Exper- ience	Masters	Pupil: Teacher	Accred- ited
Average cost	−0.04	0.98	0.75	0.40	−7.46	2.04
Reading	0.015	0.52	1.36	0	0	0
Latin pass	0.004	0.18	0.10	0	0	0
Mathematics	0	0	0.89	−1.08	0	1.41
Continuation	0.004	0	0	−0.07	−0.31	.06
Latin application	0.004	0	0	0.16	0	0.31
Attendance	0	0	0	0.03	0	0.06

[a]Enrollment and pupil-teacher ratios are expressed as units; the remaining inputs as percentages.

Table 4.5. Output/cost ratios.

	Enroll- ment	Uncrowd- ing	Exper- ience	Masters	Pupil: Teacher	Accred- ited
Reading	−.38	.59	1.81	0	0	0
Latin pass	−.10	.18	.13	0	0	0
Mathematics	0	0	1.19	−2.70	0	.06
Continuation	−.10	0	0	−0.18	.04	.03
Latin application	−.10	0	0	0.40	0	0.15
Attendance	0	0	0	0.07	0	0.03

diture on better-trained teachers translates into decreases in two outputs.

Some Illustrations

As a base line from which to compare resource allocations, costs are minimized subject to input constraints only. With this objective function, enrollments, pupil-teacher ratios, and crowding are maximized; teacher accreditation, experience, and training are minimized.

From this minimum cost allocation, supply curves are generated for each output in turn, without regard for the levels of the other outputs (Figures 4.1, a-e). Next, constraints on the levels of other outputs are introduced. A successive introduction of

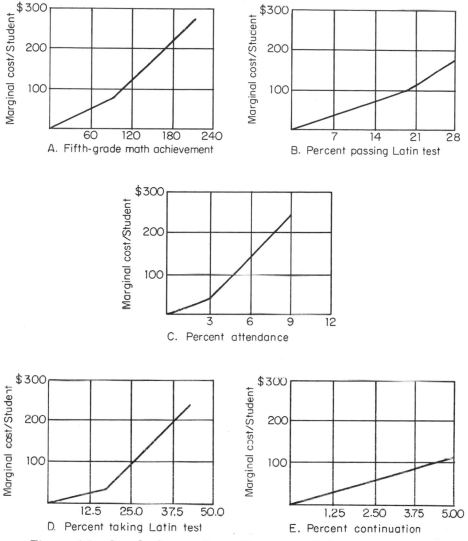

Figure 4.1   Supply Curves, Input Constraints Only.

output constraints (at their mean level) raises the constant term or minimum feasible level of output, as illustrated by the reading score supply curve (Figure 4.2). Output constraints leave the slope of the supply curves virtually unchanged.

It is important to note that the supply curves do not extend

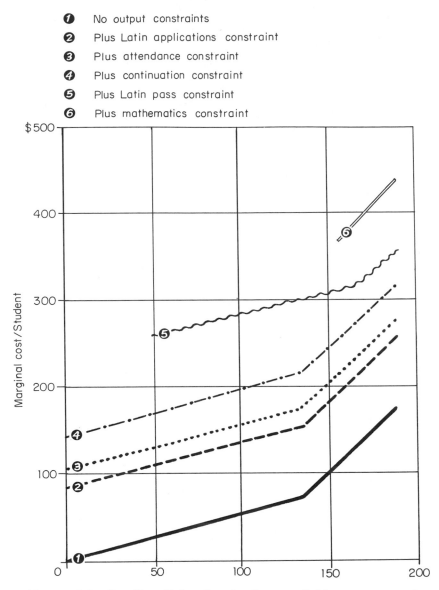

❶	No output constraints
❷	Plus Latin applications constraint
❸	Plus attendance constraint
❹	Plus continuation constraint
❺	Plus Latin pass constraint
❻	Plus mathematics constraint

Figure 4.2 Reading Gains Supply Curves. Subject to successive constraints on other outputs at mean levels observed in Boston.

infinitely in a northeasterly direction because the inputs achieve some maximal constraints because, for example, the percentage of teachers with master's degrees cannot exceed

100 percent. This limitation does not suggest that additional sums cannot be spent on schooling, for it is obvious that more buildings can be constructed, class sizes can be diminished, and expensive equipment can be purchased. Given our knowledge of the production functions, however, *it is unclear how to spend additional money effectively.*

Production Possibilities under Budget Constraints

A second approach to the output-cost relationship is to focus on alternative output bundles attainable at a given level of expenditures. To illustrate, those bundles attainable by maximizing each output in turn at an expenditure of eighty dollars above minimum costs is indicated in Table 4.6. The maximization of any single output residually determines the levels of all other outputs because of the conditions of joint production. Each row of this table indicates the output levels associated with each maximand. The production possibilities for a marginal expenditure of eighty dollars include not only these listed output bundles, but also all weighted combinations of these bundles.*

The pattern of outputs emphasizes the nature of the tradeoffs inherent in the technology of the school system under consideration. At an expenditure of eighty dollars, the two cognitive outputs, reading and mathematics scores are almost

Table 4.6. Some vertexes of the production possibilities frontier: Expenditure of $80 above minimum.

Maximand	Read.	Math.	L. pass	Att.	L. appl.	Cont.
			Levels of output			
Reading	138.	89.	10.9	0.0	0.0	−9.3
Mathematics	136.	93.	10.0	0.0	0.0	−9.3
Latin pass	48.	0.	14.4	0.0	0.0	−9.3
Attendance	0.	−80.	0.0	4.1	22.2	−10.3
Latin application	0.	−80.	0.0	4.1	22.2	−16.3
Continuation	0.	0.	0.0	0.0	0.0	−6.0

*The row of outputs associated with each maximand can be mathematically interpreted as a vertex located along one axis (that of the maximand) in six-dimensional hyperspace.

perfect complements as are Latin applications and attendance. In other words, maximization of reading scores is nearly compatible with maximization of mathematics scores, and vice versa. On the other hand, in order to obtain high reading and mathematics scores, high rates of Latin application and of attendance must be given up, and vice versa. Latin passing** is somewhat complementary to the cognitive outputs, but not to the other outputs. Finally, there seem to be substantial trade-offs between achieving high rates of continuation and any other output. Examples of these trade-offs among pairs of outputs are illustrated in Figure 4.3.

The Supply Price versus Actual Expenditures

The supply curve describes the *minimum* expenditures necessary to attain any level of output. If production were inefficient, then by definition the actual expenditures would be above the minimum. To test the efficiency of Boston's elementary school system, actual production costs are compared to the minimum costs of attaining the systems outputs. The average outputs of the system's districts (from Table 3.10, the "school" column) could be efficiently produced for $253 per student as opposed to an actual expenditure of $364. This discrepancy is consistent with the hypotheses that the Boston school system is not particularly concerned with technological efficiency; that the system is really efficient in terms of outputs not measured here; or that the system would like to be efficient, but is unaware of the production functions.

The supply curves can also be compared to the expenditure-output relationships observed in other school systems. Kiesling found this relationship to be inelastic in the higher grades and, in small school districts, at all grades.[30] For elementary grades in large districts, he calculates the annual costs per student for improving mental test scores by one grade level to be $650 to

**The percentage of students passing the Latin examination is fixed for the school system, so that it is of course impossible for the system as a whole, but not for a particular school, to increase the passing rate. The interpretation of "increasing Latin passes" then is raising the percentage of students who surpass that grade which was passing in the year our data were collected (1965–66).

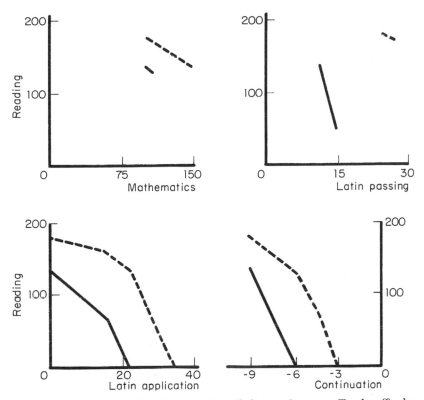

Figure 4.3 Some Production Possibilities Curves. Trade-offs be-tween reading gains and other outputs are shown at $80 and $160 above minimum costs. Dotted line represents production possibili-ties at $160; solid line, at $80.

$770, depending upon social class. Similarly, Bowles and Levin obtain relatively inelastic relationships between expenditures and performance at the twelfth grade, the annual costs per stu-dent for improving verbal ability by one grade level being $1000.*

*Samuel S. Bowles and Henry M. Levin, "More on Multi-Collinear-ity and the Effectiveness of Schools," *Journal of Human Resources,* 3 (Spring 1968), 393–401, do not estimate an expenditure-performance relationship, but provide the basis for such an estimate. The regression coefficient for teacher salary (in thousands of dollars) with respect to Negro twelfth-grade verbal scores is about 1.8. If we assume the average class size to be thirty and a year's progress equal to 6.0 points, improving scores by one grade level costs about $1,000 per student per year.

The supply curves derived here lie considerably below the observed expenditure-performance relationships. While the former curve describes the maximal output attainable by efficient use of expenditures, the latter describes the output attainable through current expenditure practices. Consequently, the supply curves indicate that the annual costs of improving reading and mathematics achievement by one grade level in elementary school are only $60 and $100, respectively.

The supply curve indicates that continuation rates can be increased by 7 percent for an annual expenditure of $165 per student. An experimental guidance program was able to reduce attrition by the same amount at the cost of $580 per student for two years. The present value of the antiattrition program, discounted at 5 percent per year to the first grade is only $690, while the present value of preventing attrition in high school by expenditures in elementary school is $1065. In this case, an intense special program is more efficient than a diffuse attempt at preventing attrition during elementary school. This finding does not contradict the earlier statement that the supply curve was derived from the most efficient resource combination *used in traditional ways*. The fact that an experimental program is cheaper than the most efficient traditional program reinforces my optimism regarding the value of experimentation.[31]

Compensatory Education

There have been many compensatory programs initiated in elementary schools in the last few years.[32] Most such programs involve the reduction of class sizes and the addition of remedial specialists to the teaching staff. Although it may be too early to evaluate such programs properly, they have hardly proven themselves to be effective. For example, at a marginal cost of $700 per student per year, the More Effective Schools program in New York City has increased reading and mathematics achievement by no more than a few months' progress. This relative lack of effectiveness is not surprising because production analyses have generally shown that variations in pupil-teacher ratios, within the range of these experiments, have little impact on learning.

An important policy use of the supply curve is to calculate the costs of a compensatory program directed at equalizing *performance* among districts. The most deprived district in Boston has fewer whites, lower income, somewhat lower occupational status, and students with lower IQ scores (see Table 4.7). Not only are per pupil expenditures lower in this district; so is performance on every single measure.

The minimum costs of bringing the deprived district up to city standards on successive outcomes is estimated in Table 4.8.

Table 4.7. Comparisons between Boston's average and most deprived district: Socioeconomic status, expenditures per student, and performance.

Socioeconomic status	City average	Deprived district
Students white (percent)	74.1	20.0
Median income, family	$5930	$3752
Income < $3000 (percent)	18.4	42.1
White collar, males (percent)	10.8	9.0
Median IQ	104	95
Expenditures/ADM	$359	$342
Performance		
Attendance	91.9	89.0
Continuation	93.5	74.0
Reading	235	205
Mathematics	418	336
Latin apply	21.9	3.0
Latin pass	8.5	0.0

Table 4.8. Minimum costs of compensatory policies for deprived district.

Performance	Expenditure per student
Status quo	$180
Plus reading standard	198
Plus Latin pass standard	220
Plus mathematics standard	238
Plus continuation standard	262
Plus attendance standard	273
Plus Latin application standard	344

Clearly, the deprived district is inefficiently organized because current outputs can be produced much more cheaply than at present ($180 as opposed to $342). Consequently, the district can be brought up to standard in all aspects but Latin applications at an expenditure level much lower than at present.

A discussion of the costs of compensatory education must be qualified by some assumptions about the supply of teachers to lower-class schools. The relatively high rates of teacher turnover in these districts, substantiated in Chapter 5, as well as intersystem comparisons of teacher quality, suggest that the premium necessary to attract teachers to lower-class districts is quite high.*

Input choices within the technological constraints provided by the Boston school system affect a wide range of outputs. This simple fact of the technology of joint production has serious political implications. Clearly, changes in output as measured on a school-wide basis do not affect all students equally. Increases in the likelihood of entering Latin School affect the marginally excellent student; increases in continuation, the marginally poor student; increases in reading scores, a whole range of students. Obviously, the parents of different caliber students have competing interests in resource allocation. In other words, the prices different parents place on different outputs are unlikely to be similar; it is unlikely, therefore, that the

---

*The elasticity of supply of teachers can be estimated under the following set of assumptions: 1) that the supply of teachers of a given quality is directly related to salary and the socioeconomic status of their students; 2) that suburbs compete for students in a single metropolitan labor market; 3) that teachers with equivalent degrees are homogeneous in quality; and 4) that suburbs set salary schedules somewhat independently and select teachers on the basis of their training. For the seventy-seven suburbs of Boston, the percentage of teachers with a master's or at least a bachelor's degree is completely insensitive to salary differentials within the observed range of $800, but these percentages are significantly sensitive to differences in community income within the range of $5000–$14,000. Since the correlation between salary levels and community income in metropolitan Boston is close to zero, these results indicate that salary differentials would have to be quite large to offset socioeconomic differences as factors attracting teachers.

same resource allocation will be viewed as optimal by all.*

CONCLUSION

The attitude of educational administrators towards technological efficiency has been rather mixed. Some have ignored the issue; others have paid rhetorical homage to the Cult of Efficiency, which few have seriously pursued. Regardless of orientation, it is quite unlikely that educators achieve much pedagogical efficiency. On the one hand, they have little knowledge of their production functions, which is the *sine qua non* of rational economizing as opposed to mindless cost cutting. On the other hand, they are so vulnerable to public pressure that they are relatively incapable of economizing even if they had the ken and the will to do so. Part of their vulnerability stems from the general unwillingness or inability of educators to develop a technical body of knowledge that might legitimize their professional authority. Vulnerability is characteristic of educators responsive to both middle-class and working-class constituencies. It would be quite accidental if the pressures of either the middle class, which values participation in school policy so highly yet which is so captivated by untested educational novelties, or the working class, which is so interested in nonpedagogical benefits from schools, were to result in policies that were pedagogically efficient or optimal. It would be equally accidental, however, if the best "professional" judgments of educators, so lightly founded on empirical knowledge, were much better.

Shifting from a behavioral to a normative discussion of efficiency, supply curves are derived from input cost and production functions. The supply curves reflect the minimum cost of

---

*One suggested way of pricing an outcome of schooling is in terms of its long-run effect on income. If a one-grade-level increase in reading ability, for example, translates into a $1000 gain in net worth, reading ability is so priced. I reject this approach outright because the consequences of schooling, social as well as private, noneconomic as well as economic, are too complex to merit such philistine treatment.

six jointly produced outputs. Since these outputs are not produced in fixed proportion, one cannot speak of a unique "educational quality supply curve." Rather, many bundles of outputs can be produced at a given cost. The evaluation of any bundle supplied is a political rather than a technical decision because there is likely to be no agreement on the proper output prices.

The supply curves generated here reflect only those input choices avaliable within a single school system; hence, these curves are short run. The true long-run supply curve requires knowing the costs and productivity of changing all factors that can possibly vary among school systems. Second, the outputs considered here are few and crude at that. In view of the complex output trade-offs inherent in educational technology, one would want to consider more outputs in the joint production model.

Knowledge of the supply curve is highly useful for rational policymaking. Rather than defining programs in terms of expenditures alone, the supply curve specifies expenditure-output packages. Consequently, the policy choice becomes more explicit than $1,000,000 for education, as opposed to $1,000,000 for health, for example. Instead, it becomes a choice between X percent gained in reading and Y percent gained in life expectancy.

Chapter 5 THE DISTRIBUTION OF EDUCATIONAL OPPORTUNITY

*The present allocation of resources may match the
distribution of political power, but it does not match the
distribution of need.*[1]
—*Alan K. Campbell*

It is characteristic of education in the United States that inequalities in access to its benefits exist. While this is not unique to education (it pertains as well to income and the things that money can buy), there is some inconsistency between inequalities in schooling and the American creed of equality of opportunity.

The present chapter is an empirical rather than a normative analysis of the distribution of educational opportunities. The empirical study of distribution as a key economic process, especially in the nonmarket sector, seems relatively neglected in the professional literature. While different resource allocations generate different income distributions, studies of allocation in the public sector often ignore the distributive consequences as if some lump sum transfer could painlessly solve the problems of equity.[2]

The study of distribution in the public sector is more difficult than the study of production. Not only are there the common problems of measuring the physical output of the service and pricing the freely distributed service; there are also problems of externalities or spillover effects. In consuming educational services, an individual may benefit not only himself but also others in the community, as well as subsequent generations.[3] Tracing all of the indirect beneficiaries of educational services is a formidable accounting problem.

There are three major issues in an analysis of the distribution of educational opportunity: defining the object which is being distributed, describing the patterns of distribution, and explaining the patterns.

The definition of equality is of more than academic interest since the courts have now assumed a major role in reducing some aspects of inequality. One of the most common objects of their concern has been the distribution of expenditures. Several "empirical" studies of distribution in the public sector *assume* that each child in a state receives equal expenditure so that benefits vary inversely with family income, the poor having more children.[4] More sophisticated studies, reviewed below, focus on actual expenditures and physical resources, which are subject to the ambiguities described in Chapter 2. Here an analysis of distribution in Boston demonstrates the possibilities and limitations of measuring the distribution of school *outputs*.

The patterns of distribution can be characterized by the overall degree of inequality and by the relationship between the quality of schools and the characteristics of the people they serve. This latter relationship can be expressed by both correlation and regression coefficients. The former describe the "goodness of fit" between schools and social characteristics. If, for example, all rich people have better schools than all poor people, the correlation is perfect. The regression coefficient indicates *by how much*, on the average, schools serving rich people are better than those serving poor people. The distinction between the two coefficients as descriptors of bias in distribution is crucial. While the correlation between income and school quality may be perfect, the quality difference between schools serving the rich and the poor may not be very large; conversely, even though the correlation between income and school quality may be small, the schools of the rich may, on the average, be far superior to the schools of the poor.

Finally, and most relevant in the development of policy, there are those factors which account for any inequalities and biases in the distribution of educational quality. Here, those factors that account for the distribution of schooling among fiscally autonomous districts are distinguished from those that account for inequalities and biases within big cities.

DEFINING OBJECTS OF DISTRIBUTION[5]

Distribution means "who gets what?" There are several operational definitions of the *what* with respect to educational opportunity, or the objects of distribution in education.

Absence of Racial Segregation

A notion of equality of educational opportunity, the limits of which are still undefined, is the right to attend a particular school without respect to race. One rationale for this principle is that de jure segregation is inherently unequal to members of minority groups who are officially stigmatized as well as deprived of the opportunity to be socialized into the majority culture.[6] In practice this principle has been applied by the courts with few exceptions to dual school systems within a single district in which students are classified and segregated by race.

Although there has been legislation outlawing de facto racial segregation within school systems, the Supreme Court so far has not ruled that either socioeconomic segregation within school systems, or segregation by race or class created by school system boundaries, is inherently unequal or unconstitutional. While there are several cases pending in which the plaintiffs challenge the constitutionality of such forms of segregation, the arguments are based on the *fiscal* consequences of segregation rather than on the ground of inherent pedagogical inequality.[7]

This narrow notion of equality can be criticized on several grounds.[8] First, there is little evidence that *racial* segregation in elementary schools is harmful to minority youngsters when "tangible" resources and the social class of their peers are held constant.[9] In other words, the integration of lower-class blacks with lower-class whites, *ceteris paribus,* is unlikely to have any pedagogical benefit for either. Second, there is better evidence that segregation on the basis of socioeconomic status, which is rampant in the American educational system at all levels, is harmful to lower-class children.[10] Finally, de jure or de facto segregation is an insufficient notion of inequality, irrelevant to school systems where race is a minor factor. On pragmatic grounds, however, racial integration is one strategy for socioeconomic integration and the equalization of physical school resources.

Equal Control over Resources

A relatively new conception of equal educational opportunity comes under the rubric of "community control." According to this principle, school systems in big cities which are run democratically according to the will of the majority overlook, sometimes maliciously, the special needs of minority group children. In some cities, at-large systems of election result in no minority representation on the school board. In Boston, for example, the School Committee is responsive to a predominantly Catholic working- or lower-middle-class electorate—groups from which most school personnel originated—and there is considerable feeling that such a system is not responsive to the needs of lower-class Negroes or upper-middle-class Yankees.[11]

An indirect pedagogical consequence of community control may be to increase parents' and childrens' sense of "fate control," which is positively correlated with academic success, according to the Coleman Report. The relationship between community control and fate control is only presumed, not demonstrated.

Equal Resources

One of the most commonly used criteria for equality of educational opportunity is the distribution of educational resources, both financial (expenditures per student) and physical. The objections to financial resources as a valid criterion were reviewed in Chapter 2. The difficulties of using physical resources are that they oversimplify the educational process (ignoring intangibles), they make untested assumptions about the effectiveness of particular resources, and they are incommensurable. Although the Supreme Court, in overturning *Plessy* v. *Ferguson* in 1954, rejected equal resources as a *sufficient* criterion of equality of opportunity, it has been used in subsequent decisions because of its simplicity, visibility, and amenability to remedy.

Equally Effective Resources

An analysis of production can identify the effectiveness of school resources with respect to particular objectives of schooling. In actual practice, however, it may be impossible to determine the effectiveness of resources in a particular school system *a priori* because we suspect that each system has its own production characteristics. Externally derived functions can, nevertheless, provide some guidance as to which resources are likely to be effective. It is possible that resources which are effective for a student of a given ability, social class, or ethnic group may not be effective for a student with different characteristics. Consequently, *equally effective* resources may be compatible with *different* resources for different students.[12]

Equal Academic Performance

The lesson of Chapter 3 is that educational performance depends upon student characteristics as well as school resources. The equalization of effective school resources will not offset differences in performance resulting from individual differences in ability or motivation. Pursuing a goal of equal performance requires prior knowledge of how student background as well as school resources affect performance.

Equal Opportunity for Maximum Development

The definition of equality in terms of results, academic or otherwise, implicitly confuses variety with inequality and sameness with equality. Susan Stodolsky and Gerald Lesser provide strong evidence that within an ethnic group, social classes differ on *levels* of ability, but that different ethnic groups differ in *patterns* of ability, which are fairly stable across class lines.

For example, Chinese students tend to surpass other groups in spatial conceptualization, while Jewish students tend to excel in numerical ability. Lower-class children in all groups have lower levels of each cognitive ability than corresponding middle-class children. Eliminating differences in ethnic patterns may be inefficient as well as unethical. Capitalizing on the comparative advantages of Chinese-American children or Jewish children may be more efficient than attempting to provide all students with an equal opportunity to become an architect or an accountant. In addition, forced homogenization beyond the level of "basic" cognitive skills is an explicit rejection of the ideal of cultural pluralism.[13]

Objects of Distribution as Social Indicators

Which object of distribution is best? The answer depends both upon one's goals and upon one's tastes. The alternative objects can be compared along several dimensions: validity, quantifiability, and controllability.

Absence of segregation (de jure or de facto) can be operationalized by a large number of arbitrary standards, depending upon community characteristics, such as no school having a substantially higher proportion of minority students than the community or no school having more than 50 percent minority members. The standard is measurable and controllable in principle, given political support. Its validity depends upon its as yet undiscovered relationship to ultimate educational or social goals.

Equal control over resources is not easily measurable or manipulable. Granting a "community" the right to elect a school board and to set budgets does not automatically translate into control.[14] The willingness and ability to participate in decisions also affects the degree of "effective" control. Again, the relationship between control and educational goals is unknown.

Some resources themselves are easily measurable. Expenditures provide a compact index of resources; in current institutions in most big cities, however, these depend upon teacher characteristics, which are relatively uncontrollable, as explained below. The validity of expenditure measures of resources is rather low because of their weak relationship with short-run and long-run student performance. Among physical resource measures, teacher turnover is highly valid yet not easily controlled within big city districts (because of the single salary schedule), while class size is fairly invalid yet easily controllable. Less measurable resources, such as teacher "attitudes," "skills," or "classroom atmosphere" may be highly valid but basically uncontrollable.

Measuring effective resources requires a prior analysis of production, which assigns productivity weights to various resources. Applying to a particular school system weights that are externally derived is dangerous because each system may have different production characteristics. The effective resources index is highly valid, being defined as the contribution of schooling to student performance, but its controllability depends upon that of the component inputs.

Equal academic performance, like equally effective resources, is valid and somewhat measurable, and it requires a prior analysis of production in order to be controllable. A court cannot order a school system to equalize performance among its schools if the causes of inequality are unknown.

The criterion of equal opportunity for maximum development implies the matching of curriculum to student ability; hence, indirectly, it encourages the tracking of students on ethnic or other grounds into programs suited to their needs. As suggested by Judge Skelly Wright in *Hobson* v. *Hansen*, tracking may be a ruse for segregation on the basis of race or class. Even in the absence of such nefarious designs, the goal of maximum development may be incompatible with the goals of integration and of equal performance, both within and between ethnic groups.

Which criterion should a court or legislature use in attempting to reduce inequality in educational opportunity? Clearly, there are trade-offs among the criteria of validity, quantifiability, and controllability. Since definitive production analysis is lacking, there is a strong temptation to focus on segregation or physical resources which are of questionable validity and controllability. One can hope that the focus of attention would be on those resources with the greatest educational consequence, such as teacher turnover and experience, which are unfortunately difficult to control under existing institutions. In the event that production functions are more perfectly specified, the criteria of equally effective resources or of equal performance, which have high validity, become controllable. Whether public policy selects as its goal equally effective resources, equal performance, or equal opportunity for maximum development is a normative rather than an empirical question.

Equality for Whom?

Although the American concept of equality of opportunity is commonly reified as equal educational opportunity, public policy is rather ambivalent as to how much, and what kinds of, equality ought to exist. In practice, public policy permits greater inequalities in education than in some other opportunities such as the right to vote and the right to a fair trial. In the exercise of these latter rights, individuals cannot be classified by sex, ethnicity, or financial status for purposes of unequal treatment.[15]

Although a widely held principle of equity in public finance is that people in equal positions be treated equally, defining who is equal is not simple.[16] "The Constitution does not require that things different in fact be treated in laws as though they were the same. But it does require, in its concern for equality, those who are similarly situated be similarly treated. The measure of reasonableness of a classification is the degree of its success in treating similarly those similarly situated."[17]

The case of tax policy may prove instructive. An individual's federal income tax burden depends upon his income, not sex, ethnicity, or other "extraneous" considerations. Tax policy, however, does classify individuals on the basis of marital status (allowing a married couple to split their income), form of housing tenure (interest on mortgage and property taxes are deductible by homeowners), and source of income (capital gains are taxable at a lower rate than salaries). Presumably such distinctions are deemed reasonable as incentives for marrying, owning homes, and investing. These exceptions aside, the tax structure provides for equal treatment of equals *as defined by gross adjusted income* and specifics a "proper" degree of unequal treatment for unequals through a progressive tax rate.[18]

In the arena of education, courts define as equals those under the same school board jurisdiction. While, on occasion, they have required a school system to treat all its students equally by some criterion, the courts permit considerable intersystem inequalities to exist. The Supreme Court ruled, in *Salsburg* v. *Maryland,* 346 US 545,551 (1954), that the Fourteenth Amendment related to the equal protection of the law "between persons as such rather than between areas." In *McGinnis* v. *Ogilvie* (No. 1033, March 24, 1969), the Supreme Court refused to hear an appeal on a ruling that intrastate inequalities in educational expenditure were not unconstitutional. In other words, the right of rich communities to spend more on schooling than poor communities is legitimate in the eyes of the law.

Proscribing *intra*system inequalities while tolerating the *inter*system ones has peculiar results that are seen most clearly in rulings on segregation. Courts and legislatures have generally placed the onus for desegregation upon school boards rather than upon metropolitan areas or states. For example, the Massachusetts Racial Imbalance Act places the burden of reducing de facto segregation upon offending cities like Boston, which enrolls 90 percent of its metropolitan area's Negro students but requires no assistance from the surrounding suburbs.[19] The likelihood that Negro children would benefit more from integration with middle-class suburban children than with lower-class urban children has no bearing on the enforcement of the law. In effect the historical accident of municipal boundaries determines what forms of inequality are legitimate and illegitimate.[20]

PATTERNS OF DISTRIBUTION

The distribution of educational resources is conditioned by technologies of scale, institutions of fiscal federalism, institutions for rationing the use of school services, and the housing market. School systems can operate efficiently at relatively low levels of enrollment. As I have shown in previous chapters, small elementary school systems operate at an optimum enrollment of two thousand, while larger systems can operate at lowest cost within the range of twenty thousand to fifty thousand students. Because the costs of operating below the optimum enrollment are not very high, many independent school systems are viable, if not technologically efficient. In this respect elementary schooling resembles many enterprises in the private sector of the economy, such as restaurants and barber shops, more than some enterprises in the public or quasi-public sector, such as atomic power plants.

Unlike services in the private sector, however, public schooling is not distributed through a price mechanism. Production decisions (How many resources? How should they be combined? What should be produced?) are influenced by groups of voters delimited by municipal boundaries rather than by individuals bidding in a market. Influential voters may include nonparents, as well as those not interested in public schools because all presumably pay taxes and are affected by their social costs and benefits. As a corollary, residents of communities outside the school system have little or no direct effect on production decisions.* In contrast, competition in the market sector may make production decisions responsive to the demands of individuals who are *potential* as well as actual customers.

Under the institutions of fiscal federalism, a major portion of the fiscal burden of elementary and secondary education is borne locally. Like the individual consumer, the community decides what resources should be allocated to education as opposed to other publicly and privately consumed goods. The amount allocated depends upon the relative costs of education and these other goods, the community's preferences, and the community's income (Figure 5.1). In general, higher income communities will vote to spend more tax dollars on education. The income-consumption curve, which relates spending on education to income can be expressed graphically (Figure

---

*This proposition is modified by the constitutional proscriptions stemming from the school desegregation cases, by state compulsory attendance laws, by state aid formulas, and more recently by federal aid programs.

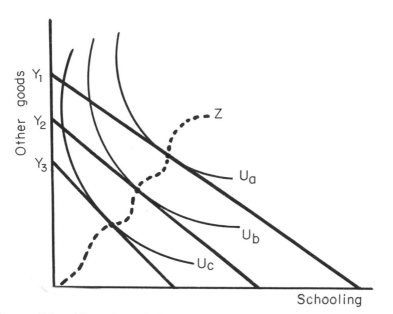

Figure 5.1   Allocation of Community Income between Schooling and Other Goods. The intercepts of Y_i indicate the per capita income levels of different communities, while the slopes indicate the relative costs of schooling and other goods. The pattern of slopes suggests that poorer communities pay relatively more for a given bundle of schooling. The locus of tangencies Z, between income Y_i and preferences U_j, generates the income-expenditure curves for both schooling and other goods.

5.2). Although this curve resembles a traditional supply curve, it is really an unidentifiable combination of supply and demand, that is, the locus of supply and demand curve intersections generated by changes in community income.

This model is somewhat modified in the case of big city school systems. Because a city-wide constituency determines how schools in each district are operated, the patrons of a particular school have a relatively small voice in influencing its policies. Unlike the suburb, the city neighborhood has no mechanism for equating supply and demand (Figure 5.3). For users of a particular school to improve its quality, they must persuade a majority of the rest of the city through a cumbersome political mechanism, or somehow elicit favor from the central administration.

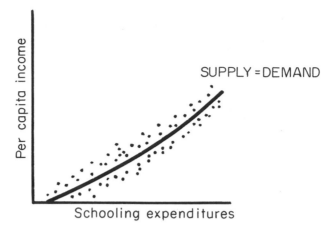

Figure 5.2   Income-Expenditure Curve for Schooling. Equilibrium expenditures on schooling at each income level are derived from Z in Figure 4.1. The solid line describes average relationship observed between income and school expenditures in small municipalities.

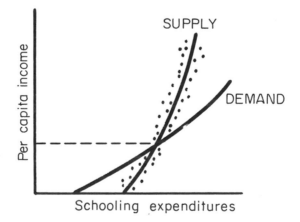

Figure 5.3   Distribution in a Big City School System. The equilibrium income-expenditure curve is assumed to be equal in both suburbs and big cities, *ceteris paribus*. Since there is no fiscal mechanism for equating supply and demand in neighborhoods, taxes and expenditures are too low for high-income voters. The sloping supply curve suggests that the distribution is slightly biased in favor of high-income voters.

116

The distribution of school services is free to those living within the district and is usually proscribed to those living outside its boundaries. Within big cities, this institution is often supplemented by a policy of "open enrollment," which permits students to transfer to other districts when there are vacancies. Few such institutions for free transfer to other school systems exist.* The principle of distribution on the basis of mutually exclusive and exhaustive attendance zones in effect grants each public school a local monopoly, a market condition quite unlike that for other small-scale enterprises. If inequalities among systems exist, "arbitrage" by transfer to the better system is often impossible, even were tuition to be paid. The principle of free distribution is not dictated by technology, for exclusion on the basis of price, such as is practiced by private and parochial schools, is possible.

The housing market segregates families on the basis of income, ethnicity, and occupation, among other things.[21] In the context of fiscal federalism, residential patterns almost guarantee that school districts will differ in their ability and willingness to pay for education, as well as in their styles of operation. To the extent that schools are financed by the state, their support is divorced from local ability to pay, and intrastate inequalities are reduced.[22]

The institutions for producing and distributing education, part of the "Municipal Services Market System," force people to consume housing and educational services jointly.[23] In practice, these institutions might reinforce housing segregation among social classes and ethnic groups. Living among poorer (or richer) families means that the level of public expenditures on education will be lower (or higher) than desired, and personal taxes disproportionately high (or low). Segregating itself through "voting by feet," the richer family can more easily obtain public support for higher taxes and expenditures on educa-

---

*In the Boston area, the Metropolitan Council for Educational Opportunity (METCO) program permits several hundred Negro children from the central city to enroll free in several suburban school systems. In this rather limited program, the tuitions are covered by foundation and federal grants.

tion, pay what it regards a "fair" (or roughly equal) share of these taxes, obtain a consensus as to how the schools should be run, and avoid having to suffer the adverse peer effects of the poorer students.

The discussion above suggests that inequalities among school systems, biased with respect to social characteristics, are likely to exist. How great are these inequalities and biases in fact? While it is preferable to answer these questions in terms of "effective school resources," the lack of data forces us to consider expenditures and physical resources for the most part.

There is no unique statistic for expressing how equal or unequal a distribution is. In fact, the statistic chosen may affect the conclusions about these matters. Here reliance is on the coefficient of variation which uses information about the complete distribution and which is relatively reliable and valid.* The coefficient of variation is defined as the standard deviation divided by the mean of a distribution. If a distribution is normal, then two-thirds of the observations lie within the limits of the coefficient of variation. For example, if the mean of a normal distribution is 50 and the standard deviation is 10, the coefficient of variation is .20, and two-thirds of the observations lie within 20 percent of the mean.

Inequalities

Expenditures. The most readily available data on inequalities in school resources measure expenditures per student. Although there are no comprehensive surveys of all schools in the nation, public and private, two studies do provide some insight. In a nonrepresentative sample of elementary school systems,

---

*For an exhaustive discussion of this issue, see Hayward R. Alker, Jr. and Bruce M. Russett, "On Measuring Inequality," *Behavioral Science*, 9 (July 1964), 207–218; and Otis Dudley Duncan and Beverly Duncan, "A Methodological Analysis of Segregation Indexes," *American Sociological Review*, 20 (Apr. 1955), 210–217. Alker and Russet find that statistics of inequality based upon extreme points of a distribution, e.g., interquartile range, are misleading, as well as uncorrelated with "full information" statistics, like the coefficient of variation. Arthur E. Wise, *Rich Schools, Poor Schools* (Chicago: University of Chicago Press, 1968), finds such shocking intrastate inequalities because he uses extreme statistics, i.e., ratio of maximum to minimum expenditures.

the Coleman Report found a coefficient of variation for expenditures per student of .42. Jerry Miner found that the same statistic for eleven hundred public school systems in a stratified random sample was .72.[24] Whether this figure would increase or decrease if data for parochial schools were included must be left to speculation.

The total variation among the nation's schools can be partitioned into between state and within state components. The coefficient of variation in expenditures among state averages is .25,[25] while the within state variation depends upon several factors, among them the relative importance of state equalization grants. For example, the coefficient in Alabama is only .05, but it is .37 in Missouri.[26] The fact that state aid tends to reduce inequalities within a state is suggested both by the study of H. Thomas James and by Miner's finding that national variations in local effort exceed variations in total (local plus state) effort, that is, 1.09 as opposed to .72.

Inequalities in expenditures per student are generally less among big city districts than among localities within a state. While the coefficient for several Massachusetts towns is .22, it is between .13 and .15 in three big cities. Consequently, big cities tend to provide relatively equal protection to citizens, as measured by educational expenditure, while the institutions of fiscal federalism permit massive inequalities.

Physical Resources. From the fragmentary data available, the inequalities in resources are of similar magnitude to inequalities in expenditures.[27] The degree of inequality in teacher characteristics and pupil-teacher ratio are similar, ranging from .30 to .40. The degree of inequality in teacher turnover, however, is much higher than for any other resource measure. Although the degree of inequality in expenditures is greater among all the nation's schools than within big city systems, the inequality in resources is fairly stable across levels of government (see Table 5.1).

Factors Contributing to Bias

The institutions for production and distribution of education on the elementary level provide the mechanism for municipali-

119

Table 5.1. Coefficients of variation in school resources: Between and within states.

Resource	Total	Interstate	Intrastate	Intracity[e]
Expenditure/student	.43[a]–.72[b]	.25[c]	.22[d]–.26	.14
Expenditure/classroom[h]	.24	—	.22–.26	—
Teacher, masters (percent)	.48[g]	—	.05–.37	.27
Teacher, experience	.40[a]	—	.60[d]	.39
Teacher, turnover (percent)	1.17	—	—	.65
Pupil:teacher	.16[c]–.41[a]	—	.12[d]–.33[f]	.43

[a]James S. Coleman *et al.*, *Equality of Educational Opportunity*, US Office of Education (Washington, D.C.: Government Printing Office, 1966), Appendixes, Caucasian students (nonrandom sample).

[b]Jerry Miner, *Social and Economic Factors in Spending for Public Education* (Syracuse, N.Y.: Syracuse University Press, 1963), 97 (random sample).

[c]National Education Association, "Estimates of School Statistics," Research Report R-13, and "Class Size in Kindergarten and Elementary Schools," Research Report R-11, 1967 (mimeo.) (complete count); William G. Mollenkopf and S. Donald Melville, "A Study of Secondary School Characteristics as Related to Test Scores," Research Bulletin 56–6 (Princeton, N.J.: Educational Testing Service, 1956, mimeo.), 9 (random sample).

[d]Massachusetts Teachers Association, "Background Data for Comparing Towns in Respect to Payment of Adequate Salaries to Teachers," Oct. 30, 1964 (mimeo.) (random sample).

[e]Average of Atlanta, Boston, and Chicago, see Table 5.8, below.

[f]Charles S. Benson *et al.*, *State anl Local Fiscal Relationships in Public Education in California* (Sacramento: Senate of the State of California, 1965) (nearly exhaustive sample); for pupil:teacher, .18 in New York State, .33 in California.

[g]Mollenkopf and Melville, "Study of Secondary School Characteristics as Related to Test Scores," 9.

[h]Adapted from Forrest W. Harrison and Eugene P. McLoone, *Profiles in School Support: A Decennial Overview* (Washington, D.C.: Government Printing Office, 1959).

ties to differ in their school resources. Residential segregation provides a mechanism of demand aggregation that systematically relates school to community characteristics.

Expenditures. The level of expenditures per student is related to income per capita, the value of nonresidential property, the proportion of children in the public schools, and the level of community education.

The estimated income elasticity for education depends upon the unit of analysis. For 1100 scattered systems, Miner found an elasticity of .26 for local expenditures with respect to local income; patterns of state aid were such, however, that the elasticity of total (state plus local) expenditures with respect to local income is zero, but the elasticity of total expenditures to state income is .23.[28] In other words, as state income rises by 10 percent, local expenditures rise by 2.3 percent.

Patterns in a particular state may diverge from these average relationships. For example, Werner Hirsch found an income elasticity of .6 for expenditures per student among St. Louis County municipalities. In contrast to fiscally autonomous units, big city school districts do not have an expenditure capacity based on district income. Consequently, I observed an income elasticity of −.31 for expenditures per student in Boston. Although they do not calculate this statistic, neither Jesse Burkhead nor Patricia Sexton demonstrate any strong positive relationship between district income and expenditures.[29]

Otto Davis related several categories of expenditures per student (teacher salary, instructional, current, total) to a large number of "political" characteristics in 134 school districts in western Pennsylvania.[30] All categories of expenditures per student were found to be negatively related to the percentage of property owners in the population, but positively related to the educational level of the population and the value of industrial and personal property per capita. These things being equal, there was no relationship between expenditures and per capita income, which is highly correlated with these other explanatory variables. The relationship between expenditures and property ownership is consistent with the broader studies of bond referenda by Banfield and Wilson and reflects the self-interests of those who bear the *direct* burden for financing the schools in low property taxes.[31] This is an interesting result because there is some evidence that home owners are assessed at lower rates than owners of multifamily dwellings, who shift the tax burden indirectly and invisibly onto their tenants.[32] The relationship between industrial property valuation per capita and expenditures reveals the degree to which a community can "exploit" nonresident taxpayers.

Since all people in a community do not benefit directly from public education or benefit in proportion to their tax payments, the support for public education seems to be related to the percentage of people interested in public education. Surprisingly, expenditures per student are *inversely* related to the proportion of students in public as opposed to private school; this means that the more parents who send their children to public school, the smaller the expenditures per student. School taxes per capita, however, increase as the proportion of public attendance increases.[33] In other words, as public attendance increases more voters are willing to pay more for public education, but not so much as to increase expenditures per student. Consequently, the existence of a private school system is a double fiscal boon to those who use the public schools; it lowers their per capita taxes, and it raises expenditures per student.

Big cities comprise families with a wider range of demands for education than suburbs, which are relatively homogeneous. One might expect the big city rich to be more reluctant to tax themselves for education than their suburban counterparts because a given tax increase for the rich has less effect on average expenditures in a big city than in a suburb, and the rich in the big city subsidize the poor. Such speculation seems borne out by the data. George Pidot finds that the per capita income elasticity of *per capita* school expenditures is only .36 in one hundred central cities, but .57 in the suburbs. In a somewhat smaller sample, Allan Campbell and Seymour Sacks find elasticities of .54 in the cities and .60 in the suburbs.[34]

Ethnic and regional factors are also adduced to explain systematic differences in expenditures per student among schools. For example, the Coleman Report found that the average expenditures on Negro students was only $380, while that on Mexican-Americans was $400 and, on Caucasians, $430. Similarly, expenditures on metropolitan Caucasian students in northern versus southern schools was $492 versus $287. One suspects that these differences are correlated with regional income differences. For example, about $500 is spent on the average Puerto Rican student. Most of these students live in the metropolitan northeastern area (mostly New York), however.[35]

Physical Resources. Data relating physical resources to social characteristics of schools are rather sparse. The Coleman Report reveals rather minor differences in the physical resources of schools serving different ethnic and regional groups of students. For example, in the nation the pupil-teacher ratio in schools with predominantly Negro pupils is thirty and, with Caucasian pupils, twenty-eight, a trivial difference in light of the production analysis. Similarly, differences in average teacher experience are quite small: thirteen years for Negro schools and twelve years for Caucasian. Regional as well as urban-rural differences are equally small. For example, in comparing urban schools for northern versus southern Causasians we find pupil-teacher ratios of twenty-six as opposed to thirty; average teacher experience of eleven as opposed to ten years. There are similar small biases in teacher salaries, which are highly related to performance; they favor nonsouthern metropolitan, Caucasian schools.

Degree of Bias

Not every rich community has better resources than every poor community. In other words, the correlation between community characteristics and educational resources is not perfect.

Expenditures. In the nation as a whole only half of the inter-system variance in expenditures per student is related to a wide range of measurable community characteristics, including income, age composition, and private school attendance, among others. Variations in per capita income explain by far the greatest proportion of the variance: about 30 percent among all schools and about 70 percent among state averages. Within states, the variance in local expenditures explained by community characteristics ranges between 38 and 56 percent. Intrastate income differences explain only from 10 to 30 percent of the variance.[36]

Physical Resources. Benson suggests that differences in expenditures per pupil are explained by differences in teacher salary, rather then differences in class size. About 75 percent of the interstate variation in teacher's salary is explained by per capita income. Similarly, among 300 school systems in California Benson found that about 40 percent of the variance in mean teacher salary and 17 percent in administrator salary was explained by variables related to income. Although negatively correlated with pupil-teacher ratio and percentage of provisional teachers, income explains only 44 and 19 percent of the variance in these resources, respectively.[37]

DISTRIBUTION WITHIN BIG CITIES

The process of distributing educational resources among fiscally autonomous school systems is easily understood in terms of the municipal services market model. Such a model, however, has little relevance to the process of distribution *within* big city school systems. When fiscal and administrative jurisdictions are coterminous, as occurs when a small town is served by a single high school, distribution is equal to all students except where there is tracking by ability. Where school systems are multiplant enterprises, as in big cities, the distributive mechanism is more complex. The users of a particular school cannot vote to tax themselves to control their own expenditures, which are determined at a central level. Users of a particular school, however, may pressure the central authorities for more resources to the exclusion of other schools in the system.

While the possibilities for unequal and biased distributions within big city systems clearly exist, it is not obvious from any theoretical considerations on what principles resources within big cities are distributed, whether major inequalities or biases result from these principles, or who would be favored by any existing bias in resource distribution.

There are three, by no means mutually exclusive, models of how distributive decisions in big cities are made. The conspiratorial model posits that an elite or "establishment" in the city decides who is to get what and has the power to enforce its decision. The biases of this elite may take almost any form: equal distribution, distribution on the basis of taxes paid (thereby favoring the rich), or distribution on the basis of ethnicity. The implication of this model is that, to change the observed distribution of school resources, one has to influence the preferences of the establishment.[38]

The second model proposes that the school administration distributes resources on the normal bases of democratic, grass roots American politics: "greasing the wheels that squeak loudest." Rather than accepting the dicta of the establishment, the school administration arbitrates among competing demands of parents and other voters. In this model votes serve as the currency exchangeable for resources; hence, to change the distribution of school resources, the distribution of power must be changed.[39]

While conspiratorial models are rather popular in American political ideology,[40] academic economists like to think of "invisible hands" regulating and coordinating the independent decisions of individuals. The municipal services market model of allocation and distribution is certainly within this tradition, and this third model of distribution in big city schools suggests that inequalities and biases can emerge from the normal functioning of internal institutions and may not result from explicit distributional policy. For example, the labor market for teachers may be the most important single institution that affects the distribution of school resources. Most cities, big and small, pay teachers according to a single salary schedule based on accreditation, experience, and training, regardless of *what* and *where* they teach. Since the single salary schedule permits no bonuses for teaching in undesirable schools, such schools can attract only those teachers with the fewest options. Specifically, schools with children from poor or Negro families will attract teachers with the least experience and training, and they will suffer the greatest turnover in staff.

A second institution, which exists in Boston as well as some other big cities, grants teachers transfer privileges in order of seniority. When an opening exists in a desirable school, the experienced teachers from other schools will fill these openings, leaving less experienced teachers to fill their place. Since seniority is positively correlated with training and accreditation, the effects of the transfer institution reinforces the effects of the single salary schedule.

Some Hypotheses: The Process of Distribution in Boston

All three models may be useful in describing the distribution of school resources in big cities. For example the schools in Boston are formally governed by a five-man committee elected at large every two years. In theory the School Committee can control the age of school buildings and district enrollment and, hence, economies of scale. In practice, new schools are rarely built, and district boundaries are rarely redrawn in the city. On the other hand, the committee can more easily control the degree of crowding, median class size, and overall pupil-teacher ratio. Although the School Committee is ultimately responsible for teacher placement, the single salary schedule and the competition of other school systems in the metropolitan area attenuate its power to control teacher quality and turnover in a particular district.

The absence of any building program in the system is consistent with the working-class belief that new buildings are frills. The unwillingness of the school administrators to manipulate district sizes, and even pupil-teacher ratios and crowding, may also be explained by their perception that these resources are not important. A supplementary explanation is that administrators operate in an environment of rapid demographic change. In the last ten years, enrollments increased by more than 10 percent in twenty-six districts, decreased by the same amount in fourteen districts, and fluctuated in the remaining sixteen districts. Generally, all three patterns of enrollment are found in neighboring districts. If the school administrators were economizers, they might shift district lines every year in order to produce the enrollment and class-size distributions consistent with their preferences, be they egalitarian or discriminatory.

It is probably much simpler for the administrators to leave the district boundaries fixed and assign teachers according to the rule of thumb of one per classroom. Rather than trying to equalize district and class sizes in response to "random" shifts in enrollment, the administrators may ride these shifts out and concentrate on other issues. As long as the voters express little dissatisfaction with the enrollment, class sizes, and crowding in their districts, the administrators have little incentive to search for more efficient resource allocations. The resulting values of these resource inputs is more a product of fortuitous demographic shifts than of design.[41]

An additional factor sustaining the unwillingness of the administration to redistrict is the demand of the Negro minority for redistricting for the purposes of "racial balance." The administration would not survive politically if it did so; hence, it avoids the issue by refusing to redistrict at all. It is quite difficult to prove that discriminatory actions or inactions are undertaken when the School Committee refuses to redistrict in the name of "higher" educational principles, namely the neighborhood school.

Some Hypotheses: Beneficiaries of Bias

The school system in Boston is predominantly staffed by Irish Catholics, especially at the higher administrative and policy levels. This pattern results from the high proportion of Irish-Americans in the city, their relative lack of success in the fairly stagnant market economy, and their extraordinary success in local politics. It is a plausible hypothesis that schools in Irish neighborhoods are favored because the School Committee distributes the resources it can control in their favor and because Irish teachers prefer to teach Irish students. On the other hand, Irish Catholics in Boston may not be particularly concerned with public school resources in their neighborhood because they tend to use parochial schools (see Table 5.2) and because they may be relatively "unimpressed with the mystique of education."[42] Nor do middle-class Irish teachers necessarily prefer to teach in the more heavily Irish neighborhoods, which are lower class and which experience considerable delinquency and school vandalism.[43] It may be that all teachers prefer upper-income schools regardless of ethnicity.

Table 5.2. Influences on participation in School Committee elections
and public school utilization: Regression coefficients
(standard errors).

Dependent variable	Population Caucasian (percent)	Median family income	Foreign stock, Irish (percent)	R^2_c
Public attendance, elementary (percent)	−0.325[a]	−0.002	−0.366[a]	.53
	(0.074)	(0.001)	(0.110)	
Voting (percent)	−0.276[a]	0.001	0.257[a]	.51
	(0.039)	(0.001)	(0.058)	

[a]Significant .05

A second plausible hypothesis is that the Boston school system distributes resources in favor of those who are most active politically or of parents who are most interested in the public schools. Several factors cast doubt on this hypothesis. For one thing, many voters have no children in public schools, and those most likely to vote are least likely to have children in public school. Such voters are probably more interested in low taxes than in better schools. A second consideration is that the parent-teacher association in the city has the reputation of being more a company union than a vehicle for imposing parental demands upon the system. Also, the elected School Committee is rather deferential to the professional administrators regarding the routine matters of school operation; they are mainly concerned with the distribution of special favors to particular individuals.[44]

The dispersion of 30 percent of the city's children to parochial schools may affect school quality in either of two ways. Districts with more parochial school children may have fewer parents interested in public education and, therefore, less pressure for good schools.[45] Alternatively, fewer public school students may translate into more resources per child, as is suggested in the intersystem expenditure studies.

The influence of income on the receipt of school services is interesting from a redistributive point of view. While residents with higher incomes generally pay higher local taxes,[46] it is not clear whether any income from a higher tax bill is recaptured in the form of better services.

The relationship between resources and race depicts more clearly the consequences of de facto segregation. The evidence of Chapter 3 suggests that segregation in Boston does not hinder Negro academic performance, school resources and student background being equal. Although segregation may not be inherently unequal to Negroes, their schools may receive worse resources.

The measures of income and public school enrollment are fairly straightforward. There are two plausible measures of both race and political power. Race can be measured either by the percentage of students who are Caucasian or by the percentage of population which is Caucasian. I selected the latter because it explains more of the variance; in other words, the distribution of resources is related more to *parental* characteristics than to student characteristics. Political power can be measured by the rate of voting participation or the number of voters per student, and the former explains more of the variance. While there is no direct measure of the number of people who consider themselves Irish (a majority of Bostonians reputedly do), we can measure the percentage of foreign stock who were either born in Ireland or who are of Irish parentage. This measure assumes that first and second generation Irish-Americans live in the same neighborhoods as older settlers.

Each of the recipient measures is subject to wide variation (see Table 5.3). Unfortunately, there is considerable multicollinearity among these variables, for both voting participation and public school attendance depend upon race, income, and parentage (see Tables 5.2 and 5.4). The degree of multicollinearity is not so high as to obscure the identification of the model, however.

Distribution of Resources in Boston

The distribution of school resources is weakly related to the characteristics of the recipients (see Table 5.5). Only teacher turnover and expenditures per student are significantly related

Table 5.3. Dispersion of social factors influencing the distribution of resources.

	Mean	Standard deviation	Minimum	Maximum
Voting participation (percent)[a]	49.1	7.4	34.8	69.9
Population Caucasian (percent)[b]	87.1	22.1	18.3	100.0
Median family income[b]	$5791	1079	3542	8324
Public attendance (percent)[b]	69.6	14.7	38.5	97.9
Irish, foreign stock (percent)[b]	22.4	13.2	1.4	46.6

[a]*Annual Report of the Election Department,* City of Boston, 1966, for School Committee election, Nov. 1965.

[b]US Census of Population, 1960, *Boston Standard Metropolitan Statistical Area, Final Report PC (3)-1D* (Washington, D.C.: Government Printing Office, 1960).

Table 5.4. Correlations among social factors influencing distribution.[a]

	1	2	3	4	5
1. Voting (percent)	.56[b]	−.60	−.21	−.18	.16
2. Caucasian (percent)		.75[b]	.53	−.69	.40
3. Median family income			.31[b]	−.48	.31
4. Public elementary (percent)				.45[b]	−.56
5. Irish (percent)					.59[b]

[a]$|X'X| = .111$
[b]R^2 of variable with four other variables.

to these characteristics. No single social characteristic consistently induces a bias in the distribution of these resources.

It was hypothesized earlier that teacher characteristics in a particular district were relatively uncontrollable by the central administration; they depended mostly upon the characteristics of the students. The data are consistent with these hypotheses. Upper-income districts have more accredited teachers and less turnover, although they have fewer with master's degrees. Dis-

Table 5.5. Distribution of resources as a function of social factors: Regression coefficients (standard errors).

School resources	Voting (percent)	Caucasian (percent)	Median income	Public (percent)	Irish (percent)
Accredited (percent)	.742	.212	.003	.169	-.028
	(.249)	(.111)	(.001)	(.130)	(.124)
$R^{2a} = .24$					
Masters (percent)	.085	.176	-.003	-.119	-.322
	(.029)	(.130)	(.002)	(.153)	(.145)
$R^2 = .07$					
Experienced (percent)	.173	.276	.001	.039	.188
	(.316)	(.141)	(.002)	(.166)	(.158)
$R^2 = .19$					
Uncrowded (percent)	.066	-.143	-.003	-.524[b]	-.378
	(.366)	(.163)	(.002)	(.192)	(.183)
$R^2 = .20$					
Pupil : teacher	.264	.070	.001	.060	.036
	(.101)	(.045)	(.001)	(.053)	(.051)
$R^2 = .26$					
Teacher turnover (percent)	.347	-.131	-.002	.113	.111
	(.196)	(.087)	(.001)	(.103)	(.098)
$R^2 = .50$[b]					
Enrollment	4.382	-.687	0.186[b]	9.111	9.027
	(9.200)	(4.101)	(0.051)	(4.826)	(4.606)
$R^2 = .29$					
Age of building	0.066	-.181	-.006	-.040	.331
	(.433)	(.193)	(.002)	(.227)	(.218)
$R^2 = .15$					
Current expenditures/pupil	.656	-.055	-.019[c]	-2.416[c]	-2.680[c]
	(1.365)	(.609)	(.008)	(.716)	(.684)
$R^2 = .23$[c]					

[a]R^2 (corrected for degrees of freedom).
[b]Significant .05 (one-tail, 8 tests).
[c]Significant .05 (one-tail, 1 test).

131

tricts with greater percentages of Caucasians have more accredited, more highly trained, and more experienced teachers,
with lower rates of turnover. Given these characteristics, teachers are unaffected by the degree of Irishness of the student
body.

The degree of voting participation and utilization of the public schools has a rather mixed effect on teacher quality. While
districts with high participation have better teachers, they also
have higher teacher turnover. The former finding might reflect
the responsiveness of the School Committee to the demands of
the parents. On the other hand, "authoritarian" teachers may
not like to teach in districts with great parental interest in the
schools, and this might account for the higher turnover.*

Of the resources which the central administration can and
does control, there seems to be no coherent pattern of bias.
The pupil-teacher ratios (and class sizes, not shown here) are
higher in the actively voting, more Caucasian, and higher-
income districts, a finding markedly inconsistent with the conspiratorial hypothesis. These same districts are not significantly
less crowded than the others.

District size, pupil-teacher ratio, and crowding can be explained in terms of demographic change and the school policy
of stable district boundaries. All three inputs are highly correlated with the absolute growth in enrollment in recent years,
from 1960 to 1964 (.48, .54, and .48, respectively). Consequently, changes in expenditures per student are negatively
correlated with changes in enrollment (see Table 5.6). The
districts which are undergoing the most rapid growth, however,
have no identifiable income or ethnic characteristics.

Of those resources which the central administration can, but
does not, in practice control, there seems to be some bias in
the direction suggesting conspiracy. Higher-income and more

*This notion is not farfetched. An assistant superintendent once told
me that the ideal student in the eyes of the Boston teachers was one who
was highly motivated (hence, the income or social-class effect) but
whose parents did not "interfere" in school affairs (hence, the voting
participation effect). Teachers in Boston may view the Negro student
as the antithesis of this ideal — "culturally deprived," with "troublemak-
ing" parents.

Irish districts have larger enrollments, thereby benefitting from economies of scale. Districts with more Caucasians and higher income have newer buildings. It is highly unlikely that conspiracy is at work here because the School Committee has not undertaken significant redistricting or construction in years. The upper-income, white areas of the city have newer schools because they are newer areas of the city with respect to all construction. The fact that less than 10 percent of the capital stock has been replenished since World War II is hardly suggestive of a replacement policy for rich whites only.

Table 5.6. Changes in expenditures per pupil as a function of changes in total expenditures and changes in enrollment, 1960–1954.[a]

Dependent variable	Zero-order correlation	Partial correlation	Regression coefficient	t
Δ Enrollment	−.53	−.83	−.200	−10.89
Δ Expenditure	.18	.77	.0004	8.67

[a]$R^2_c = .68$.

There are several ways of summarizing the bias in the distribution of resources. First, we focus on the pattern of signs of regression coefficients. The politically active, upper-income, and more Caucasian districts are favored in the distribution of only five of eight physical resources; public school-oriented districts, in only four resources; Irish districts, in only two. None of these patterns are unexpected on a chance basis.

A second approach is to focus on expenditures per student which are the function of physical resources. Expenditures are significantly related to the set of social characteristics. They are inversely related to the income, Irishness, and public school participation in the district. Expenditures, however, are not strongly related to student performance in Boston.

The third, and most useful, approach is to sum the resources by the coefficients of the production function. Then we can measure inequalities and biases in the distribution of educational *quality* or effective school resources (see Table 5.7). This

Table 5.7. Distribution of school quality as a function of social factors: Regression coefficients (standard errors).

Quality measure	Voting (percent)	Caucasian (percent)	Income	Public (percent)	Irish (percent)
Attendance	.011	.031[b]	.003	−.005	−.022
$R^{2a} = .39$[b]	(.026)	(.012)	(.001)	(.003)	(.014)
Continuation	−.042	−.010	.009[b]	.049	.060[b]
$R^2 = .20$	(.047)	(.021)	(.003)	(.025)	(.024)
Reading	.192	.468	.910	−0.384	−.490
$R^2 = .21$	(.561)	(.256)	(3.090)	(0.295)	(.282)
Mathematics	.359	.728	.015[b]	.022	−.500
$R^2 = .44$[b]	(.180)	(.321)	(.004)	(.379)	(.359)
Latin application	.189	.117[b]	.001[b]	.044	−.049
$R^2 = .29$	(.094)	(.042)	(.000)	(.048)	(.049)
Latin pass	−.035	.031	.001	−.086	−.076
$R^2 = .21$	(.095)	(.042)	(.001)	(.050)	(.047)

[a]R^2 (corrected for degrees of freedom).
[b]Significant .05 (one-tail, six tests).

method reveals the pattern much more clearly than the two previous ones. The distribution of quality is biased in favor of upper-income districts for all six measures of output and in favor of Caucasian districts for five outputs. On the other hand, the distribution of five outputs is biased against the Irish districts. The effects of voting participation and public school utilization on bias are mixed.

How do we reconcile the finding that quality measures are biased in favor of upper-income and Caucasian districts with the finding that expenditures are biased against these districts? Returning to the distribution of physical resources we observe that these districts have larger classes and more crowding, a situation which has little effect on output but reduces costs per student. In addition, these districts have less turnover, which improves productivity but has no effect on costs. On the other hand, better teachers cost more. Although the cost effects cancel, the output effects do not. Consequently, the efficiency or output per dollar of these districts is greater. (This result can be arrived at by regressing output per dollar against district characteristics.)

Why is the distribution of resources unrelated to the voting strength of a district? The answer is that the intent rather than the magnitude of the vote is what the School Committee responds to. Voting participation is directly related to income and Irishness, but the utilization of public schools is inversely related to these factors. This means that many voters have no stake in improving the quality of the public schools. These voters are perhaps more interested in keeping taxes low than in obtaining better resources for schools in their districts. O'Connell suggests that Irish working-class voters are, in addition, more interested in obtaining jobs and favors from school politicians than in quality of resources. Finally, by the 1965 election, there was a negative relationship between voting and percent Caucasian, *ceteris paribus*. Although quite vocal, the Negro community during the period under consideration was demanding integration rather than more resources for their segregated schools.

Distribution in Other Big Cities

Inequality. There have been relatively few systematic studies of the distribution of educational resources within big city school systems. In the landmark case of *Hobson* v. *Hansen,* the Court cites rather unconnected tidbits of information about inequalities and biases in Washington, D.C., which are nevertheless more comprehensive and comprehensible than those presented in most rulings on educational inequality. In a study of Detroit, Sexton found some inequalities in resources, but she did not present the parameters of the distributions, much less correlation and regression coefficients. In contrast, a study done by Jesse Burkhead, Thomas Fox, and John Holland presents the coefficients of variation in high school resources, which differ according to the dimension measured and the school system studied. The degree of inequality in Boston is not too different from that in Chicago and Atlanta, which Burkhead studied (see Table 5.8). The three cities are strikingly

Table 5.8. Inequality of school resources in three big cities: coefficients of variation.

Resource	Boston	Chicago	Atlanta
Current expenditure/pupil	.13	.15	.14
Masters degree (percent)	.23	.26	—
Experience[a]	.24	.69	.25
Pupil : teacher	.30	.09	—
Median class size	.24	.05	.11
Enrollment	.32	.30	.46
Age of buildings	.32	.53	.77

[a]Average experience in Chicago and Atlanta, percent with more than ten years experience in Boston.

similar in the relatively equal distribution of expenditures per student.[47]

Bias. The evidence on distributional bias is rather mixed, varying from city to city. Sexton found that, in Detroit, resources (class size, teacher quality, facilities) were distributed in favor of the upper-income, relatively white school districts. In *Hobson* v. *Hansen,* the Court reported that in Washington, D.C., schools with higher percentages of Negroes had fewer permanent teachers, slightly larger classes, and, hence, lower expenditures per student. In addition, among schools with more than 85 percent Negroes, those in high-income areas had more permanent teachers and newer buildings. Burkhead, on the other hand, found relatively little bias with respect to income in either Chicago or Atlanta. In Atlanta, upper-income high schools had newer buildings and smaller classes; in Chicago, such districts had newer buildings and more experienced teachers. In neither city were expenditures per student biased.

The regression and correlation coefficients in Boston are comparable to those computed from the *Hobson* decision. While the coefficient of determination for percentage accredited is .24 in Boston, the coefficient in Washington is .22 (race only). The regression coefficient for race in Boston is .21, while it is .33 in Washington, which is an upward bias because there is no control for income. While pupil-teacher ratios are slightly larger in white districts in Boston, they are slightly smaller in Washington. In both cities, there is almost no correlation between age of building and race (−.18 and −.03), but there is a significant negative correlation with income (coefficient unreported for Washington). There is a major difference between the cities in the relationship between expenditures per student and income. In Boston, the elasticity is −.31; in Washington, .42.

The fact that there are only trivial resource biases in both Atlanta and Chicago is striking in light of their different power structures: the aloof "establishment" in Atlanta as opposed to an old style "machine" in Chicago.[48] It is more surprising that there is as great a bias against the poor in Detroit, which is reputedly a "good" working-class town, as in the then voteless city of Washington, D.C. The few systematic biases that do exist seem more easily explainable by the "invisible hand" than by any other factor. Higher-income areas in all four cities have newer schools because they are newer neighborhoods with respect to all capital facilities (stores, houses). Higher-income areas in Chicago and Detroit also have more experienced teachers in the schools because of the operation of the single salary schedule.

CONCLUSION

How serious are inequalities in educational opportunity? While the answer depends ultimately on the firmness of one's moral convictions about inequality, three points come to mind. First, inequalities in educational attainment, measured by school years completed, are less than inequalities in income, wealth, health expenditures, or housing quality.[49] Second, equalization of school quality will not go very far in equalizing educational performance. It was discovered in Chapter 3 that equalization of school resources would reduce *interschool* variance in academic performance by 20–50 percent. The Coleman Report, moreover, suggests that equalizing resources would reduce *individual* variations in performance by only about 5 percent.[50] Third, the equalization of school achievement would reduce individual variations in income and occupation by only 1 and 25 percent, respectively.[51] Equalizing the quality of schooling, or even the quality of student performance, would not go very far, therefore, in equalizing individual levels of well-being. I am not arguing that it is unimportant or unnecessary to equalize educational opportunity. Besides being symbolically important, equalizing school quality is probably politically easier than equalizing income.

Which criterion of equality should be used? Ideally, the criterion should be valid in the sense of being causally related to what is learned in school. Clearly, expenditure equalization is insufficient to equalize school resources because middle-class districts can attract more qualified teachers than lower-class districts at a given price. Presumably, the extra salary lower-class districts have to pay in order to attract teachers from middle-class districts would be substantial. Perhaps a fortuitous source of teachers may be ardent, young teachers and administrators who find the problem of lower-class urban schools challenging. Zealots, however, may seek new causes when the problems of compensatory education prove intractable and may be a less reliable resource than matrons who volunteer as aides in the suburban schools. Integration as a criterion suffers from being unclearly related to achievement and from being of limited use in school systems that are ethnically homogeneous. Physical resources also suffer from lack of clear relationship to performance.

Ultimately, a normative approach to equality requires a prior analysis of production in which family, peer, and resource effects are specified. Such an analysis would presumably identify that increment in resources which would compensate for segregation if its elimination were politically unfeasible. If the criterion is equal performance, a production analysis is necessary, *a fortiori*, to determine that increment in resources which would compensate for an impoverished family background.

With respect to what community should education be equalized? Although there are some intrasystem inequalities, big city school systems do a fairly good job of equalizing educational opportunity within their jurisdiction. Inequalities within and among states are much greater. Therefore, placing the burden for equalization upon the big cities will have little positive impact on global equality, which in fact may get worse were migration to the suburbs induced. Although placing the burden of equalization on the states will go far in reducing global inequality, interstate differences in social class and in school resources still account for a substantial proportion of inequality in school achievement.

Chapter 6   RESTRUCTURING BIG CITY SCHOOL SYSTEMS

The confusion between state provision and state financing is so prevalent in most discussions of the welfare state that we might pause a moment firmly to establish [the] distinction. For example, to show that many people cannot afford to educate their children beyond the statutory leaving age at best establishes a case for a cash grant by the state, an income tax rebate, or a personal loan from the public authorities, but has absolutely nothing to do with the issue of private versus public ownership of schools . . . External benefits, parental incompetence, and equality of opportunity do not stand up as arguments for state-provided education.[1]
—Mark Blaug

Structural reform is a commonly proposed remedy for institutions performing below expectation. As an institution of this sort, the big city school system perennially draws the attention of reform mongers, many of whom view school reorganization as the key to remaking society. Currently, the most conspicuous proposals for correcting the ills of education are metropolitanism, decentralization, and tuition grants for private schooling. While there are innumerable varieties of hybrids, the main focus here is on those "ideal types," which present the starkest contrast.

Believing that the power of the pen can be much exaggerated, I do not suggest any particular reform. Instead, I prefer to explore some of the potential consequences of each alternative. The discussion that follows is mostly speculative because reforms tend to function in ways not anticipated by the most careful social engineers, and often contrary to their intention.

The most important criteria for comparison and evaluation of the many consequences of institutional change include: technological efficiency, technological progress, consumption efficiency, equality of opportunity, and integration.

Technological efficiency, the subject of Chapter 4, is defined as obtaining specific pedagogical objectives at the lowest cost. Technological progress is defined as a shift in the production function which permits the attainment of traditional outputs at lower cost or the invention of new functions for producing different outputs.

Consumption efficiency is the provision of that output bundle most highly valued by the consumer-client. Preconditions for the attainment of efficiency in consumption are either *responsiveness* on the part of the producer to the demand of consumers or the *freedom of choice* to patronize that producer whose output the consumer values most highly. For example, suppose all schools can produce two different kinds of outputs, A and B, for a given expenditure. Were a given consumer to prefer A, his consumption would be inefficient if all schools insisted upon producing B or if he were restricted from patronizing that school which in fact produced A.

Equality of opportunity for the sake of this discussion is defined as equality of resources. Integration is defined as the degree of heterogeneity of the student body of a school, defined on any dimension of interest, such as ethnicity, social class, ability. In addition to considering the effects of institutional revision on these several criteria, I estimate the distributive impact of each proposal on several interest groups in the metropolitan community: the suburban rich, the big city rich, the urban poor, ethnic minorities, and the "Educational Establishment."

The analysis hints that a choice among these institutional alternatives cannot be made on a technical basis. There are trade-offs both among the several goals and among the interest groups. In other words, it is unlikely that any reform explored here can result in the attainment of more of *all goals* or can make *all interest groups* better off than an alternative proposal.

CURRENT ORGANIZATION OF BIG CITY SCHOOLS

The major institutions which the reforms discussed here would alter are the mechanisms of financing, of administrative decision making, and of student placement. With respect to these institutions, big city schools can be characterized in the following way: tax expenditure decisions are made jointly by a city-wide constituency rather than by the patrons of a particular school or school district. Second, decisions as to the type of resources (for example, salary schedule), style of administration (upper middle class versus working class), and to some extent goals (college preparatory versus vocational) are generally made on a city-wide rather than on a district basis. Third, each school is circumscribed by an attendance zone, which may include culturally diverse students depending upon patterns of residential segregation.

These three institutions are not inextricably bound to each other by the technology of schooling. It is feasible for neighborhoods to raise their own school taxes, or for schools to charge tuition. Even if schools were centrally financed, neighborhoods could determine administrative policy with as much autonomy as suburban districts have now. Whether or not a big city school system is fiscally and administratively centralized, there is no technological necessity to keep students from attending schools in other neighborhoods or even in the suburbs.

Although suburban school systems formally have similar municipal-wide fiscal, administrative, and placement institutions, they usually have less diversity in income and in subcultures owing to their size. Suburban voters, who have similar incomes and tastes, generally share a single senior and junior high school, and occasionally a single elementary school. Collective choice under those circumstances has different implications than under the size and heterogeneity of the multiplant, big city school systems.

Consumption Efficiency

When a diverse constituency decides upon fiscal and administrative questions, the interests of all parties cannot be simultaneously implemented. To illustrate, suppose two ethnic groups with equal income have different views as to the proper method of school administration and as to the desired combination of goals. If neither group particularly cared about the *modus operandi* of schools not serving their children, then each group would be better off if it had the right to run its own schools (Figure 6.1). If the two groups were residentially

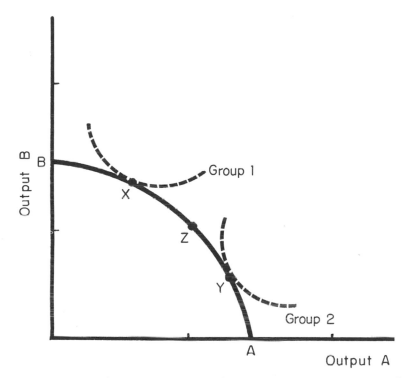

Figure 6.1 Preferred Resource Allocations: Communities with Different Preferences. Assume ethnic groups differ in their preferences toward alternative school outputs (for example, college preparation, remedial reading). One group is best off at X; the other, at Y; while integrated communities will choose some point Z intermediate between X and Y. Assuming no peer effects, segregating the decision-making process by ethnicity benefits both groups.

segregated, then fiscal and administrative decentralization would provide a means for each group to obtain its most favored form of schooling without the necessity for compromise.

The reduction in consumer satisfaction as a result of institutionalized need to compromise is lessened by the degree of homogeneity of the constituency determining school policy. Since suburbs tend to be more homogeneous than big cities, the effective responsiveness of school systems to individual desires is greater. This does not imply, however, that the complete decentralization of big city school systems will benefit everybody. Big city populations are diverse not only in tastes, but in income.

Equality

The fact that different income groups in big cities must compromise on the level of public school expenditures affects not only consumer efficiency but also the equality of opportunity. Among fiscally autonomous suburbs, rich communities have the freedom to spend more on education than poor communities. Within big cities, wealthy neighborhoods have no such freedom. Consequently, the degree of inequality among districts serving different income groups is less within big cities than among suburbs with comparable income (see Table 6.1). For example, the three wealthiest districts in Boston receive no greater expenditures per student than middle-income and low-income districts. The same salary schedule applies to all districts within the city, and the percentage of highly trained teachers is nearly equal in all. In contrast, the spread in expenditures per student, in salary schedules, and in teacher training between high- and middle-income suburbs is considerable. In addition, the level of school expenditures in poor districts of big cities tends to be higher than in suburbs of comparable income, while the expenditure in rich districts is lower. Despite interdistrict inequalities and biases in resource allocation, therefore, big cities more effectively narrow the gap in educational opportunity than do the multitude of autonomous suburbs.

144

Table 6.1. Comparisons of school resources among Boston school districts and Massachusetts towns matched for income and size of public elementary school enrollment, 1964.

	Median family income	White collar (percent)	Expenditures per student	Maximum B.A. salary	Masters degrees (percent)	Public elementary (percent)
High-income districts						
Highest-income Boston districts[a]	$7934	50.4	$337	$7860	45.0	62.3
Upper-middle-income towns in Massachusetts[b]	7926	60.7	470	7691	25.0	83.9
Low-income districts						
Medium-income Boston districts[c]	5283	30.8	349	7860	53.0	71.4
Lowest-income towns in Massachusetts[d]	5157	36.6	405	7200	17.5	80.6
Lowest-income Boston districts[e]	3757	16.5	449	7860	55.0	85.8

Source: Massachusetts Teachers Association, "Background Data for Comparing Towns in Respect to Payment of Adequate Salaries to Teachers," Oct. 30, 1964 (mimeo.).

[a]Districts #56, 55, 50.

[b]Bedford, Belmont, Hingham, Melrose, Reading, Sharon (all are Boston suburbs).

[c]Districts #6, 18, 23, 38, 44, 48.

[d]Adams, Ayer, Bourne, Chelsea, Lynn, Revere (the last three are suburbs).

[e]Districts #10, 15, 17.

Integration

Parents with different tastes would be better off in patronizing separate schools if all schools had equal access to resources and students did not reciprocally influence each other's academic performance. In fact, the first condition does not hold. Within big cities, middle-class districts obtain more experienced teachers and suffer less turnover than lower-class districts. Among suburbs, resource differences are even more striking. Whether or not fiscal or administrative autonomy is granted to neighborhoods, the segregation of students of differing social class by attendance boundaries results in resource inequalities.

Even if all schools had equal resources, it is not clear that parents of different subcultures would all be better off if their children went to different schools. The normative implications depend upon which model of peer interaction best describes educational reality.

The integrationist model presumes that heterogeneity benefits all students, that is, that the production possibilities frontier is further out in heterogeneous schools than in homogeneous schools. This shift does not imply that integration necessarily benefits everybody. Integration diversifies not only the student body but also the parents to whom the educators are responsible. As a result, the *potential* pedagogical gains to all parties may not offset losses due to compromising administrative decisions (Figure 6.2).

The apartheid model presumes that heterogeneity harms all students. Consequently, there are no pedagogical gains to diversifying the student body and, *a fortiori*, the parental constituency.

The asymmetric model, which has the most popular adherents as well as some scientific support, suggests that integration helps the lower-class student while it harms the middle-class student.[2] Were this true, integration would shift the production possibilities frontier for the former outward and for the latter inward. For the middle class, the losses from integration and from compromising administrative decisions make them unequivocally worse off. For the lower class, the

146

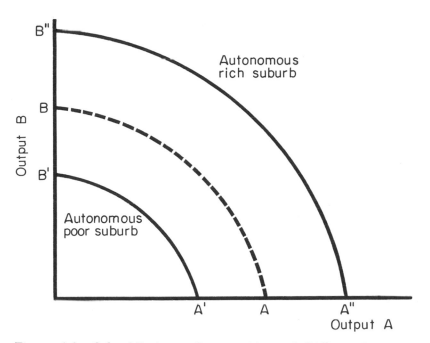

Figure 6.2 School Budgets: Communities with Different Incomes. Fiscally autonomous suburbs expend resources on education in proportion to their income. Fiscal unification of school districts differing in income, as exists in the big cities, results in budgets, such as AB, intermediate between those of autonomous districts.

gains to integration may or may not offset the losses due to compromise.

A variant of the asymmetric model holds that, when a few lower-class children are integrated into a middle-class environment, their achievement improves without damaging that of the majority. For example, Hanushek suggests that the achievement of Negro students declines as the percentage of Negroes in a classroom surpasses 45 percent.[3] Since the achievement of whites is not hindered until the percentage of Negroes surpasses 75 percent, the shifting of Negroes from classes in which they are a majority to classes in which they are a substantial minority might make them better off without harming the achievement of whites. If, however, the school shifted its emphasis from goals desired by middle-class whites to goals

147

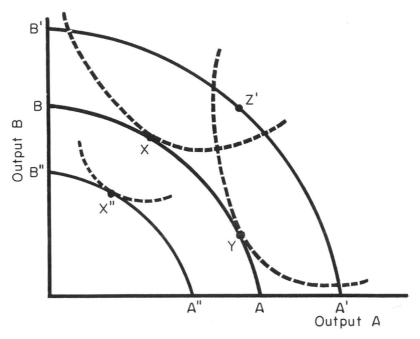

Figure 6.3   Preferred Resource Allocations: Peer Effects.

Integration model: integration shifts the opportunity locus for both rich and poor out to A'B'. Some output compromise, such as Z', may make both groups better off than if both the schooling and the decision-making processes were segregated.

Apartheid model: integration shifts the opportunity locus for both rich and poor in to A"B". Neither can be made better off by integrating either the schooling or decision-making processes.

Assymetric model: integration shifts the opportunity locus for the poor out to A'B', for the rich in to A"B". While the rich are worse off when schooling and decision-making are integrated, the gain to the poor by integrating schooling may be offset by the loss from integrating decision making.

desired by lower-class blacks, then integration would not be mutually beneficial.

Distributional Consequences

Upper-middle and middle classes. Despite biases in the distribution of school resources in their favor, the urban middle classes receive worse public schooling than they are willing to pay for (see Table 6.1, above); the expenditures per pupil are much greater in upper-income suburbs than in big city districts of equal socioeconomic status. Second, and perhaps more important, the upper middle classes do not receive the style of education they would like with respect to both the means and ends of the school system. Their dissatisfaction with the quality of public schooling available in the big city is expressed by their relatively low rate of public school utilization; for example, 60 percent in Boston as compared to 80 percent in suburbs of similar income.

Third, the middle classes in the big city are given the major burden of financing the schooling of the lower classes. Nationally, about 60 percent of all public school revenue is levied through property taxes, and in some areas, like Boston, this is closer to 90 percent. While property taxes tend to be regressive, wherein the *rate* of taxation varies inversely with income, the total *tax bills* tend to vary directly with income. Because school taxes tend to be more responsive to differences in income than school expenditures received, "the property tax on balance tends to redistribute income from the rich to the poor."[4] Perhaps an unusual case, school expenditures in Boston vary *inversely* while tax bills vary directly with income.[5] Because property taxes are limited by municipal boundaries, the middle classes can escape these subsidies by fleeing behind the fiscal "Berlin wall" of suburbia. In other words, while school taxes in the city are practically based upon ability to pay, these taxes in the suburbs are generally proportional to benefits received.[6]

Finally, the existence of "open enrollment" raises the possibility that upper-middle-class schools will be inundated with lower-class transfers. Because most middle-class people believe that the resulting peer effects would be deleterious to their own children, they have a further incentive to leave the urban public school system.

Consequently, the institutions for producing, distributing, and financing big city schooling are not fiscally neutral with respect to the residential choices of the upper-income groups. Faced with two equally desirable houses, one in the big city, one in a high-income suburb, the upper middle class has three incentives to choose the suburb: they are more likely to find schools with desired expenditures and style of operations; there is less burden of subsidy; and there is no fear of lower-class students transferring across municipal boundaries. Consequently, residential patterns are likely to be distorted in the direction of oversuburbanization and oversegregation. The exercise of the option to use private schools or to go to the suburbs has results incompatible with urban renewal goals of increasing the stake of the middle class in the central city. The institutional structure of urban schooling, then, may play a critical role in creating the current "urban crisis."

Minorities. Lower-class minorities are an additional group damaged by the current organization of big city schools. Much of the bias against schools with lower-class students emerges from the teacher placement mechanism. The single salary schedule, used in most big cities, permits no extra compensation for teaching in these allegedly more difficult schools. Consequently, teacher turnover and vacancy rates are higher, and teachers with greater training and experience, hence with greater choice in the labor market, tend to teach elsewhere.

Subtler expression of bias against minorities, such as prejudice on the part of teachers, guidance counselors, and administrators, may hinder student performance more than bias in the distribution of high quality teachers. The centralized mechanism for placing personnel does not permit minorities to weed out hostile teachers in their own schools.

Finally, the centralized control of school policy may frustrate the special educational demands of the minorities. For example, a school system like that in Boston, which is run by the Irish Catholic lower-middle- and working-class, may have little sympathy when the Negroes demand black studies.*

*Boston's electoral system weakens the ability of Negroes to offset these biases. Because school committee seats are filled by at-large elections, the less than 10 percent of the electorate who were Negro were unable to save the seat of a white sympathizer, much less elect a candidate of their own race in 1965. As long as education in the big city involves racial issues, as has been true in Boston since 1963, the Negro minority may find the white voters polarized against any attempts to alleviate bias.

The Poor. Although the upper-income families in big cities subsidize their schooling, the poor may be overburdened in the process. School systems are generally financed by local property taxes, the incidence of which tends to be shifted from landlords to their poor tenants.[7] Because they live near higher-income families who are willing to spend more on education, the poor (especially the elderly) may be forced to pay for higher quality schools than they would choose under fiscal autonomy. This would be true if the marginal disutility of additional taxes exceeded the marginal utility of the better schools.

Big cities contribute considerably more to equality in educational opportunity than do the multitude of suburbs and small towns in a state. As a mechanism for expressing consumer preferences, a big city school system fails to provide wealthier groups with the opportunity for upgrading their own public schools or minorities with the power to grapple with their peculiar educational needs. As a mixture-producing mechanism, it is limited to the degree that residential heterogeneity exists and to the degree that upper-income and Roman Catholic parents patronize private rather than public schools. The municipal boundary around a city inhibits the mixing of children from the city's low-income families with those from the higher-income suburbs. Consequently, it is not at all obvious that big city school systems, as presently organized, are efficient instruments for simultaneously achieving racial integration, equalizing educational opportunity, and expressing consumer choice.

PATCHING AND REPAIRING THE CURRENT SYSTEM

To what extent can a reorganization of education in large cities increase the degree of equality of opportunity without further impairing the free expression of consumer choice? Conversely, to what extent can freedom of choice be enhanced without exacerbating the inequalities? Is integration compatible with either of these two goals? Are there ways of patching up the current system to improve performance on *all* these criteria?

Altering Placement Policies

Suppose we attempted to alter teacher placement institutions in order to equalize the teacher quality of all big city schools. For example, extra compensation for teaching in undesirable schools would probably improve the quality of staff and lower the turnover rates in those schools. Such a policy, however, would probably not improve the attitudes of teachers and administrators toward students of those schools. One clear consequence of the policy would be to drain some of the quality teachers from the more desirable schools. More upper-income parents might respond by moving to the suburbs or enrolling their children in private schools. If the financing for such an arrangement came from the state or federal governments, the staffs of the undersirable schools might be improved without undermining the quality of the desirable schools.

An alternative policy for equalizing teaching quality is by consciously assigning teachers of equal caliber to all schools. Under such an arrangement, the teacher turnover rates in the poor areas would still be relatively high. Teacher morale might fall in reaction to the constraints on teacher choice, and the turnover rates for the whole system might consequently rise.

Although the teacher placement institutions produce bias, they are in some sense impartial. Educators have little discretion to favor or disfavor certain schools in the system. A more conscious and discretionary policy of teacher placement, by fiat or by compensatory bonus, is a two-edged sword. An administrator of bad faith or of practical political sense would have the power to reward his friends and punish his enemies even more than he now can. In the context of racial tension, white voters might force administrators to assign the better teachers to their own areas, to the detriment of the Negro areas.

Complete Integration

Instead of tinkering with teacher placement institutions, suppose the administration integrated schools with respect to all ethnic and socioeconomic characteristics present in the big city. Because every school would reflect a similar cross section, good teachers would not favor any particular school because of the composition of the study body. Even a conspiratorial administrator would have difficulty in favoring certain groups because all groups would share all schools. Still, teachers in classrooms might single out students of certain ethnic or income groups for abuse, a phenomenon very difficult to control. The policy of integration, then, is one which maximizes the equality of educational opportunities for all groups in the big city.

There are several flaws in this mechanism for providing equality. First, the policy eliminates any possibility for upper-income groups to upgrade their own educational levels. As the gap between actual and desired quality of public schools increases for this group, they have greater incentives to secure better schooling elsewhere. Second, if all schools were of uniform quality, more than ever the educational needs of minorities might be suppressed in favor of the needs of the majority. As mentioned before, different socioeconomic groups tend to value different educational goals. As suggested by the production analysis above, these goals compete for resources and cannot all be maximized simultaneously. Under such conditions, the fate of minority interests is in doubt.

If racial, and perhaps socioeconomic, integration is perceived as a means of equalizing educational opportunity, we can ask whether there are not other means with less costly by-products. If racial integration is perceived as an end in itself, we ought to explicitly catalog both its costs in consumer freedom and its burden to different groups in the big city. Conceivably, the burden would be most inequitably distributed, and the educational benefits would be most insignificant if lower-income Negroes were to be integrated with lower-income whites who have less resources to flock to private or suburban education than their upper-income compatriots.

Federal and State Financial Aid

Rather than altering any of the administrative institutions, the state or federal government may attempt to equalize resources of all districts, suburban and urban, by block grants. Because of large interstate differences in income, the federal government is in a better position than the states to produce national equalization.

A conservative method of federal aid is a flat grant of X dollars per student enrolled in each district. This system would provide a fiscal floor below which no district could fall. Because districts would probably augment school expenditures through local taxation, wealthier suburbs would still spend more than poorer suburbs.

A system of federal grants inversely proportional to income would permit poor districts to spend as much on schooling as wealthier districts. Because lower-class districts have to pay more to obtain a given level of teaching resources, the system of grants should result in poorer districts spending a greater total on schooling than rich districts.

A more radical method of federal aid sets minimum standards of performance which students from all schools are expected to attain, such as finishing high school or reading at a certain level of competence. Relatively "culturally advantaged" districts, of course, require fewer school resources to attain a given standard, and the discussion of the supply curve in Chapter 4 suggests a method of calculating the compensatory grant for the "deprived" districts.

Federal financing spreads the burden for upgrading the poor from the shoulders of the rich in the big city to those of upper-income groups throughout the state and nation. The rich would no longer escape the burden of financing the education of the poor by moving to the suburbs. These subsidies, however, in no way provide the rich in the city with a mechanism for the upgrading of or the minorities with the power to control the style of their own education.

DECENTRALIZATION

Decentralizing the administration and control of schooling might better reconcile the goals of equality of educational opportunity and freedom of consumer choice. Suppose that big city school systems were split into neighborhood districts with fiscal and administrative autonomy. Let each district raise its own school taxes and hire its own personnel in accord with the income and preferences of the voters.[8]

Because educational opportunities among small towns tend to be less equal than among big city districts, complete fiscal decentralization would undoubtedly lower the educational opportunities of the poor. If, in addition to this structural change, more of the financial burden were shifted to state and federal governments, there is no reason for the education of the poor to be downgraded. The fiscal and administrative autonomy of the neighborhood district permits different socioeconomic groups to add to the basic grant according to their preferences and income.

There are several advantageous by-products from the operation of the proposed institutions. First, autonomous school districts might be more sensitive to the needs and aspirations of the local populace than a city-wide bureaucracy. Conflicting interests of residentially segregated groups could be satisfied without compromise, thereby reducing intergroup tensions.

Second, the locality might have greater control over school personnel. Negroes could more easily weed out prejudiced and unsympathetic teachers and administrators. This control would be limited to the degree that current tenure and seniority rights were respected. In Boston, for example, 60 percent of the permanent teachers have been with the system for ten years or more, which suggests that replacing an entire faculty by normal attrition is time consuming.

Third, school boards in working-class districts would be in a better position to give local residents the "jobs, recognition, and protection" that is so important to these voters. The upper-middle-class school boards would be in a greater position to run the schools with "impartiality, consistency, and efficiency," which are the values of the middle-class voters.[9]

Finally, neighborhood school systems might make it easier for state and federal programs aimed at certain groups to hit the target. At present, compensatory grants to big cities to help the poor may be diffused to all residents of the city by

155

being absorbed centrally as overhead. If grants were made to poor neighborhood districts, it is less likely that the benefits will spill over to more affluent districts.

While decentralization may be radical in the big cities, it is commonplace in the suburbs. A historical accident gives suburbs the right to control their schools while denying this right to big city neighborhoods, which are often larger in population.

Technological Efficiency

Because small school systems operate most efficiently at enrollments of 2000 and larger systems at 20,000-50,000, full fiscal and administrative decentralization would not incur economic costs.[10] Without sacrificing technological efficiency, Boston could be divided into about thirty small, independent subsystems comprising two or three larger systems, the latter of which may provide specialized services too costly for the smaller systems.

Participation

Advocates of decentralization argue that such a proposal will increase parental participation in the schooling process, which is presumed to be desirable on democratic grounds. The evidence for this argument is rather weak. While smaller school districts generally have higher turnouts in school tax and bond elections, the participation rate rarely exceeds 40 percent, which is only a few points higher than in larger districts.[11] Also, the few people who consistently vote tend to be strong supporters of quality education, while those marginal voters who contribute to "high" turnouts usually appear to vote down school expenditures. Finally, people are more likely to vote when local property taxes comprise the greater share of school revenues. If decentralization is combined with a dependence on more outside funds, as it must for poor districts to survive, participation in school affairs is likely to fall.

Integration

School decentralization does not necessarily circumscribe the goal of racial or socioeconomic integration. Of course, the notion that a local board has the sole responsibility for integration would have to be abandoned.[12] Rather than coercion, which has been notably unsuccessful, financial incentives could be offered a local board to enroll heterogeneous students from other districts. For example, suppose a state defines the "racial balance point" as that percentage of Negroes in a school which matches their percentage of school children in a given city, county, or metropolitan area. The balance defined for the city of Boston in such terms is 25 percent. The state might offer a bounty of Y percent above the cost per student for any policies a school board might undertake to reduce racial imbalance, that is, for white districts accepting Negro transfers. The bounty per student might increase with the percentage of Negroes in the district, up to the balance point. Because whites seem more resistant to admitting Negroes to their schools than vice versa, the method compensates whites for not expressing their prejudice, or at least specifies the costs of segregation to themselves.*

Decentralization would work best if the big city were segregated into completely homogeneous subcultural areas.[13] This solution overlooks the facts of metropolitan ecology: even tiny neighborhoods contain diverse subcultures, and compact suburbs are not immune to normative conflict.[14] Consequently, subcultural minorities may fare worse in a decentralized district, in which they are heavily outvoted, than in a more centralized system in which they have allies.

There is a more profound difficulty with decentralization or decollectivization as a policy for benefiting everybody in a pluralistic society. Since all subcultures presume that schools are effective socializing agents, they are concerned not only with the normative patterns learned by their own children, but also those learned by others. In economic jargon, decisions about resource allocation and socialization involve externalities. The fact that each subculture believes

---

*The federal rent subsidy program is a precedent for this policy. Both lower- and middle-income families are given grants to live in a particular project; the former because they need the money, the latter as an incentive to live with lower-income neighbors.

its own superior norms are worthy of universalization pre-
scribes any technical solutions to the optimal unit of educational decision making. We observe in practice that educational
enterprises in the United States have always been highly regu-
lated, as evidenced by compulsory attendance laws, state
controls on curriculum and texts, and accreditation.

METROPOLITANISM

Contrary in direction to decentralization, metropolitanism is
the central city school system writ large.[15] While metropolitan
government is often advocated on the presumption of scale
economies or spillovers in urban services, no such economies
in elementary or secondary schooling justify a metropolitan
school system. Rather, for purposes of equalizing school resources and integration, the metropolitan system "captures"
those who would flee behind suburban boundaries.

As an institution for equalizing support per student among
districts, metropolitanism is inferior to state or federal subsidies, which draw on a wider tax base. More important, if the
metropolitan system should have a single salary schedule (and
it is most likely to), impoverished districts in large cities might
attract relatively or absolutely *worse* resources than they now
do. Under existing "Balkanization," big cities may be able to
compete for teachers with some of the poorer suburbs because
they offer higher salaries (see Table 6.1, above).

A metropolitan system may increase the degree of integration only marginally if simply based upon "open enrollment."
Elementary school children probably would not be permitted
by their parents to travel very far for better schooling, even if
the bussing were publicly financed. Large-scale cross-bussing,
even if politically feasible, would be extremely costly, especially
in cities like Chicago where middle-class Caucasian and lower-
class Negro neighborhoods are widely separated.

The most radical variant of metropolitanism is the "educational park," a complex of schools which draws large numbers
of children from a wide area.[16] While such a proposal maximizes the degree of equality among public schools and the

degree of racial and social integration, it is not without its costs. Aside from the expense in time and money in transporting large numbers of children, the educational park completely eliminates the freedom of choice inherent even in the current organization of schooling.

Metropolitan school systems are likely to magnify many of the flaws of the present big city system. First, aspirations for local control and responsiveness to local needs, especially among the minorities who will be more heavily outnumbered, are severely circumscribed if not thwarted. It is unlikely that the Negroes, who will soon obtain political hegemony in many big cities, would be willing to share with a metropolitan constituency the control of big city schools, and the jobs, protection, and recognition such control entails. Second, freedom of choice regarding the quality and style of public schooling is reduced by the necessity for compromise among the diverse metropolitan constituency. While current Balkanization and even the use of private schools serves to reduce conflict, the metropolitanization of schools might exacerbate these conflicts by closing the surburban escape hatch.*

This second objection is met by the hope that big city systems can be raised to the excellence of some of the suburban schools, rather than the contrary. Potentially, metropolitan schools could be made so good that even the wealthy would want to enroll their children.

This argument overlooks the politics of public finance. The wealthy suburbanites already have the quality of schooling they are willing to pay for. To raise all metropolitan schools to this level would require higher taxes and expenditures, which contribute nothing to their immediate welfare. While much of the tax burden will fall on the wealthy, the poor will also have

---

*Yankee suburbanites of Boston, for example, would shudder at the thought of an educator like Louise Day Hicks directing their children's education, just as her ancestors chafed under the proselytizing Yankees several generations earlier. See Peter H. and Alice S. Rossi, "Parochial School Education in America," Dædalus, 90 (Winter 1961), 61–78, on the withdrawal of Irish Catholics from the public school system in the nineteenth century.

to pay more taxes, and the costs may more than offset their perceived gain in terms of school quality.

Upper-middle-class individuals often vote against their narrow self-interest on local matters over which they have some control.[17] Thus, they *may* vote to raise the quality of all metropolitan schools to the pinnacles. Doing so would require immense subsidization of the poor, but the rich have not demonstrated much willingness to subsidize them through state aid. Indeed, in the few metropolitan areas in the United States that have adopted some form of regional government, upper-income suburbs have succeeded in excluding schooling as a regional function.

Even if metropolitanism existed, a plausible strategy for the rich would be to vote against school taxes altogether and to favor private education, as many currently do in large cities. As suggested in Chapter 5, a group abandoning the public schools confers two immediate benefits on the rest of the community; per capita taxes tend to fall and per pupil expenditures to rise. If the rich abandon the public schools, inequalities will be somewhat reduced, but socioeconomic integration then becomes infeasible and the major rationale for metropolitanism is jeopardized.

TUITION VOUCHERS

While there were good evolutionary reasons for the traditional role of government in education,[18] not all forms of government intervention are necessarily adaptive today. The most radical proposal for school reorganization, most cogently proposed by Milton Friedman, is turning over the production of educational services to the private or market sector of the economy.[19]

The need for government intervention in education to equalize opportunity and to ensure national unity does not logically justify public *production* of educational services. It is quite possible for the government to meet those objectives without engaging in any production. Friedman proposes for example, that the federal government "require a minimum level of schooling, financed by giving parents vouchers redeemable for

specified maximum sum per child if spent on approved education." Under this system parents can supplement these
vouchers with private expenditures, and the role of government is simplified to financing and insuring minimum standards of quality.

The Nature of the Market

The consequence of grants to parents is the "privatization" or
the desocialization of education, with all of its ramifications.
First, profit-seeking entrepreneurs could enter the education
industry on terms equal to the current public "entrepreneurs."
Currently, competition between public and private educators is
on unequal terms because the latter, unlike the former, has to
meet expenses through user charges. Under the alternative
system, all would compete for consumer dollars in order to
survive. Like producers in the private sector, educators would
become responsive to consumer demand because they would
no longer monopolize public education. In turn, the consumer
would have greater freedom of choice, without having to "vote
by feet" or to persuade a community to alter its collective
policies.

Under the current organization, a well-defined constituency
has more or less direct control over a single school system. In
large cities, as we have mentioned, this constituency has diverse interests and includes those who have no positive stake
in educational quality. Under the tuition voucher system, no
school would be directly controlled by such a constituency.
Individuals would exercise indirect control over a whole set of
schools via the market, for those schools which are unrespon-
sive to consumer demands will fold. Whether direct or indirect
control provides greater responsiveness to consumer needs is
debatable. Consumers may be apathetic or as manipulable by
profit-seeking educators as by vote-seeking educators. Dema-
goguery in politics has its economic counterpart in "demand
creation" through advertising.[20]

Technological Efficiency

Friedman argues that the extension of the market system to

primary and secondary education will produce technological efficiency because of the profit motive. Greater efficiency would translate into either lower costs or greater quality for the consumer, and inefficient schools would succumb, unlike the immortal monopolies of today.

This line of reasoning is highly implausible. First, invention and innovation in education are probably inherently more difficult than in manufacturing. Even the rate of technological progress in the profit-making service enterprises, like barber shops, is not outstanding.[21]

Second, the selection pressures toward efficiency in education are rather weak. Producers are hardly more able to distinguish frills from essentials than are consumers. Neither is likely to have well-founded beliefs about the value of alternative resource allocations. The most likely result under any regime is the kind of professional paternalism that exists in medicine and auto repairing, in which the producer makes judgments of value as well as of fact for the nominally sovereign consumer. Either professional ethics or venality invariably dictates higher levels of service than a fully knowledgeable consumer would want.

Attempting to introduce an effective evaluation system brings the public into direct conflict with the professional ethic of educators. Public accountability is incompatible with peer accountability. The unhappy developments in the National Educational Assessment Program suggest that the educational establishment is powerful enough to prevent a meaningful evaluative system that would compare the performance of students in different schools, that would identify the relationship between resources and student performance, and that would, finally, permit an evaluation of the effectiveness and efficiency of particular school systems.[22]

The enemy of evaluation is not bureaucracy but professionalism. Such diverse "market-oriented" occupational groups as lawyers, physicians, and electricians prefer esoteric systems of peer ratings, and they avoid quality competition and public accountability. Even in the industrial sector, competition is usually on the basis of styling and quality rather than by invidious comparison on criteria such as safety or price.

Third, immanent in most free market proposals are the factors that undermine competition. For example, a metropolitan teachers' union may achieve greater strength vis-à-vis a multitude of small, independent schools than current unions vis-à-vis big city school boards. One result may be a high single salary schedule which would limit the ability of schools catering to lower-class children to offer "combat pay."[23] Or, independent schools might be forced to adopt standards of accreditation and administration that would inhibit any meaningful experimentation.

Another kind of efficiency is likely to emerge from the voucher scheme, however. Under the current institutions, the purchase of a home and the option to attend public school are indivisible. Residential location often depends, therefore, upon the quality of this option. Privatization through tuition vouchers separates residential and schooling decisions, making educational policy more fiscally neutral with respect to land use. The optimization of residential patterns is consequently unconstrained by educational considerations: good schooling becomes obtainable without the purchase of an expensive home; homes can be chosen with little consideration to the quality of the closest school. Consequently, housing segregation might diminish somewhat.[24]

Integration

Privatization reverses the traditional public policy of denying subsidy to schools controlled by "divisive" or separatist minorities. Without getting involved with the constitutional aspects of church-state relations, we can speculate on the impact of this reversal on class, racial, or religious segregation in the schools and, ultimately, on national unity.

If one were to design a system for maximizing segregation on those dimensions, he could not substantially improve upon the existing municipal services market mechanism. The voucher system is likely to increase educational segregation to a minor extent because consumer freedom extends to choice of peers as well as to choice of tangible inputs. First, a new breath of life would be given to parochial school systems were they to be eligible for the private funds. Second, the most ambitious children in a lower-class "ghetto" might flee the neighborhood public school, leaving behind a more impoverished peer group. Third, the little progress toward desegregation in the South would probably be undone. Nondiscriminatory admissions policies may have little effect on these tendencies if segregation is self-imposed on ideological or pedagogical grounds.

If tuition vouchers were to lead to a marginal increase in school segregation and to a marginal decrease in residential segregation, it is important to ask how divisive such events might be for the social order. Although nineteenth-century nativists looked upon the common public school as a vehicle for assimilating divisive minorities, many minorities resisted such assimilation. German-Americans in the Midwest were denied public support for German-language schools which were intended to perpetuate the culture and eventually lead to the creation of German-speaking states. In response, a Lutheran school system was established, and it still survives although the language of instruction is now English. Similarly, the creation of the Catholic school system by the Irish was a response to proselytizing efforts of Protestants in the public schools.[25]

At least in the case of Catholic education, segregation does not seem to produce divisiveness. Comparisons between Catholics who had parochial instead of public education show little difference in community involvement, tolerance, and interaction with non-Catholics.[26]

Apparently, the American fear of tolerating cultural variants in public schools is subsiding. New federal programs provide funds for instruction in several European, Oriental, and American Indian languages as a vehicle for the eventual teaching of English. The aim of these bilingual programs, however, is not cultural pluralism but more rapid assimilation. Whether this logic is borne out by events remains to be seen. At any rate, there is little firm evidence to confirm or refute the proposition that school systems based on cultural premises that vary from the American norm would result in the dissolution of the social order. We must recognize that any system of financing, such as tuition vouchers, which would promote educational variety involves risks.

CONCLUSION

Because the degree of technological efficiency and progress is not likely to vary with respect to institutions for producing and distributing elementary and secondary schooling, the four alternative structures are compared with respect to consumption efficiency, equality, and integration. Although different features of each organization may be combined, the four ideal types may be characterized as follows:

1) Status quo: multidistrict systems in a big city would be under central control, with the neighborhood school "monopoly" tempered by open enrollment with transportation costs privately borne (no "bussing"); suburban systems would be fiscally autonomous; no intersystem transfers would be permitted without payment of tuition.
2) Decentralization: big city districts would assume the same autonomy as suburban systems; no open enrollment.
3) Metropolitanism: all schools in a metropolitan area would be centrally financed and administered; educationsl parks would draw students from a wide area.
4) Tuition vouchers: students may add supplementary private funds.

To make the four organizations comparable, we assume that the average level of state-federal support per student is identical under all plans and that there are no programs with integration as the primary purpose (see Table 6.2).

In terms of the goals of equality and integration, metropolitanism ranks highest because all public schools would be of equal quality. An indeterminate number of families would seek much better private education, however, thus producing a bimodal distribution of overall quality. On the other hand, privatization produces the greatest inequality and segregation. In terms of freedom of choice, or consumer efficiency, privatization ranks highest and metropolitanism, lowest. The status quo

Table 6.2. Rankings of educational organizations: Attainment of policy goals and preferences of interest groups.

Organization	Policy goals			Interest groups			
	Equality	Consumer freedom	Integration	City rich	Suburb rich	Minority poor	Educational establishment
Status quo	2	3	2	4	1	4	1
Decentralization	3	2	3	2	3	?	3
Metropolitanism	1	4	1	3	4	?	2
Tuition vouchers	4	1	4	1	1	?	4

166

and decentralization rank midway between these two other systems with respect to all three criteria.

The four major interest groups are likely to have widely divergent orders of preference. The rich in large cities would favor privatization because it permits them to live where they want without compromising their preferences, inordinately subsidizing the poor, or sharing facilities with them. Decentralization might be their second best option because they could control their own schools. Metropolitanism would give them some suburban allies but it would have most of the disadvantages of the status quo.

The suburban rich are probably indifferent to a choice between the status quo and private schools, which may be no better than schools in exclusive suburbs. While decentralization in the city leaves them unaffected, they could only lose by metropolitanization.

The educational establishment, like all establishments, would probably resist any change. Metropolitanism is probably the least noxious change because size tends to reduce the interest of voters and to foster civil service "professionalism." In addition, another level of administration provides opportunities for promotion. Privatization would be the greatest threat if unionism were abandoned in favor of "free market" forces. On the other hand, if teachers' organizations survived, they might have greater bargaining power vis-à-vis the many independent schools.

The preferences of the poor and of the minorities are less clear. Decentralization or privatization gives them control but no integration; metropolitanism gives them integration but no control. The status quo provides neither. How they would choose among the first three systems is unclear.

It is not obvious whether some combination of decentralization, metropolitanism, and privatization could be reached that would benefit all of the major interest groups more than the status quo. For example, vouchers might be given to all students on the basis of income (the poor would get more). All students would have a choice of attending a private school or the fiscally autonomous public schools, which would be locally controlled. A metropolitan public agency might coordinate interschool student exchanges, serves as an employment exchange for teachers, disseminate information on the relative quality of different schools, operate an educational television station, or offer "cooperative purchasing services." Finally, the state or metropolitan government might offer fiscal incentives for integration.

It is sterile to evaluate the four organizations on technical grounds. No organization dominates any other with respect to all three criteria; nor is so dominated. Ultimately, the choice among organizational forms is a political one.

Chapter 7   THE BURDENS ON BIG CITY SCHOOLS

It is absolutely crucial to understand that the society cannot continue to write reports accurately describing the failure of the educational institutions *vis-à-vis black people without ultimately taking into account the impact those truths will have on black Americans. There comes a point when it is no longer possible to recognize* institutional failure *and then merely propose more stepped-up measures to overcome these failures—especially when the proposals come from the same kinds of people who administered so long the present unacceptable and* dysfunctional policies and systems [*emphasis mine*].[1]
— Charles Hamilton

The American school has traditionally been viewed as an agency of both social change and individual mobility. In the past the school has successfully educated the masses in the workings of democracy, disseminated the fruits of technology, and acculturated hordes of immigrants. The present generation has given the school even more Herculean tasks, yet it has grave misgivings about the school's capacity to meet the challenge.[2]

The shibboleths of our time—the space race, automation, and the war on poverty—suggest the tasks. While the problems of teaching languages and science to "catch up with the Russians" and of retraining workers in dying industries are common to all communities, the burdens of giving a "head start" to "disadvantaged" infants and of molding the racial attitudes of the next generation fall especially on the big cities. Paradoxically, it is in the big cities that the misgivings about the school's capacity to perform any of these tasks are greatest.

In this chapter, I hope to summarize the arguments developed in the book, to clarify some of the problems of big city schools, and to distinguish between those common to all social service enterprises and those peculiar to schooling. In contrast to those who look toward more resources or administrative reorganization as a way out of the educational crisis, I suggest that a search, first, for new educational technologies and, second, for new curricula for educational administrators is a potentially more fruitful mode of action, however undramatic it may be.

SUMMARY

School systems have traditionally been evaluated in terms of the propriety of the procedures by which they are administered, the magnitude of the resources they consume, or the performance of their students, but rarely in terms of how much they teach. Because school performance depends upon the characteristics of both the home and the school, it is possible for children in poor schools to perform well or children in excellent schools to perform poorly. Since so little is known about the relationship between particular school resources and student performance, there is little reason to assume that schools consuming higher levels of resources are more effective. Indeed, in the profit-making sector of the economy, increased use of resources may indicate decreased efficiency. Knowledge of the resource-performance nexus, or the educational production function, is the *sine qua non* of evaluation and prescription.

Most econometric studies of educational production functions have been inconclusive. They suffer from fractional measurement of the multitude of educational goals, from high correlations among school resource and social class variables that make the identification of distinct resource effects impossible, and from a lack of substantial variation in school resources that beclouds any attempts to predict effects of radical resource changes on performance. These shortcomings result from the inability of researchers, for political and ethical rea sons, to perform controlled educational experiments. Nevertheless, a review of statistical "natural experiments" suggests that *many resources which are presumed to have a major impact on how much children learn—age of building, class size, teacher's academic degrees—are fairly unimportant.*

Production functions for Boston are estimated by relating measures of student performance to the school resources and social class characteristics of each of the city's fifty-six elementary school districts. In addition to expenditures per student, the following measures of school resources are observed: percentage of teachers accredited, percentage of teachers with at least a master's degree, percentage of permanent teachers with more than ten years of experience, percentage of students in uncrowded classes, pupil-teacher ratio, annual rate of teacher turnover, district enrollment, and age of school building.

The above resources are related to several measures of student performance by the statistical technique of regression analysis: two measures of holding power or the attractiveness of schooling (attendance rates, continuation or nondropout rates); two measures of cognitive development (reading gains, level of mathematics achievement); and two measures of academic achievement (percentage of sixth graders taking and percentage passing the examination for entry to the elite Latin High Schools).

The regression coefficients relate the numerical change in per formance to numerical changes in school resources. In general, changes in a given input do not affect all performance measures. In other words, in order to influence a given measure of performance only expenditures on particular inputs have any effect. Teacher turnover, accreditation, and experience, lack of crowding, and levels of enrollment have a strong effect on some measures of performance, while teacher training, class size, and the age of building have a negligible effect. Because many expensive resources, like small classes or new buildings, have little impact on learning, we observe that expenditures per student are weakly related to performance.

From the equation for each performance measure, an index of quality can be calculated. The sum of school resources weighted by their regression coefficients can be interpreted as the contribution of schooling to student performance. An index of this type comes closer to our intuitive notions of school quality than any other. Because indexes based on different performance measures are not highly correlated and because different groups in the community do not always agree as to the importance of variance aspects of performance, *there is no technically deducible method of evaluating school quality.*

The impact of school resources on performance can be expressed in three ways. From the quality index one finds, for example, that, in Boston, school resources contribute an average of 55 percent to the *level* of reading gains. The responsiveness or *elasticity* of reading gains to school resources is 0.5, which means that a 10 percent increase in all effective resources translates into a 5 percent gain in reading. Finally, about 42 percent of the *variance* in reading gains is explained by school resources. In other words, if school resources were distributed equally among districts, then the variance in reading gains would decline by 42 percent.

The effect of the school's racial composition on performance can be examined only when both school resources and social class are held constant. In Boston, students in the predominantly Negro schools do not perform worse than students in the predominantly white schools, *ceteris paribus.* In addition, students in integrated schools perform, on the average, like those in white and Negro schools, *ceteris paribus.* This is not to say that racial segregation is not educationally harmful in some circumstances, but such does not seem to be the case in Boston where the correlation between race and social class is fairly insubstantial.

Of the many measures by which the distribution of educational opportunity can be characterized, the most valid is an index of resources weighted by the coefficients of the production functions. Because of the unreliability of generally derived production functions as descriptions of particular school systems and because of the lack of sufficient data, little can be said of the distribution of quality of the nation's schools. At best we can describe the distribution of expenditures of physical resources on a national, interstate, and intrastate basis.

Fortunately, the availability of relatively reliable production functions and data from Boston permits the proper calculation of the inequalities and biases of that school system. In Boston, the degree of inequality in school quality is rather minor. In addition, there is a low but statistically significant correlation between resources, either weighted or raw, and the social characteristics of the school districts. *Districts with higher income and more Caucasians tend to have more effective resources*, but there is little bias in favor of Irish or politically active districts. Three big cities—Boston, Chicago, and Atlanta —which have been intensively studied are remarkably similar in the degree of inequality of resources, and Boston exhibits the least inequality.

The degree of equality of resources tends to be greater among big city school districts than among independent systems within a state and than among the averages of all the states. In general, communities with higher income spend more on school resources, although the correlation is far from perfect. Whether more expenditures translate into more effective resources cannot be determined without detailed knowledge of particular systems.

THE BURDENS

Big city school systems are facing a crisis because of their ineffectiveness and inefficiency in meeting educational objectives, because of their lack of responsiveness to the demands of their clients, and because of their unequal treatment of low income and minority groups. What is the role of technology, institutions, and politics in resolving these crises?

Effectiveness and Technological Efficiency

Major problems of ineffectiveness plague all school systems. First, the objectives of schooling are neither easily identifiable nor measurable. The important long-term consequences of schooling, such as "earning power," "thinking ability," or "citizenship" cannot be easily related to any resource characteristics of schooling or even to more proximate indicators of student performance, such as test scores.

Second, the input-output technology of education, a *sine qua non* of economizing, is poorly understood. While many parents and educators believe that smaller classes, newer buildings, and teachers with more academic training are superior, there is little evidence that these resources have any significant effect on students. On the other hand, less measurable and less controllable resources, such as teacher turnover, verbal ability, and expectation, have a major impact on performance. Dissemination of some of the findings reviewed here will, I hope, guide the public and educators toward resource choices that are in line with their productivity and cost effects.

Third, because of vagueness of the objectives and of technology of education, school administrators have less ability to economize than producers in the manufacturing sector. Because consumers are less able to evaluate services with long-term consequences than to evaluate goods, and because schools are generally nonprofit institutions, educators have less *incentive* to economize. Consequently, they are likely to "satisfice," or perform up to the expectations of consumers.[3] In Boston, for example, the average output of the schools could be produced 30 percent more cheaply if educational efficiency were the prime goal of the system.

While many of these problems plague all government service activities, there are additional problems peculiar to some big cities, which further compound their difficulties in remaining solvent. First, a disproportion of urban voters have relatively little stake in the efficiency of public schooling. Parents of parochial school children may be more interested in low taxes while working-class voters may be interested in the job provision function of schooling. Politicians catering to these interests tend to view School Committee posts as stepping-stones to higher office rather than as positions of public responsibility and service.[4]

Second, big cities tend to have greater difficulty in recruiting quality personnel than do most suburbs. Better teachers, those with the greater freedom of job choice, often prefer positions in middle-class suburbs rather than in central cities strained by problems of poverty, race, inbred administrations, and hostile parents. In addition, with the suburbanization of the middle and lower middle classes, from which most female teachers come, locational considerations make big city schools decreasingly attractive. It is not surprising, then, that few graduates of the best schools of education in metropolitan Boston teach in the central city. Despite the city's high salary schedule, the caliber of the faculty it attracts is not of commensurate repute.[5]

Because of greater inefficiency and higher resource costs, the expenditure on a given level of school output is probably higher in big cities than in the suburbs. Consequently, city voters, who get less per educational dollar than equivalent suburbanites, would prefer to substitute expenditures on other goods for higher expenditures on education, *ceteris paribus*.

Responsiveness

The lack of responsiveness of educators to the demands of their clients stems partly from the nature of educational institutions but also partly from the way in which education in the United States has been perceived. Educators cannot be responsive to each demand from every constituency because many of the demands are incompatible, as, for example, devoting more attention to deprived students as opposed to advanced students. Much of the unresponsiveness of this type might be remedied if constituencies with diverse tastes or problems did not have to decide collectively about school policy. Administrative decentralization in the context of residential segregation would at least provide the educator with a more nearly unanimous constituency to which he could respond, a constituency more like that of a small town.

It is not clear how responsive America's culturally dominant white Protestant middle class wants schooling to be to demands of minorities. The prohibition of foreign-language schools and of subsidies to parochial schools since the nineteenth century suggests that pluralism is not one of the goals of the public school system. Indeed, the ideal was that of the *common school*, which would mold foreign, lower-class children into the "typical" American image. Current patterns of state curriculum regulation maintain this tradition.

Equality

All school systems face the problem of obtaining financial resources from voters. Schools compete for funds with alternative uses of a community's resources. The sum a municipality will spend upon schooling depends upon its income, its preferences, and the relative costs of schooling vis-à-vis other goods and services.

The big cities have three peculiar solvency problems, as illustrated by Boston (see Table 7.1). Like most core cities, Boston has a lower median income than its suburbs. As a result, the big city has lesser fiscal capacity to match suburban school expenditures in the absence of state or federal aid.

Boston also has a disproportion of poor and Negro families, presumably the most disadvantaged in the metropolitan area.

Table 7.1. Socioeconomic characteristics of Metropolitan Boston, central city versus suburbs, 1960.

Characteristic	Central city (a)	Suburbs (b)	a:b
Income, median family	$5747	$7300	.79
Families, income less than $3000 (percent)	16.6	9.1	1.83
Population, Negro (percent)	9.0	0.8	11.25
Public school students, Negro (percent)	25.0	2.0	12.50
Professional, male (percent)	15.3	30.8	.49
Population, "ethnic" (percent)	21.0	14.9	1.41
Private school enrollment, elementary (percent)	33.1	19.5	1.70

Source: U.S. Census of Population, 1960, *Boston Standard Metropolitan Statistical Area, Final Report PC(3)-1D* (Washington, D.C.: Government Printing Office, 1963), Tables 1-3; Massachusetts Department of Education, *Racial Census of Schools, 1965* (mimeo.).

Since home and school are complementary agents of education, the big city schools have to do more for their students than suburban schools in order to elicit a given level of performance. With some set of "minimum standards" of *performance* in mind, the "needs" of the big city school systems are greater than those of the suburbs.

Besides having greater needs but fewer resources than the suburbs, the big city is more likely to comprise an electorate relatively indifferent or hostile to public education. Banfield and Wilson distinguish two opposing systems of consumer-voter values and preferences: the "public-regarding" who tend to favor spending for their perception of the "public interest" and the "private-regarding" who tend to oppose public spending unless they benefit materially. Yankees (northern white Anglo-Saxon Protestants), Jews, and professionals tend to fall in the public-regarding category, while foreign stock Irish-, Italian-, and Polish-Americans, especially of the lower middle and working classes tend to fall in the private-regarding category.*

Like most central cities, Boston comprises relatively more private-regarding voters than its suburbs. Consequently, there is relatively less support for schools among those receiving no direct benefit: those with no children in the public schools. One reflection of the private-regarding tastes of Boston's population is that the rate of private school utilization is relatively higher than in suburbs.

All school systems must decide in whose benefit its resources are to be utilized. Because of the output trade-offs inherent in the educational production functions, an implicit or explicit choice is made between the interests of students differing in aptitude, aspiration, and achievement. Abstracting from the rather ambiguous peer effects, those resource bun-

---

*Edward C. Banfield and James Q. Wilson, "Public-Regardingness as a Value Premise in Voting Behavior," *American Political Science Review*, 58 (Dec. 1964), 876–887. They identify the residual "private-regarding" voters as the very poor, largely Negro, who tend to favor public spending because they *perceive* that they have nothing to lose. As renters, to whom the incidence of property taxation shifts, this class in fact has much to lose by an increase in the tax rate.

dles which do the most to prevent dropouts do the least to serve students aspiring to college.

A choice is also made between the interests of students and those of school personnel. As mentioned earlier, "private-regarding" voters are more concerned with "jobs, favors, and protection," than with the quality of services. In Boston, for example, school custodians, secretaries, and teachers have considerable power to establish high salary schedules, to create and and preserve jobs, and to exclude outsiders from employment.[6] Whether the exercise of these powers is compatible with quality education is doubtful.

Unlike small homogeneous communities served by a central school or a few schools, the big cities must divide resources among schools in dispersed neighborhoods that tend to differ in socioeconomic and ethnic composition. Because of its multiplant nature, the big city system inextricably binds distributive and allocative decisions. In concrete terms, the resources devoted to a given school benefit directly only residents of the neighborhood.

Studies of distribution reviewed earlier suggest that schools in white and upper-income neighborhoods tend to be better than those in Negro and lower-income neighborhoods. Of course, all schools in white, upper-income neighborhoods are not better than all schools in black, lower-income neighborhoods, and even the average differences are quite small.

Although the law on this matter is changing, the courts, in insisting on equal educational opportunity *within* a municipality, place the major burden for equalization and integration on the big cities rather than on the states. What is seldom recognized is that disparities among school districts in a big city are usually less than those among suburbs, and certainly less than those among states, with comparable income differences. In the global context of the metropolitan community, big city school systems contribute to relative equality of educational opportunity.

The tendency for big cities to assume the major burden in equalizing educational opportunity has consequences that weaken its viability in transforming resources and satisfying consumer aspirations. First, a considerable share of administrative energy must be devoted to conflict resolution as opposed to economizing. Second, the fact that school quality is fairly equal among big city districts has the corollary that the upper middle classes are not receiving the superior public schooling they are willing to pay for. In response, this class utilizes private schools to a greater degree in the city than in the suburbs. The incentives for this class to move to the suburbs or to utilize public schooling would increase if the large cities were forced to equalize and to integrate more than at present, while allowing inequality and segregation to exist among suburbs.

THE PROMISE

While structural reorganization may make schools more responsive to parents, or more equal and less biased, they are unlikely to make schools "better" in the sense of teaching children more things we think they should know. Failures of effectiveness cannot be remedied without taking at least the following three steps: developing reliable and valid indicators of educational progress; identifying the *current* technological relationships between the characteristics of schools and student performance, as measured by these indicators; and inventing and disseminating *new* technologies. Not until these technologies become known does the issue of incentives toward efficiency in using these technologies become meaningful.

National Educational Assessment

The first step in this agenda has been initiated by the establishment of a continuing program of National Educational Assessment.[7] With the express purpose of gathering information useful in policy formulation, over 100,000 individuals will be tested annually in ten subject areas: science, citizenship, writing, music, mathematics, literature, social studies, reading, art, and vocational education.

Although the validity of the tests can be criticized, there are more serious reasons why this program will provide little information about policy choices. First, performance measures will not be related to characteristics of schools and of students in any meaningful way. No information about school resources will be collected, and only the grossest social characteristics will be recorded (region of the country, size of the city, whether or not poor). It would be impossible, therefore, to make any statements about the effect of educational policy on student performance.

There are more serious difficulties even if detailed school and family characteristics were recorded. As indicated by the experience of Project TALENT and the Equal Educational Opportunity Survey, social reality rarely generates data in a pattern tailored to the requirements of experimental design. For one thing, schools are not sufficiently different, at least with respect to the characteristics that are most measurable and manipulable. For example, there are too few schools with extreme class sizes of, say, ten and fifty, that are similar in all other respects so that we could test nonexperimentally the effects of radical policy changes in class size. In addition, school and student characteristics are so highly correlated that it is difficult to find schools that differ in only one major respect. For example, it is difficult to find upper-class children attending small classes who have poorly trained teachers; most such children have highly trained teachers. Consequently, we cannot distinguish among effects of various school characteristics, like teacher training and class size. These two difficulties, insufficient range of data and multicollinearity, are the plague of educational survey research, and they are not obviated by larger or better-chosen samples.

The Need for Inventions in Education

The social services sector of the economy, especially the schools, desperately needs more effective technologies. While in the past educators have devoured innovations, or *new* techniques, they have done relatively little to invent *effective* ones and much less to evaluate existing ones.

The skills and temperament of educators notwithstanding, local school systems have ignored these functions for rational reasons. First, research and development is expensive, perhaps beyond the fiscal capacity of all but the largest systems. Even in the largest industrial corporations, the government subsidizes a large proportion of research and development expenditures.[8] Second, and more important, social technologies are nearly pure public goods: the local system cannot recapture the costs of inventions by "selling" its discovery; moreover, it can obtain for free any inventions made elsewhere.[9] This means that local systems have little incentive for research and development *at their own expense.*

A possible source of innovation is profit-making enterprises which produce textbooks, audiovisual aids, and other learning devices. Such firms have an incentive to develop *marketable* educational innovations. While greater effectiveness or efficiency may be a strong selling point, educator-customers are relatively unable to evaluate the claims of the producers. Consequently, these firms may emphasize the salable, and possibly educationally irrelevant, aspects of their products, which may bias reports of their efficacy. In addition, private enterprise has an incentive to develop only those techniques that can be embodied in materials vendable on the market. They may tend to underinvest in research on techniques, while over-investing in research on materials.

A second source of innovation can be quasi-public agencies such as universities and research institutions, which may be uniquely situated for research into disembodied techniques and ideas. In addition, the federal government, foundations, or professional societies might maintain a "consumer union" to prevent the dissemination of misleading claims by firms in the private sector.

There is, finally, the need for a new breed of school administrator, a public service entrepreneur skilled in decision making for the nonprofit sector of the economy. If not as actual producers, these new educators should at least be trained as intelligent consumers of educational research.

CONCLUSION

Our understanding of schooling today is no further advanced than was medicine at the turn of the century, when, reputedly, a random patient treated by a random physician had a 50 percent chance of ending up no worse for the encounter. Altering school resources within the constraints of present technology may be no more effective than changing the doctor to patient ratio a century ago. There have been few major innovations *of proven effectiveness* in the technology of imparting information in school since the invention of movable type five hundred years ago, and school children of that era probably learned to read as they do today. We have hardly explored this ancient technology much less the new media through which the technology is being transmitted (such as audiovisual aids), and we know little of the relative effectiveness of private tutoring, small seminars, or large lectures—all ancient instructional forms.

A revolution of Darwinian, Einsteinian, or Freudian proportions has yet to occur in education. Perhaps it will take place in the form of computerized instruction or, more fantastically, in direct chemical transfer of knowledge.[10] Until the "Revolution," an economics of education can guide us toward making the best choices within the narrow constraints of a rather lame technology.

APPENDIXES, NOTES, AND INDEX

APPENDIX A

MISCELLANEOUS DATA PROBLEMS

The data from which the production functions are developed are cross-sectional observations on the city's fifty-six school districts. For each district, which comprises several schools, performance and resources characteristics arc available for the academic year 1964-65. Because no contemporary social characteristics were available, these had to be estimated from coterminous census tracts for 1960.

Methods of Calculating School Variables

The peculiar grade structure of the Boston Public Schools complicates data analysis. School authorities generally publish data on the basis of districts, which may contain up to five elementary schools under a single principal. Forty-four of the districts range from kindergarten to the sixth grade (K-6), and twelve of the districts range from kindergarten to the eighth grade (K-8). Because the seventh and eighth grades have unusual costs for shops and specialized personnel, cross-sectional comparisons which do not correct for these different types of elementary districts can be misleading. Table A.1, for example, shows the average spread of costs per pupil in the various types of districts.

To standardize for eight grades, I had to estimate the costs and physical resources used in educating students from K-6 districts in the seventh and eighth grades. While some students from K-6 districts go to K-8 districts for those grades, most

Table A.1. Comparisons of costs and master's degrees among various categories of school districts.

Category	Current costs per ADM	Masters (percent)
K–6	$327	
All elementary	341	36
K–8	399	
Junior high school	449	52

Sources: Annual Report of the Business Manager to the School Committee of the City of Boston, School doc. No. 4–1965, Table 2; percent masters 1965–1966 reported verbally by the Business Manager.

feed into one of the city's sixteen junior high schools. As school policy on feeder patterns is ambiguous, I had to make estimates by comparing maps of elementary districts and junior high districts. In several cases, corroborated by school authorities, some districts apparently send students to several junior highs.

Costs and physical resources for the seventh and eighth grades are assumed proportional to the number of students in these grades as a fraction of the total enrollment in the three-year junior high school. An elementary district's share of these resources was assumed to be proportional to its estimated share of junior high students. This latter share is proportional to the elementary enrollment of the districts feeding in.

Method of Calculating Socioeconomic Variables

The socioeconomic data were mostly compiled from the US Census, Population for the Boston Standard Metropolitan Statistical Area (SMSA), 1960.[1] There are three difficulties in making socioeconomic data comparable to educational data. First and least serious, the city's 155 census tracts have few boundaries in common with the 56 elementary school districts. I had to assume that the characteristics of the tract were distributed uniformly within its borders. A map of the school districts was superimposed onto a map of the census tracts, and a district's share of the various tracts was visually estimated to the nearest ¼ by area. The socioeconomic data was aggregated according to these visually estimated shares. Because 95 percent of the city's public school children attend within their home districts, I have some confidence that the two sets of data refer to the same population.

The second problem is that several of the social indicators are expressed as medians in the census data. For lack of any alternative, I weighted the medians in proportion to census tract population in the course of aggregation. For two of the variables characterized by medians—income and education—there are alternative measures, percentage of families with income less than $3000 and percentage of adults completing high school. The high correlations between the weighted medians and the corresponding percentages suggest that the results of weighting medians are not too farfetched.

The third and most serious problem is the time gap between the two sets of data. The 1960 census is the only available source of socioeconomic data. Unfortunately, detailed school data is available only for later years, from September 1964 to October 1965. Clearly, both the schools and the city changed rapidly during the period 1960-1965. According to the Massachusetts census of 1965, the city population fell from 697,000 to 615,000 in that period. From my own projections of the rate of Negro population growth, the nonwhite proportion rose from about 10 percent to 13 percent of the total population. The racial census shows that the percentage of Negroes in the public schools rose even faster, from 16.6 percent to about 25 percent.[2]

There is a rapid turnover of students among districts: only 80 percent of those registering in September are in the same district by February.[3] If turnover were a Markov process, less than 20 percent of the original registrants would be present in a district for eight years of elementary schooling. Residential turnover is somewhat less: 50 percent live in the same house, and 82 percent stay in Boston within a five-year period.[4] Despite the magnitude of turnover, there is some evidence that the process replaces those who leave with persons of similar characteristics. In particular, the correlation by district between the percentage of the total population that was white in 1960 and the percentage of the school population that was white in 1965 is .92.

The effect of these difficulties would seem to randomize the data so that the multiple correlations are lowered. The very fact that some of our correlations are so high suggests that the two sets of data are not weakly related.

APPENDIX B

THE USE OF MENTAL TEST SCORES IN REGRESSION ANALYSIS

All of the major studies of educational production measure output by mental test scores. Such scores are intuitively appealing because they presumably sample skills important in later life. While it is possible to compute the means, variances, and covariance and regression coefficients for these scores, the interpretation of such parametric statistics is not at all clear.

Scores are generally arrived at by administering multiquestion examinations to a representative sample of youngsters at each grade level. As predicted by the central limit theorem, the number of correct answers tends to be normally distributed, unless an artificial ceiling is built into the test. The mean score for a particular grade becomes the grade norm. Raw scores are transformed into grade units by administering the same test to children in another grade. The mean of the second group's raw score serves as an anchor which sets the length of a whole grade unit. These grade units then serve as the magnitude for measuring the effectiveness of schooling.

There is serious doubt whether such a procedure is sufficient to permit the meaningful calculation of any parametric statistics involving mental test units. It is not clear that the normality of test scores implies anything about the normality of any mental ability. Any distributional statement implies that there is a scale of measurement with well-defined units. "Number of correct answers" has that property; however, it may not have any interesting relationship with mental ability. For example, we probably agree that a person who obtains more correct answers has greater ability, but we do not know whether mental differences between ten and fifteen correct answers are equal to mental differences between fifteen and twenty correct answers. Falling back on the extreme operationalist position that mental ability is what the mental tests measure does not avoid the problem. To draw an analogy from physics, we may attempt to compare three rocks on their "hardness." It is clear that we can rank the rocks relative to each other simply by seeing which rocks are capable of scratching the others. We can also observe the percentage of N other test materials each rock can scratch, and naturally find that the rocks rank the same on both tests. Are we then justified in defining a scale of hardness in terms of "percentage scratches" and thereby assign a cardinal magnitude to each rock? Surely we cannot because there is no way of knowing the differences in hardness among the test materials. Although we can calculate all sorts of parameters concerning "percentage scratches," there may be no correspondence between this magnitude and any interesting aspect of reality.

Returning to mental test scores, we have no assurance that equally computed grade unit differences imply equal mental differences. There is no way of determining by the method above whether normal improvement from the fourth grade to the fifth grade equals that between the fifth grade and the sixth grade; or that students with achievement levels 4.9 and 5.1 are equally distant from the fifth grade norm. If in truth "number of correct answers" is analogous to "percentage scratches," the only meaningfully derived measure of central tendency is the median, not the mean. The mean number of "correct answers," and "scratches" can undoubtedly be computed, just like the mean number on the backs of football players (even if assigned on the basis of some property like height or weight), but they have no empirical validity. If the mean cannot be computed, neither can any other parametric statistics.

One way to overcome this difficulty is by treating ranges of mental test scores as discrete variables. The existence of resource-performance relationships can then be established by cross-tabulation and nonparametric statistics such as Chi-square. If there are discontinuities in the production functions, as there may very well be, the treatment of mental test scores as discrete variables may be an advantage.

Despite the impossibility of deducing the equality of mental score intervals, such equality may be approximated on empirical grounds. If the assumption of a correspondence between mental score and intelligence units leads to good predictions, then the assumption may be pragmatically justifiable.[1] In practice, linear models work fairly well;[2] however, the goodness of fit is not extraordinarily high.[3]

Bloom suggests an alternative method of deriving mental units.[4] First he assumes that mental ability in youngsters is a stock variable that grows just like height or weight. Such an assumption implies that the correlation among individual scores between any points in time (t^1 and t) takes the following fuctional form:

$$ r_{t't} = \frac{\sigma_t + r_t(t' - t)\sigma(t' - t)}{\sigma_{t'}} $$

If we assume that gains between any two time periods are uncorrelated then:

$$ r_{t't} = \sigma_t / \sigma_{t'} $$

This last assumption seems plausible in light of evidence about growth in height and weight.

Finally, we assume that the variance in scores at any age is proportional to the (unknown) mean intelligence in absolute units:

$$ r^2_{t't} = \frac{\sigma^2_t}{\sigma^2_{t'}} = \frac{X_t}{X_{t'}} $$

$$ r_{t't} = \sqrt{(X_t/X_{t'})} $$

Consequently, the ratio of mental development at any two time periods is a function of their correlation. This model leaps the hurdle of defining equal units and defines a point of zero development.

We attempted to test some of the assumptions of this model with cross-sectional test scores from grades one to six in the Boston School System. First, reading gains tend to be uncorrelated with first-grade scores, at several final-grade levels. These correlations are: $-.45$ (second grade); $.05$ (third grade); $-.20$ (fourth grade); and $.00$ (sixth grade). Similarly the correlation between second-grade scores and gains to the sixth grade are only $.24$, which is not significantly different from zero. Thus, about 84 percent of the variance in sixth-grade reading scores is explained by gains from the first grade; 70 percent, by gains from the second grade.

The first assumption being satisfied, there is no way to test the heteroscedasticity property except by analogy to variances in height and weight observed in children. If we are willing to take this logical leap, then we can estimate a growth curve in the mental ability of Boston's youngsters by showing simple correlations between district reading scores in the sixth and other grades.

In addition, external evidence on the growth of mental abilities is provided by correlations in grade point averages

Table B.1. Percentage of sixth-grade mental ability attained by specified grade.

Grade	Observed		Expected	
	Reading[a]	Grade points[b]	Grade level[c]	Age[d]
6	100	100	100	100
5	—	54	83	91
4	49	41	66	82
3	42	37	50	73
2	36	31	30	64
1	36	—	16	55

[a]From correlations among median reading scores by school district.
[b]From correlations among median grade point averages.
[c]Assuming that grade levels are mental units.
[d]Assuming that ages are mental units.

among students in Negro schools at different points in time (truly longitudinal).[5] Estimates of mental growth based on the longitudinal data seem to fit well with the cross-sectional estimates.

We can compare the mental growth curves based on reading scores and grade point averages to those based on the alternative assumptions that age or grade levels comprise mental units. The latter assumption fits with the data better, at least for the grade range of interest in this study (See Table B.1).

APPENDIX C

SPECIFYING AN EDUCATIONAL PRODUCTION FUNCTION

The major methodological issues in specifying an educational production function are specifying the proper mathematical form of the function, choosing a statistical technique, and verifying whether the data under consideration adhere to the assumptions of the model and the statistical technique.

Functional Forms

The mathematical relationship between the independent variables (social background, school resources) and the dependent variable (student performance) may take many plausible forms, each with its particular properties. There are no hard and fast rules for choosing the "best" functional form, although parsimony or simplicity is one criterion.

Two of the simplest functional forms are the purely linear and the purely multiplicative model:

1) $O = \text{constant} + \sum_i a_i S_i + bC + e$

2) $O = \text{constant} \times \prod_i S_i{}^{\alpha i} C^{\beta} e$

Each of these functional forms has its relative advantage. The multiplicative model, the well-known Cobb-Douglas function, expresses a log-linear relationship between inputs and outputs. The coefficients of the function (α_i) express the percentage change in output produced by a change of one percentage point in input. If there were diminishing returns, which

194

might be a property of educational production functions, the coefficient would be less than one. Pure linear models assume that there are no diminishing or increasing returns, for all independent variables are implicitly raised to the first power. Only by adding higher power terms can nonlinear returns be expressed in linear models.

Multiplicative models express output as a product of input; consequently, the impact of a particular input depends upon the magnitude of the other inputs. Pure linear models do not have this property, known as interaction, because changes in inputs are assumed to have additive effects. Interaction can be expressed in linear models by the addition of cumbersome interaction terms, which may be rather costly in terms of degrees of freedom. In an additive model with i independent variables, there are $2_i - 1$ possible interaction terms of the first degree, for example, a $X_1 X_2$, b X_1 X_2 X_k. The choice of linear or multiplicative models depends upon one's a priori hypotheses about the importance of interaction among school resources and social background in influencing performance.

Multiplicative models have a major disadvantage in assuming that, if one independent variable takes a zero value, then the value of the output is zero, regardless of the value of all other independent variables. This property does not seem plausible for the kind of educational inputs we consider, which include percentage of teachers with master's degrees.

Linear models have the prime advantages of computational simplicity and, for most people, comprehensibility. To perform regressions with multiplicative models, all variables have to be transformed into logarithms. Since the logarithm of zero is undefined, one must either eliminate observations with this magnitude or assume, as we do, that the magnitude is truly some small positive number, such as, 0.1. Furthermore, multiplicative models are not readily adapted to the simplest optimizing techniques, such as linear programming.

In addition to these formal characteristics, linear and multiplicative models can be compared on the basis of their predictive capacity in the cases at hand. First, we find for each performance measure the best linear model, that is, that set of independent variables which produces the lowest standard error of estimate of the dependent variable. Similarly, we find the best multiplicative models, which generally include the same independent variables. Then we compare the standard errors of estimate for each output:

$$F_i = \frac{(\text{standard error}_L)^2}{(\text{standard error}_M)^2}$$

Standard errors are a function of the average residuals from the regression. In linear models, residuals are:

$$\text{actual } O - \text{expected } O$$

In multiplicative models, residuals are:

$$\text{actual log } O - \text{expected log } O, \text{ or actual } O/ \text{ expected } O$$

To compare linear and multiplicative models we must use a consistent definition of the residual. Since our null hypothesis is that linear models are preferable, we define residuals as actual − expected.

For every performance measure the *F*-ratio of residuals is nearly unity, suggesting that additive and multiplicative models have equal predictive capacity (see Table C.1). Since, on a priori and predictive grounds, multiplicative models are not superior, simplicity and comprehensibility favor the linear models of educational production.

Statistical Techniques

There are three major statistical techniques for specifying the structure of joint production: ordinary least squares (OLS),

Table C.1. Linear residuals of linear and multiplicative models.

	Standard errors of estimate		
Dependent variable	Linear	Multiplicative	F-ratio
Attendance	2.29	2.31	.98
Continuation	3.25	3.25	.98
Reading	33.4	35.6	.88
Mathematics	32.1	33.0	.94
Latin application	8.73	10.4	.71
Latin pass	6.61	6.61	1.00

canonical correlation (CC), and three-stage least squares (TSLS).

OLS, the best known of these techniques, requires little comment. Each equation is estimated separately, ignoring the existence of the other equations and the correlations of the stochastic components. While OLS generally produces the best linear unbiased estimates, its application to joint production may lead to inconsistency or asymptotic bias.[1] It is doubtful, however, whether asymptotic or large sample properties are of practical interest.

Canonical correlation, a less well-known technique, permits the specification of all joint production functions simultaneously.[2] The technique finds a set of weights that maximizes the correlation between the inputs (S_i) and the outputs (O_i). A number of orthogonal sets of weights (A, B) can be extracted, equal to the rank of the S or O matrix, whichever is smaller. The relationships between input and output can be expressed thus: [3]

$$AO = rBS$$
$$O - A^{-1}rBS - CS$$

where $A^{-1} = A'(AA')^{-1}$, a pseudoinverse when A is not square.

Taking the first $(p = .01)$ and then the first two $(p = .06)$ canonical correlations, we compare the set of production coefficients to those attained by OLS (see Table C.2). Although there are no significance tests for elements of the latent vectors in canonical correlation, we find that the derived coefficients are not generally different from those of OLS. Consequently, CC provides no different information from OLS, which has better-known small sample properties and statistical tests.

Three-stage least squares takes into consideration the possibility of correlation of the stochastic components among equations.[4] This technique which specifies all equations simultaneously, provides more efficient estimates than OLS, if *all* equations are specified correctly. If one equation is incorrectly specified, then the coefficients in all equations may be biased. TSLS is most advantageous when there is interdependence or simultaneity in an equation system, or there are high correla-

Table C.2. Several production functions: Beta coefficients, alternative methods.

	Accredited	Masters	Experience	Uncrowded	Pupil: teacher	Turnover	Enrollment	Age of building	SES
Attendance									
OC[a]	.00	.02	.01	.02	−.01	−.01[e]	.02	.02	.00
TC[b]	.02	.04	.06	.07	−.03	.09[e]	.09	.05	.10
BMR[c]	.25	.13	.00	.00	.00	−.42	.00	.00	−.14
FMR[d]	.37	.13	.01	−.08	−.15	−.41	.00	−.07	−.16
	(.20)	(.19)	(.16)	(.17)	(.21)	(.16)	(.20)	(.15)	(.17)
Continuation									
OC	.07	−.10	.05	.01	.00	−.14	.02[e]	−.08	.26
TC	.12	−.04	.15	.13	−.06	−.30	.17	−.01	.47
BMR	.14	−.18	.00	.00	−.30	−.17	.32	.00	.43
FMR	.04	−.22	.13	.04	−.27	−.19	.29	−.08	.46
	(.17)	(.15)	(.14)	(.13)	(.18)	(.13)	(.13)	(.13)	(.14)

Reading

OC	.03	−.05	.02[e]	.00	.00	−.06	.01	−.04	.12
TC	.15	.07	.26	.29	.12	−.46	.35	.12	.63
BMR	.00	.00	.37	.16	.00	−.23	.12	.11	.33
FMR	−.10	.00	.36	.21	.10	−.24	.12	.14	.36
	(.16)	(.05)	(.13)	(.13)	(.16)	(.12)	(.14)	(.12)	(.13)

[a]OC = one canonical correlation.
[b]TC = two canonical correlations.
[c]BMR = best multiple regression.
[d]FMR = full multiple regression/(standard error of beta).
[e]Different from FMR coefficients, p = .05, two-tail.

tions among stochastic terms. Since neither condition holds (see Table C.3), TSLS has no advantage over OLS and incurs risks of biasing coefficients.

Six production functions are derived by OLS. Because we are testing the regression coefficients for six equations simultaneously, usual tests of significance underestimate the probability of a type I error. In general, if $(1-a)$ is the probability of not making such an error in one test, then $(1-a)^n$ is the probability of not making any such errors in n tests. In practice, to be 95 percent sure of not making any type I errors in testing six hypotheses, we must be 99 percent sure for each single hypothesis.

Error Terms

The error term in the production functions can have three by no means mutually exclusive interpretations: unreliability of measuring tools, omission of important variables that could not be measured, and an indeterminacy reflecting the "Uncertainty Principle."

First, the measurement of performance and resources for Boston's school districts is fairly reliable. Although a particular

Table C.3. Residuals from best linear models: Intercorrelations, factor loadings associated with largest latent root.

	Att.	Cont.	Read.	Math.	L. appl.	L. pass	Factor loadings
Attendance	1.00	.17	.06	.27	−.17	.17	.35
Continuation		1.00	−.16	−.16	.23	−.01	−.11
Reading			1.00	.20	.11	.30	.62
Mathematics				1.00	−.09	.27	.57
Latin application					1.00	.46[a]	.44
Latin pass						1.00	.83
							1.73[b]

[a]Significant .10 (two-tail). See Allen L. Edwards, *Experimental Design in Psychological Research* (New York: Holt, Rinehart, and Winston, 1968), Table Xa; $t_{.05} = 3.23$ (55d.f.; 6 variables).

[b]Latent root; equals 29 percent of trace.

test score may be unreliable, the group mean score, which we measure, is quite reliable. Resources at a given point in time, however, are a less reliable surrogate for the history of resources available during the period of elementary schooling. Additional historical errors may result from migration patterns which upset the relationship between social class measured in 1960 and social class measured over the period of elementary schooling. Computations described in Appendix A suggest that the latter errors are relatively unimportant.

Second, many factors related either to school or to social class have not been measured, including administrative ability and student motivation, among others. If such factors were an important source of error, then the residuals of the several production functions should be highly correlated with each other and with the unmeasured common factor(s). In fact, the intercorrelations among residuals are rather low; moreover, less than 30 percent of the variance among residuals can be "explained" by one common factor or latent root, while the two largest latent roots explain only 53 percent of the residual variance (see Table C.3). Unmeasured variables do not, therefore, seem to be an important source of error common to all equations.

Third, some of the residual variance may be "inherent" in the production relationship even if all important variables are known. There is probably an educational analogue to the "Uncertainty Principle" in particle physics: the operations of measurement affect the state of the system in random directions. School systems which are being observed and evaluated may behave differently from those which are not: the former may try harder or conceal unfavorable information from the observer. There is little likelihood that the data from the Boston school system is distorted, most of it being collected on a systematic basis in which the observer (the central administration), has the power to verify any information on resources. Even if the testing of students encouraged the teachers to work harder (which, by the way, is a good thing if the tests are valid), all schools in the system are subject to similar incentive.

Behavioral Assumptions

The identifiability of the production function depends critically upon the assumption that independent variables such as school resources are uncorrelated with the error term. Whether this is true depends upon the validity of one's assumptions about managerial behavior. In a classic article, Jacob Marschak and William Andrews argue that well-managed firms will use different resource bundles and will grow relative to poorly managed firms.[6] Consequently, managerial ability—an unmeasured factor reflected in the error term—is correlated both with the level and pattern of inputs, so that the least-squares model overestimates the impact of resources. Such a bias is unlikely, however, to apply to the estimation of educational production functions *within school systems*. If we assume that school administrators differ in their ability to economize or use resources wisely, that they have an incentive to economize, and that they have discretion over the inputs to the school system, the kinds of inputs chosen by administrators will correlate with their managerial ability, which is not directly measurable. Consequently, production coefficients will be upwardly biased, the effect of resources confounded with this unmeasurable ability.

It is unlikely that these assumptions are reasonable. First, school administrators have only the vaguest notions of production possibilities. (In fact, if they knew these possibilities, this analysis, as well as those reviewed in Chapter 2 would have been unnecessary.) Second, even if they know the production and cost coefficients, they have little incentive to optimize although perhaps they must give the illusion of optimizing in order to satisfy their clientele. Third, even if they had the knowledge and incentive to optimize, *district* administrators within big city systems have almost no control over local resources. Finally, districts that are better managed do not grow at the expense of those that are poorly managed. Therefore, the econometric assumption of no correlation between exogenous variables and the disturbance term is satisfied.

The rejection of an optimizing decision model is not incompatible with the specification of a production function strictly defined: the *maximum* output attainable from a given set of inputs, *physically defined*. Suppose that the true production relationship were unknown to the school administrator, who chose resources at random. On the assumption that the resource is actually utilized, whereby the teacher stands in front of students in a classroom, the true production laws can be estimated from the observed data.

If the true relationship is stochastic, then production coefficients reflect the maximum *expected* outputs obtainable from *controllable* inputs. This seems to be a reasonable interpretation of coefficients of educational production functions. We obtain unbiased estimates of the coefficients and have little interest in the additional output under contingencies we can neither measure nor control.

The optimization model, however, is essential in identifying the maximum output obtainable from inputs *defined by costs*. Regressing output against costs specifies a relationship descriptive of administrative behavior, not a true production function. The coefficient of such a model would be upwardly biased in proportion to the degree of inefficiency in the system.

This model is not unreasonable in the educational context. Once resources are given, the school administrator has little choice as to how to use them in the elementary school; there is not much to do with a teacher (who tends to be nonspecialist) but to put them in front of a classroom. The possibilities of gross misallocations, as are possible in the high school—giving the gym teacher all the poetry classes, and the English teacher the gym classes—just do not exist on the elementary level.

We are not saying that good administrators are not important. On the contrary, they may affect the morale and cohesiveness of the organization, which may affect student learning. Rather, we are saying that management bias is not an econometric problem in this study.

NOTES

1. INTRODUCTION

[1]James Q. Wilson, "Dilemmas of Police Administration," *Public Administration Review, 28* (Sept. 1968), 410.

[2]US Department of Health, Education, and Welfare, *Towards a Social Report* (Washington, D.C.: Government Printing Office, 1969) 33–34; René Dubos, *The Mirage of Health: Utopias, Progress, and Biological Change* (Garden City, N.Y.: Doubleday Anchor, 1959), 31–32; Charles Perrow, "Hospitals: Technology, Structure, and Goals," in *Handbook of Organizations*, ed. James G. March (Chicago: Rand McNally, 1965), 916–946; Hans J. Eysenck, "The Effects of Psychotherapy," *International Journal of Psychiatry, 1* (Jan. 1965), 97–178; US Department of Health, Education, and Welfare, Subcommittee of Evaluation of Mental Health Activities, *Evaluation in Mental Health* (Washington, D.C.: Government Printing Office, 1955).

[3]Wilson, "Dilemmas of Police Administration"; Walter B. Miller, "The Impact of a 'Total Community' Delinquency Control Project," *Social Problems, 10* (Fall 1962), 168–191; Martin T. Katzman, "The Economics of Defense against Crime in the Streets," *Land Economics, 44* (Nov. 1968), 431–440.

[4]US Commission on Civil Rights, *Racial Isolation in the Public Schools* (2 vols., Washington, D.C.: Government Printing Office, 1967), I, 128–139; David K. Cohen, "Compensation and Integration," *Harvard Educational Review, 38* (Winter 1968), 114–137.

[5]Edward C. Banfield, "Why Government Cannot Solve the Urban Problem," *Dædalus, 97* (Fall 1968), 1231–1241.

[6]Charles E. Lindblom, "The Science of 'Muddling Through,'" *Public Administration Review, 19* (Spring 1959), 79–88; and Charles L. Schultze, *The Politics and Economics of Public Spending* (Washington, D.C.: Brookings Institution, 1968), 35–54.

[7]For a discussion of the inherent difficulties of studying social phenomena, see Morris R. Cohen, "Reason in Social Science," in *Readings in the Philosophy of Science*, ed. Herbert Feigl and May Brodbeck, (New York: Appleton-Century-Crofts, 1953), 663–673.

[8]See Roland N. McKean, *Efficiency in Government through Systems Analysis* (New York: John Wiley & Sons, 1958), and Charles J. Hitch and Roland N. McKean, *The Economics of Defense in the Nuclear Age* (Cambridge, Mass.: Harvard University Press, 1960), 160–165, on "suboptimization."

[9]René Dubos, *The Mirage of Health;* Avedis Donabedian, "Evaluating the Quality of Medical Care," *Millbank Memorial Fund Quarterly, 44* (July 1966), 166–203.

[10]Talcott Parsons, ed. *Essays in Sociological Theory* (New York: Free Press, 1964), 34–49.

[11]See Aaron Wildavsky, *The Politics of the Budgetary Process* (Boston: Little, Brown, 1964) on incremental budgeting.

[12]*Ibid.*

[13]Daniel P. Moynihan, *Maximum Feasible Misunderstanding: Community Action in the War on Poverty* (New York: Free Press, 1969), 167–203, on the role of social scientists in the formulation of social policy. Cf. Jeanne Chall, *Learning to Read: The Great Debate* (New York: McGraw-Hill, 1967), 89–93.

[14]Thomas Kuhn, *The Structure of Scientific Revolution* (Chicago: University of Chicago Press, 1962), chap. vii, on the resistance of scientists to unpredicted facts.

[15]Dubos, *The Mirage of Health,* 129–143, 176–181.

[16]Raymond Bauer, *Social Indicators* (Cambridge, Mass.: MIT. Press, 1967), chap. i, on the functions of data routinely generated by organizations.

[17]Peter Marris and Martin Rein, *Dilemmas of Social Reform: Poverty and Community Action in the United States* (New York: Atherton Press, 1967), 191–207, discuss the difficulties inherent in evaluating any social program, particularly an experimental one. The successes of the research director and project directors of social service enterprises may be incompatible; a project failure may signify a publishable rejection of a hypothesis to the former but job failure to the latter.

[18]The tribulations such as Galileo's on grounds of heresy for his scientific discoveries are ancient history in the natural sciences; see Thomas Kuhn, *The Copernican Revolution: Planetary Astronomy in the Development of Western Thought* (Cambridge, Mass.: Harvard University Press, 1957). Compare, in the biological sciences, ideological implications of scientific findings, for example, the popular interpretation of the Darwinian concept of natural selection as a justification for "survival of the fittest" under capitalism. For a discussion of "heresy" trials of those whose findings contravene ideology, see Walter Miller, "The Elimination of the American Lower Class as National Policy: A Critique of the Ideology of the Poverty Movement of the 1960's," in *On Understanding Poverty*, ed. Daniel P. Moynihan (New York: Basic Books, 1968), 260–315. For examples, see Lee Rainwater and William Yancey, *The Moynihan Report and the Politics of Controversy* (Cambridge, Mass.:

MIT Press, 1967), and comments on the work of Arthur R. Jensen, "How Much Can We Boost IQ and Scholastic Achievement," *Harvard Educational Review, 39* (Winter 1969), 1–123 and "Discussion," *ibid.* (Spring 1969), 273–356.

[19]Daniel Patrick Moynihan, "Sources of Resistance to the Coleman Report," *Harvard Educational Review, 38* (Winter 1968), 23–26, discusses the "Establishments" threatened by report findings. Although there is legitimate scientific doubt as to what the report did find, it still has polemic usefulness.

[20]There is considerable literature on the unwillingness of businessmen to maximize profits, such as William Baumol, *Economic Theory and Operations Analysis* (Englewood Cliffs, N.J.: Prentice-Hall, 1961). Rational decision making can of course be hampered by unsound accounting practice; see James Earley, "Recent Developments in Cost Accounting and the 'Marginal Analysis,' " *Journal of Political Economy, 63* (June 1955), 227–242.

[21]References in nn. 2–4, above. The controversy surrounding the Coleman report on education and the Moynihan report on the Negro family are examples of research findings of the first type; see "Equal Educational Opportunity," Special Issue, *Harvard Educational Review, 38* (Winter 1968), and Lee Rainwater and William Yancey, *The Moynihan Report and the Politics of Controversy* (Cambridge, Mass.: MIT Press, 1966).

[22]See Raymond Bauer, *Social Indicators* (Cambridge, Mass.: MIT Press, 1966), chap. i; US Department of Health, Education, and Welfare, *Towards a Social Report*; Martin T. Katzman, "Social Indicators and Urban Public Policy," in *Planning 1968*, Yearbook of the American Society of Planning Officials, 85–94.

[23]For example, see Joseph A. Kershaw and Roland N. McKean, "Systems Analysis and Education," RAND, RM–2475FF (Santa Monica, Calif., 1959); Guy H. Orcutt *et al., Microanalysis of Socioeconomic Systems: A Simulation Study* (New York: Harper and Row, 1961).

[24]A.R. Prest and Ralph Turvey, "Cost-Benefit Analysis: A Survey," *Economic Journal, 75* (Dec. 1965), 683–735, reviews the applications of such analysis, which has been used in fields with a well-defined technology such as planning of water resources. Aaron Wildavsky, "The Political Economy of Efficiency: Cost-Benefit Analysis, Systems Analysis, and Program Budgeting," *Public Administration Review, 26* (Dec. 1966), 292–310, argues perceptively that cost-benefit analysts all too often make value judgments about distribution, time preference, and other factors in deriving "objective" results.

[25]Herbert J. Gans, *The Levittowners* (New York: Random House, 1967), 24.

[26]Walter B. Miller, "Lower Class Culture as a Generating Milieu of Gang Delinquency," *Journal of Social Issues, 14* (Dec. 1958), 5–19;

Gans, *Levittowners,* and *The Urban Villagers: Group and Class in the Life of Italian-Americans* (New York: Free Press, 1961), and "Culture and Class in the Study of Poverty," in Moynihan, *On Understanding Poverty,* 201–228, on the life styles, focal concerns of the lower, working, lower middle, and upper middle classes, and their political implications; Gerhard Lenski, *The Religious Factor: A Sociological Study of Religion's Impact on Politics, Economics, and Family Life* (New York: Doubleday, 1961); Edward C. Banfield and James Q. Wilson, "Public-Regardingness as a Value Premise in Voting Behavior," *American Political Science Review,* 58 (Dec. 1964), 876–887.

[27]William Dobriner, *Class in Suburbia* (Englewood Cliffs, N.J.: Prentice-Hall, 1963), 113–126.

[28]*Ibid.;* Gans, *Levittowners,* chap. iv.

[29]Few of the recent books on large city schools have had anything favorable to say about them, especially those run by the working class. See Jonathan Kozol, *Death at an Early Age: The Destruction of the Hearts and Minds of Negro Children in the Boston Public Schools* (Boston: Houghton Mifflin, 1967); Peter Schrag, *Village School Downtown: Boston Schools, Boston Politics* (Boston: Beacon Press, 1967); David Rogers, *110 Livingston Street: Politics and Bureaucracy in the New York City School System* (New York: Random House, 1968); James Herndon, *The Way It Spozed to Be: A Report on the Classroom War behind the Crisis in Our Schools* (New York: Simon and Schuster, 1965); Edgar Z. Friedenberg, *Coming of Age in America: Growth and Acquiescence* (New York: Random House, 1963).

[30]Banfield and Wilson, "Public-Regardingness."

[31]*The Levittowners,* chap. iv.

[32]Banfield and Wilson, "Public-Regardingness."

[33]Notable exceptions are the empirical work of Victor Fuchs, *The Service Economy* (New York: National Bureau of Economic Research, 1968), and the speculations of Roland N. McKean, "The Unseen Hand in Government," *American Economic Review,* 55 (June 1965), 496–506, and Anthony Downs, *Inside Bureaucracy* (Boston: Little, Brown, 1967), which focus on distributive choices among competing parties rather than upon technological efficiency, that is, choice among competing means to achieve a given end. See Downs's bibliography.

2. EVALUATING EDUCATIONAL QUALITY

[1]See Theodore Abel, "The Operation Called *Verstehen,*" *American Journal of Sociology,* 54 (Nov. 1948), 211–218, for a critique of this method of hypothesis testing.

[2]See the fascinating study of Robert Rosenthal and Lenore Jacobson, who produced a self-fulfilling expectation among teachers in the "supe-

riority" of a randomly selected group of students, *Pygmalion in the Classroom* (New York: Holt, Rinehart, Winston, 1968); cf. G. F. Peaker, "A Regression Analysis of the National Survey," in Central Advisory Council on Education, Lady Bridget Plowden, Chairman, *National Survey of Parental Attitudes and Circumstances Related to School and Pupil Characteristics* (2 vols., London: Her Majesty's Stationery Office, 1967), II, chap. iv.

[3]Talcott Parsons, ed., *Essays in Sociological Theory* (New York: Free Press, 1964), 34–39; Everett C. Hughes, "Professions," in *Dædalus, 92* (Fall 1963), 655–667, on the comparison between professional-client relationships where "credat emptor" is the dominant principle rather than the business principle of "caveat emptor"; Milton Friedman, *Capitalism and Freedom* (Chicago: University of Chicago Press, 1962), 137–160; and Henrik Blum, "Introduction to Comprehensive Planning for Health" (University of California, Berkeley, Mar. 1968, mimeo.).

[4]Werner Z. Hirsch, "Measuring Factors Affecting Local Government Services," in *Exploring the Metropolitan Community*, ed. John C. Bollens, (Berkeley: University of California Press, 1961), 317–352.

[5]Alma S. Wittlin, "The Teacher," *Dædalus, 91* (Fall 1963), 745–763.

[6]See Frank Riessman, *The Culturally Deprived Child* (New York: Harper & Row, 1962), on the misperception of the needs and abilities of lower-class children by middle-class teachers.

[7]A basic problem in anthropological research is comparing the validity of perceptions of those within to those outside the culture; see Clyde Kluckhohn, "Universal Categories of Culture," in *Anthropology Today: Selections*, ed. Sol Tax (Chicago: University of Chicago Press, 1962), 304–320, and *Culture and Behavior* (New York: Free Press, 1965), 286–300.

[8]See Charles V. Hamilton, "Race and Education: A Search for Legitimacy," *Harvard Educational Review*, 38 (Fall 1968), 669–684.

[9]Paul R. Mort and Orlando F. Furno, *Theory and Synthesis of a Sequential Simplex: A Model for Assessing the Effectiveness of Administration Policy*, Institute of Administrative Research, Columbia University, Study No. 12 (New York: Teachers College Press, 1960), provides the most complete guidelines for evaluating school systems on the basis of inputs. The guidelines themselves, however, are not evaluated, but accepted on faith.

[10]Werner Z. Hirsh and Elbert W. Segelhorst, "Incremental Income Benefits of Public Education," *Review of Economics and Statistics*, 47 (Nov. 1965), 392–399; cf. the less conclusive study of Finis Welch, "Measurement of the Quality of Schooling," *American Economic Review, 56* (May 1966), 379–391, which is consistent with Hirsch and Segelhorst; and comments by Alice Rivlin, *ibid.*, p. 393–395.

[11]For example, see Patricia Cayo Sexton, *Education and Income: Ine-*

qualities of Opportunity in our Public Schools (New York: Viking Press, 1961).

¹²For example, see Hirsch, "Measuring Factors Affecting Local Government Services," 317–352.

¹³For a comprehensive discussion of scaling, see "Mathematics, Measurement, and Psychophysics," in *Handbook of Experimental Psychology*, ed. S. S. Stevens (New York: John Wiley & Sons, 1951), chap. i.

¹⁴Basil Bernstein, "Social Class and Linguistic Development: A Theory of Social Learning," in *Education, Economy, and Society*, ed. A. H. Halsey, Jean Floud, and C. Arnold Anderson (New York: Free Press, 1961), 288–314; Fred L. Strodtbeck, "The Hidden Curriculum of the Middle-Class Home," in *Urban Education and Cultural Deprivation*, ed. C. W. Hunnicutt (Syracuse, N.Y.: Syracuse University School of Education, 1964), 15–31.

¹⁵See, for example, work of Ungar, reported in *The New York Times*, Apr. 17, 1968.

¹⁶D. O. Hebb, *A Textbook of Psychology* (Philadelphia: Saunders, 1957).

¹⁷B. F. Skinner, *Science and Human Behavior* (New York: Macmillan, 1953).

¹⁸*Ibid.*, 27–29.

¹⁹J. McV. Hunt, *Intelligence and Experience* (New York: Ronald Press, 1961), is an exhaustive review of the effects of early experience on child development.

²⁰Benjamin S. Bloom, *Stability and Change in Human Characteristics* (New York: John Wiley & Sons, 1964), chaps. i and ii, describes how such estimates are determined.

²¹Hunt, *Intelligence and Experience*, reviews in great detail the work of Jean Piaget, who has studied stages in the development of a wide range of abilities in children; and Eric H. Lenneberg, *Biological Foundations of Language* (New York: John Wiley & Sons, 1967), chap. iv, esp. 158–160.

²²B. F. Skinner, *The Technology of Teaching* (New York: Appleton Century-Crofts, 1968); A. A. Lumsdaine and Robert Glaser, eds., *Teaching Machines and Programmed Learning* (Washington, D.C.: National Educational Association, Department of Audio-Visual Instruction, 1960), esp. 215–246, 425–436.

²³For comparable production functions, see Eric A. Hanushek, "The Education of Negroes and Whites," unpublished doctoral dissertation, Massachusetts Institute of Technology, 1968, 14; and Samuel S. Bowles, "Towards an Educational Production Function," manuscript presented at National Bureau of Economic Research Conference on Education and Income, Nov. 1968, 3.

²⁴Robert Dreeben, *What Is Learned in School?* (Reading, Mass.:

Addison-Wesley, 1968); James S. Coleman, "Academic Achievement and the Structure of Competition," *Harvard Educational Review, 29* (Fall 1959), 330–351; Talcott Parsons, "The School Class as a Social System: Some of Its Functions in American Society," *ibid.*, 297–318; Alex Inkeles, "A Note on Social Structure and the Socialization of Competence," *ibid., 36* (Summer 1966), 265–283; Robert Dreeben, "The Contribution of Schooling to the Learning of Norms," *ibid., 37* (Spring 1967), 211–237; "Political Socialization," Special Issue, *ibid., 38* (Summer 1968); Robert J. Havighurst and Bernice L. Neugarten, *Society and Education* (3d ed., Boston: Allyn and Bacon, 1967), chap.v.

[25]James W. Trent and Leland L. Medsker, *Beyond High School: A Study of 10,000 High School Graduates* (San Francisco: Jossey-Bass, 1968); Samuel A. Stouffer, *Communism, Conformity and Civil Liberties* (New York: Doubleday, 1955).

[26]See Frank Barron, "Some Personality Correlates of Independence of Judgment," *Journal of Personality, 21* (Mar. 1953), 287–297, and "The Disposition Toward Originality," *Journal of Abnormal and Social Psychology, 51* (Nov. 1955), 478–485.

[27]For the effect of years of schooling when ability is held constant, see Dael Wolfle and Joseph Smith, "The Occupational Value of Education for Superior High School Graduates," *Journal of Higher Education, 27* (Apr. 1956), 201–213; W. Lee Hansen, "Total and Private Rates of Return to Investment in Schooling," *Journal of Political Economy, 71* (Apr. 1963), 128–140.

[28]Otis Dudley Duncan, "Ability and Achievement," *Eugenics Quarterly, 13* (Mar. 1968), 1–11.

[29]Manuel Zymelman, "The Relationship between Productivity and the Formal Education of the Labor Force in Manufacturing Industries" (UNESCO, forthcoming); Mordecai Kreinen, "Comparative Labor Effectiveness and the Leontieff Scarce-Factor Paradox," *American Economic Review, 55* (Mar. 1955), 131–140.

[30]Marion F. Shaycoft, *The High School Years: Growth in Cognitive Skills,* University of Pittsburgh, School of Education, Interim Report 3, Project TALENT (Pittsburgh, Pa.: University of Pittsburgh Press, 1967).

[31]J. Allen Thomas, Efficiency in Education: A Study of the Relationship between Selected Inputs and Mean Test Scores in a Sample of Senior High Schools," unpublished doctoral dissertation, Stanford University, 1962.

[32]William G. Mollenkopf and S. Donald Melville, "A Study of Secondary School Characteristics as Related to Test Scores," Research Bulletin 56–6 (Princeton, N.J.: Educational Testing Service, 1956, mimeo.)

[33]Samuel M. Goodman, *The Assessment of School Quality* (Albany, N.Y.: New York State Education Department, 1959).

[34]Charles S. Benson *et al., State and Local Fiscal Relationships in*

Public Education in California (Sacramento: Senate of the State of California, 1965).

[35]Herbert J. Kiesling, "Measuring a Local Government Service: A Study of School Districts in New York State," unpublished doctoral dissertation, Harvard University, 1965.

[36]Jesse Burkhead, Thomas G. Fox, and John W. Holland, *Input and Output in Large-City High Schools* (Syracuse, N.Y.: Syracuse University Press, 1967).

[37]James S. Coleman *et al.*, *Equality of Educational Opportunity*, US Office of Education (Washington, D.C.: Government Printing Office, 1966).

[38]Kiesling, "Measuring a Local Government Service," identified different production functions for several occupational classes; see also Gerald Lesser *et al.*, "Mental Abilities of Children from Different Social Class and Cultural Groups," *Child Development Monographs, 20,* (No. 4, 1965).

[39]Samuel S. Bowles and Henry M. Levin, "The Determinants of Scholastic Achievement—An Appraisal of Some Recent Evidence," *Journal of Human Resources, 3* (Winter 1968), 1–24, and "More on Multi-collinearity and the Effectiveness of Schools," *ibid.* (Spring 1968), 393–401; Eric A. Hanushek, "The Education of Negroes and Whites"; and John F. Kain and Eric A. Hanushek, "On the Value of 'Equality of Educational Opportunity' as a Guide to Public Policy," Harvard University, Program on Regional and Urban Economics, Discussion Paper No. 36, 1968.

[40]G. F. Peaker, "The Regression Analysis of the National Survey."

[41]Alexander W. Astin, "Undergraduate Achievement and Institutional 'Excellence,'" *Science, 161* (Aug. 1968), 661–668. Cognitive achievement was measured for a highly select sample (undergraduates taking the National Merit Scholarship Examination) at thirty-eight highly selective institutions. The lack of resource effects may be due to the relatively narrow variation in both student achievement and institutional characteristics. Because of the multicollinearity among characteristics of individuals, their peers, and their colleges (good schools select good students), it may be impossible to identify the production coefficients.

[42]These data are also consistent with the hypothesis that the poorer students dropped out, thereby raising the average cognitive gains of those remaining in school. It is true that lower aptitude students are more likely to drop out than higher aptitude students, but the caliber of students taking the National Merit exam is so high that attrition is probably not selective with respect to aptitude for this group. See Trent and Medsker, *Beyond High School.*

[43]Maureen Woodhall and Mark Blaug, "Productivity Trends in British Secondary Schools, 1950–63," *Sociology of Education, 41* (Winter 1968), 1–35.

3. PRODUCTION IN BOSTON'S ELEMENTARY SCHOOLS

[1]Daniel Patrick Moynihan, *Maximum Feasible Misunderstanding: Community Action in the War on Poverty* (New York: Free Press, 1969), 161.

[2]*Annual Statistics of the Boston Public Schools, School Year 1963–64* (School Doc. No. 8) is one of a series of reports issued by the Boston School Committee (Board of Education) containing information on registration, membership, and attendance.

[3]The number of school dropouts by census tract were collected for "Operation Second Chance," administrated by Action for Boston Community Development, the local antipoverty agency. Census tract figures were adjusted to coincide with school districts, as described in Appendix A. The numerator of the dropout rate is the number of students dropping out of public schools in the academic year 1962–63. The ages and grade level of these dropouts are unknown, but the former is probably sixteen or more, as required by law. The denominator is the expected number of students in the grades from which students drop out. This is calculated as one-half the number of students in grades one through eight, in 1960, two years earlier on the assumption of 1) rectangular age distributions within this range and 2) four grades from which students drop out.

[4]US Commission on Civil Rights, Massachusetts Advisory Committee, *Report on Racial Imbalance in the Boston Public Schools* (Washington, D.C.: Government Printing Office, 1965). The second-grade tests are Gates Primary Reading Test, Form 1—sentence reading and paragraph reading. The sixth-grade tests are Stanford Intermediate Achievement Tests, Form 2—word meaning and paragraph reading. The fifth-grade mathematics tests are Stanford Intermediate Tests, Form 1—computation, concepts, and applications.

[5]Benjamin Bloom, *Stability and Change in Human Characteristics* (New York: John Wiley & Sons, 1964), chap. ii, suggests that a mental score at a particular grade level tends to be highly correlated with *changes* between earlier tests and the present level, a speculation borne out by my own calculations in Appendix B. The fifth-grade mathematics score is thus a fair proxy for mathematics gains from the first to the fifth grade. On the other hand, Bloom suggests that there is little development in mathematical abilities before the fifth grade, so that the fifth-grade score may reflect more of initial ability than of value added through schooling.

[6]The numbers taking and passing the Latin School Examinations in March 1965 were compiled by an associate superintendent from reports of the two headmasters (principals).

[7]US Commission on Civil Rights, Massachusetts Advisory Committee, *Report on Racial Imbalance in the Boston Public Schools*, contains

information on experience and training of teachers in elementary schools only. Similar characteristics for seventh- and eighth-grade teachers in the junior high schools were obtained from the Business Manager.

[8]School Committee of the City of Boston, "Memorandum on New Teachers Hired as of Fall 1965" (unpublished, mimeo) lists new employees by district assignment. Under the fairly safe assumption that the number of teachers remains fairly stable over a two-year period, these figures can be translated into teacher turnover estimates.

[9]School Committee of the City of Boston, *School Census,* is an unpublished report on the number of students in every class room in the city, the accreditation status of teachers, and the number of specialists as of October of every school year.

[10]"Boston's Schools—1962" (Sargent Report), Boston Redevelopment Authority, 1962 (mimeo.).

[11]*Annual Report of the Superintendent of School Buildings,* City (Boston) Doc. No. 20, 1963, Appendix 5. Such a measure was used in the study of Burkhead and was cited in *Hobson* v. *Hansen* with similar rationale.

[12]See Donald E. Farrar and Robert R. Glauber, "Multicollinearity in Regression Analysis: The Problem Revisited," *Review of Economics and Statistics, 49* (Feb. 1967), 92–107.

[13]Eric A. Hanushek, "The Education of Negroes and Whites," unpublished doctoral dissertation, Massachusetts Institute of Technology, 1968, 37, 64–65, 73, 91–95.

[14]Alan B. Wilson, "Educational Consequences of Segregation in a California Community," in US Commission on Civil Rights, *Racial Isolation in the Public Schools* (2 vols., Washington, D.C.: Government Printing Office, 1967), II, 165–206.

[15]Nancy Hoyt St. John, "Minority Group Performance under Various Conditions of School Ethnic and Economic Integration: A Review of Research," US Office of Education (mimeo.); summarized in *Information Retrieval Center for the Disadvantaged, Bulletin, 4* (May 1968).

[16]For a discussion of problems of allocating fixed or constant factors, see John R. Meyer and Gerald Kraft, "An Evaluation of Statistical Costing as Applied to Transportation Industries," *American Economic Review, 51* (May 1961), 313–334.

[17]John F. Kain and Eric A. Hanushek, "On the Value of 'Equality of Educational Opportunity' as a Guide to Public Policy," Harvard University, Program on Regional and Urban Economics, Discussion Paper No. 36, 1968.

[18]Alan B. Wilson, "Educational Consequences of Segregation in a California Community," 184–186, observes that the effects of peer social class are more substantial than those of race on performance for both whites and blacks.

4. EFFICIENCY AND THE COSTS OF EDUCATIONAL QUALITY

[1]Edward C. Banfield, "Political Implications of Metropolitan Growth," *Dædalus, 90* (Winter 1961), 70.

[2]Armen Alchian, "Uncertainty, Evolution, and Economic Theory," *Journal of Political Economy, 58* (June 1950), 211–221.

[3]For a description of the middle-class ideology, see Edward C. Banfield and James Q. Wilson, *City Politics* (New York: Random House, 1963), chap. xii–xiv; cf. Charles E. Bidwell, "The School as a Formal Organization," in *Handbook of Organizations,* ed. James G. March (Chicago: Rand McNally, 1965), 972–1022, which assumes that a middle-class model of administrative behavior describes reality.

[4]Simon N. Patten, educational reformer and president of the American Economic Association in 1908, quoted in Raymond E. Callahan, *Education and the Cult of Efficiency* (Chicago: University of Chicago Press, 1962), 48.

[5]Excerpt from *Bulletin* of High School Teachers Association of New York City (Jan. 1912), cited by Callahan in *ibid.,* 58.

[6]*Ibid.,* preface.

[7]*Ibid.,* 40.

[8]*Ibid.,* 58–70.

[9]See, for example, David Krech and Richard S. Crutchfield, *Elements of Psychology* (New York: Alfred A. Knopf, 1965), 424–430.

[10]See, for example, Gary Becker, *Human Capital* (New York: Columbia University Press, 1964).

[11]Callahan, *Education and the Cult of Efficiency,* chap. ix, esp. 238–248.

[12]Selig Perlman, *Theory of the Labor Movement* (New York: Augustus M. Kelley, 1949), chap. i.

[13]Lawrence W. O'Connell, "The Citizen Reform Group in Central City School Politics: The Boston Experience, 1960–1965," unpublished doctoral dissertation, Syracuse University, 1968; cf. Banfield and Wilson, *City Politics,* chap. xv.

[14]O'Connell, "Citizen Reform Group," *passim.* In a continuing study of the Boston schools, Joseph Cronin has uncovered much evidence of the enormous political power of custodians, one product of which is a salary schedule comparable to that of teachers.

[15]*Ibid.* My own attendance at School Committee meetings confirmed this impression.

[16]*Ibid,* 52; *Annual Statistics of the Boston Public Schools, School Year 1963–64* (School Doc. No. 8);

[17]O'Connell, "Citizen Reform Group," 66–75; for a general discussion, see Joseph A. Kershaw and Roland N. McKean, *Teacher Shortages and Salary Schedules* (New York: McGraw-Hill, 1962).

[18]O'Connell, "Citizen Reform Group," 56, 124, *et passim.*

[19]Alan Rosenthal, *Pedagogues and Power: Teacher Groups in School Politics* (Syracuse, N.Y.: Syracuse University Press, 1969).

[20]Commonwealth of Massachusetts, Department of Education, *Teacher's Salary Survey Report, School Year 1964–65* (mimeo.). In 1964, the annual salary of a temporary (unaccredited) teacher in Boston was $3000, regardless of training or experience. The base salary for a permanent teacher was $5000, with a bonus of $480 for a master's degree and an increment of $240 for each year of experience up to ten.

[21]From J. Johnston, *Statistical Cost Analysis* (New York: McGraw-Hill, 1960), chaps. iv and v, esp. page 72.

[22]Herbert J. Kiesling, "Measuring a Local Government Service: A Study of School Districts in New York State," unpublished doctoral dissertation, Harvard University, 1965; and US Department of Health, Education, and Welfare, "High School Size and Cost Factors," Project Number 6–1590, 1968, prepared by Herbert J. Kiesling (mimeo.). In the former study Kiesling considers composite test scores at a wide range of grade levels; in the latter, a wide range of test scores of high school students. The U-shaped output-size relation seems to hold only for the New York State high schools. In no other case are scale effects clear, but there are weakly perceptible diseconomies. Perhaps this is because, in considering widely varying school systems, the only school characteristic Kiesling measures is expenditures per student. With so many aspects of these schools varying, it is hard to interpret his results.

[23]Charles S. Benson *et al., State and Local Fiscal Relationships in Public Education in California* (Sacramento: Senate of the State of California, 1965), 55, considers fifth-grade median reading scores as the output.

[24]Jesse Burkhead, Thomas G. Fox, and John W. Holland, *Input and Output in Large-City High Schools* (Syracuse, N.Y.: Syracuse University Press, 1967), 48–56, considers four major outputs (after high school plans, dropouts, IQ, and reading scores). In a parallel study of Atlanta in the same volume, Burkhead on pages 68–72, finds some diseconomies over the range 500–2700, but places little credence in his own findings because all the large schools were Negro.

[25]John Riew, "Economies of Scale in High School Operation," *Review of Economics and Statistics,* 48 (Aug. 1966), 280–287, relates total current expenditures per student to enrollments, holding other inputs constant; however, outputs are not held constant.

[26]A. D. Swanson, in his *The Effect of Size on School Costs* (Buffalo: State University of New York, 1967), observes a minimum expenditure per student where 20,000 to 50,000 are enrolled. Werner Z. Hirsch, "Expenditure Implications of Metropolitan Growth and Consolidation," *Review of Economics and Statistics,* 41 (Aug. 1959), 235–239, finds a

minimum for administrative costs per student at enrollment levels of 44,000; in a study of total current costs per student, however, he finds no scale effects ("Determinants of Public Education Expenditures," *National Tax Journal, 13* [Mar. 1960], 29–40). Nels W. Hanson, "Economies of Scale as a Cost Factor in the Financing of Local Public Schools," *National Tax Journal, 17* (Mar. 1964), 92–95, observes an average minimum in total current expenditures per student among several state systems at 50,000 students. George B. Pidot, Jr., "The Public Finances of Local Government in the Metropolitan United States," unpublished doctoral dissertation, Harvard University, 1965, observes decreasing costs per student as enrollments increase to 20,000. Although these studies consistently find minimum costs per student where 20,000–50,000 students attend large school systems, none of these studies control the quality of either input or output factors. For a comparison of scale economies in several public services, see Werner Z. Hirsch, "The Supply of Urban Public Services," in *Issues in Urban Economics*, ed. Harvey S. Perloff and Lowdon Wingo, Jr. (Baltimore: Johns Hopkins Press, 1968), 477–526.

[27]Roger G. Barker and Paul V. Gump, *Big School, Small School: High School Size and Student Behavior* (Stanford, Calif.: Stanford University Press, 1964), chap. ii.

[28]For a perceptive discussion of the social importance of personalities suited to team work and group leadership in the economic and political spheres, see David Riesman, Nathan Glazer, and Reuel Denney, *The Lonely Crowd: A Study of the Changing American Character* (Garden City, N.Y.: Doubleday, 1953).

[29]For a brilliant account of the contrasting styles (focal concerns, principles of personnel selection and promotion, patterns of authority) of the Boston school administrators and their reformer adversaries, see O'Connell, "Citizen Reform Group"; for a journalistic account, which was substantially based on O'Connell's work, see Peter Schrag, *The Village School Downtown* (Boston: Beacon Press, 1967). For comparisons of alternative styles of administration, see Marilyn Gittell and T. Edward Hollander, *Six Urban School Districts: A Comparative Study of Institutional Response* (New York: Frederick A. Praeger, 1968).

[30]Kiesling, "Measuring a Local Government Service."

[31]Burton A. Weisbrod, "Preventing High School Dropouts," in *Measuring Benefits of Government Investments*, ed. Robert Dorfman (Washington, D.C.: Brookings Institution, 1965), 117–149.

[32]For a review of these programs, see US Commission on Civil Rights, *Racial Isolation in the Public Schools*, (2 vols., Washington, D.C.: Government Printing Office, 1967), I, chap. iv; David K. Cohen, "Compensation and Integration," *Harvard Educational Review, 38* (Winter 1968), 114–137; "The Controversy Over the More Effective Schools: A Special Supplement," *Urban Review, 2* (May 1968), 15–34.

5. THE DISTRIBUTION OF EDUCATIONAL OPPORTUNITY

[1]"Inequities of School Finance," *Saturday Review* (Jan. 11, 1969), p. 48.

[2]See, for example, the essays in Robert Dorfman, ed., *Measuring the Benefits of Government Investments* (Washington, D.C.: Brookings Institution, 1965).

[3]Burton Weisbrod, *External Benefits of Public Education* (Princeton, N.J.: Princeton University Press, 1964); Werner Z. Hirsch, Elbert W. Segelhorst, and Morton J. Marcus, "Spillover of Public Education Costs and Benefits," Institute for Government and Public Affairs, UCLA, 1964 (mimeo.).

[4]Richard A. Musgrave and Darwin W. Daicoff, "Who Pays Michigan Taxes?" in *Michigan Tax Study Staff Papers*, ed. Harvey Brazer (Lansing, 1955), 131–183; Oswald H. Brownlee, *Estimated Distribution of Minnesota Taxes and Public Expenditure Benefits*, University of Minnesota Studies in Economics and Business, No. 21, 1960; Harold M. Groves and W. Donald Knight, *Wisconsin's State and Local Tax Burden*, University of Wisconsin Tax Study Committee, 1959; W. Irwin Gillespie, "Effect of Public Expenditures on the Distribution of Income," in *Essays in Fiscal Federalism*, ed. R. A. Musgrave (Washington, D.C.: Brookings Institution, 1965), 122–186.

[5]Most of the cases cited in the following section are discussed in David Kirp, "The Poor, the Schools, and Equal Protection," *Harvard Educational Review*, 38 (Fall 1968), 635–668; and in Arthur E. Wise, *Rich Schools, Poor Schools* (Chicago: University of Chicago Press, 1968).

[6]For a review of some school desegregation cases and the equal protection clause of the Fourteenth Amendment to the Constitution, see Owen M. Fiss, "Racial Imbalance in the Public Schools: The Constitutional Concepts," *Harvard Law Review*, 78 (Jan. 1965), 564–617; Harold W. Horowitz, "Unseparate but Unequal—The Emerging Fourteenth Amendment Issue in Public School Education," *UCLA Law Review*, 13 (Aug. 1966) 1147–1172; *Brown* v. *Board of Education*, 347 US 483, 74 Sup. Ct. 686, 98 L. Ed. 873 (1954); *McLaurin* v. *Oklahoma State Regents*, 339 US 637, 70 Sup. Ct. 851, 94 L. Ed. 1149 (1950).

[7]The Racial Imbalance Act in Massachusetts is the first such law which is based on the notion that de facto racial segregation, *within a school system*, is unequal. See *In re Skipwith*, 14 Misc. 2d 325, 180 NYS 2d at 864 (Dom. Rel. Ct. 1958) in which the argument of unconstitutionality is explicitly rejected; Kirp, "The Poor, the Schools, and Equal Protection," 663.

[8]For a critique on constitutional grounds, see Arthur E. Wise, "The Constitution and Equal Educational Opportunity," and Phillip B. Kurland, "Equal Educational Opportunity, or The Limits of Constitutional

Jurisprudence Undefined," in *The Quality of Inequality: Urban and Suburban Public Schools,* ed. Charles U. Daly, University of Chicago Center for Policy Study (Chicago: University of Chicago Press, 1968). Wise argues that the fiscal consequences of socioeconomic segregation among school systems violates the principles of equal protection implied in the desegregation, reapportionment, and right-to-counsel decisions in pages 27–46 of the work. Although Kurland expects the Supreme Court to extend the equal protection clause to fiscal inequalities, he opposes doing so on grounds of prudence (e.g., the abandonment of public schools by the well to do), as covered in pages 47–72 of the work.

[9]The "evidence" that the Supreme Court cited in the Brown decision has not withstood subsequent scrutiny—e.g., Max Deutscher and Isidor Chein, "The Psychological Effects of Enforced Segregation: A Survey of Social Science *Opinion* [italics mine]," *Journal of Psychology,* 26 (Oct. 1948), 259–287. The evidence since 1954 is still rather inconclusive; see Nancy H. St. John, "Minority Group Performance Under Various Conditions of School Ethnic and Economic Integration: A Review of Research," US Office of Education, Contract No. 6–10–240; summarized in *Information Retrieval Center on the Disadvantaged, Bulletin, 4* (May 1968).

[10]The findings on the effects of socioeconomic segregation are somewhat inconclusive because of the absence of proper controls for school resources and self-selection factors; for example, see Alan B. Wilson, "The Educational Consequences of Segregation in a California Community," in US Commission on Civil Rights, *Racial Isolation in the Public Schools* (2 vols., Washington, D.C.: Government Printing Office, 1967), II, Appendix C 3.

[11]It was the intent of Progressive reformers at the turn of the century that at-large municipal elections would reinforce "public" rather than localistic concerns, perpetuated by the ward system. This electoral reform had the effect of reducing the representation of minorities, such as the Yankee reformers themselves. See Edward C. Banfield and James Q. Wilson, *City Politics* (New York: Random House, 1963), chap. vii; Lawrence W. O'Connell, "The Citizen Reform Group in Central City School Politics: The Boston Experience, 1960–1965," unpublished doctoral dissertation, Syracuse University, 1968.

[12]Stephan Michelson, "Equal Protection and School Resources," *Inequality in Education,* (Dec. 1969), 9–15.

[13]Susan S. Stodolsky and Gerald Lesser, "Learning Patterns in the Disadvantaged," *Harvard Educational Review,* 37 (Fall 1967), 546–593.

[14]See Matthew Edel, "The Mexican Ejido: A Lesson in Community Control for the U.S.," Department of Economics, MIT (mimeo., 1969), on the emergence of the "cacique" or local boss in Mexican community organizations and the dangers of bossism in local American politics.

[15]See Wise, "The Constitution and Equal Educational Opportunity," and Kurland, "Equal Educational Opportunity," for a review of the decisions regarding reapportionment and voting rights, and indigents and the administration of justice, e.g., *Gideon* v. *Wainwright*, 372 US 335 (1962), *Griffin* v. *Illinois* 352 US 12 (1956).

[16]Richard A. Musgrave, *The Theory of Public Finance* (New York: McGraw-Hill, 1959), chap. viii, and John F. Due, *Government Finance* (rev. ed., Homewood, Ill.: Richard D. Irwin, 1959,), 102–120, for a discussion of equity concepts in public finance.

[17]Joseph Tussman and Jacobus ten Broek, "The Equal Protection of the Laws," *California Law Review*, 37 (Sept. 1949), 344.

[18]For a readable and informative discussion of classifications permitted in tax policy and the history of such policies, see Jerome Hellerstein, *Taxes, Loopholes, and Morals* (New York: McGraw-Hill, 1963).

[19]For a discussion of the history and meaning of this act, see Frank S. Levy, "An Essay on the Massachusetts Racial Imbalance Act," unpublished doctoral dissertation, Yale University, 1969.

[20]*Hobson* v. *Hansen*, 269 F. Supp. 401 (D.C.D.C. 1967), is the first case in which a judge challenged the legitimacy of such restrictions. Washington, D.C., whose school system is over 90 percent Negro in enrollment, was ordered to undertake metropolitan planning, in hopes of inducing cooperation from the neighboring states. The states, however, were not forced to accept this remedy. See Kirp, "The Poor, the Schools, and Equal Protection," 653–666.

[21]See, for example, Otis Dudley Duncan and Beverly Duncan, "Residential Distribution and Occupational Stratification," *American Journal of Sociology*, 60 (Mar. 1955), 493–503; Karl Taeuber and Alma Taeuber, "The Negro as an Immigrant Group," *American Journal of Sociology*, 69 (Jan. 1964), 374–382, on segregation by social class and ethnicity.

[22]H. Thomas James, "School Revenue Systems in Five States," Stanford University, School of Education, 1961; Jerry Miner, *Social and Economic Factors in Spending for Public Education* (Syracuse, N. Y.: Syracuse University Press, 1963).

[23]Charles M. Tiebout, "A Pure Theory of Local Public Expenditures," *Journal of Political Economy*, 64 (Oct. 1956), 416–424; and Robert Warren, "A Municipal Services Market Model of Metropolitan Organization," *Journal of the American Institute of Planners*, 30 (Aug. 1964), 193–204.

[24]James S. Coleman *et al.*, *Equality of Educational Opportunity*, US Office of Education (Washington, D.C.: Government Printing Office, 1966), Appendixes; and Miner, *Social and Economic Factors in Spending for Public Education*, 97.

[25]US Department of Commerce, *Statistical Abstract of the United States, 1964* (Washington, D.C.: Government Printing Office, 1964), Table 163 and Figure IX.

[26]Adapted from Forrest W. Harrison and Eugene P. McLoone, *Profiles in School Support: A Decennial Overview* (Washington, D.C.: Government Printing Office, 1959), which presents expenditures per classroom distributions in terms of percentiles by each state. Assuming that distributions are normal, the mean and standard deviations can be estimated from percentiles.

[27]See Coleman *et al., Equality of Educational Opportunity,* Tables 1–6, Appendixes; National Education Association, "Estimates of School Statistics," Research Report R-13, and "Class Size in Kindergarten and Elementary Schools," Research Report R-11, 1967 (mimeo.).

[28]Miner, *Social and Economic Factors in Spending for Public Education,* 48–65, 107, reviews the literature on this topic.

[29]Werner Z. Hirsch, "Determinants of Public Education Expenditures," *National Tax Journal, 13* (Mar. 1960), 29–40; Jesse Burkhead, Thomas G. Fox, and John W. Holland, *Input and Output in Large-City High Schools* (Syracuse, N.Y.: Syracuse University Press, 1967); Patricia Cayo Sexton, *Education and Income: The Inequalities of Opportunities in our Public Schools* (New York: Viking Press, 1961).

[30]Otto Davis, "Empirical Evidence of Political Influence upon Expenditure Policies of Public Schools," in *The Public Economy of Urban Communities,* ed. Julius Margolis (Baltimore: Johns Hopkins Press for Resources for the Future, 1965); Seymour Sacks and William F. Hellmuth, Jr., *Financing Government in a Metropolitan Area: The Cleveland Experience* (New York: Free Press, 1961).

[31]Edward C. Banfield and James Q. Wilson, "Public-Regardingness as a Value Premise in Voting Behavior," *American Political Science Review, 58* (Dec. 1964), 876–887. On the other hand, Alan K. Campbell and Seymour Sacks, *Metropolitan America: Fiscal Patterns and Governmental Patterns* (New York: Free Press, 1967), 137–147, find no relationship between home ownership and school expenditures on the metropolitan level.

[32]Oliver Oldman and Henry Aaron, "Assessment-Sales Ratio under the Boston Property Tax," *National Tax Journal, 18* (Mar. 1965), 36–49.

[33]Sherman Schapiro, "Some Socioeconomic Determinants of Expenditures for Education: Southern and Other States Compared," *Comparative Education Review, 6* (Oct. 1962), 160–166; Miner, *Social and Economic Factors in Spending for Public Education,* 98; Otto Davis, "Empirical Evidence of Political Influence upon Expenditure Policies of Public Schools"; Seymour Sacks and David Ranney, "Suburban Education: A Fiscal Analysis," *Urban Affairs Quarterly, 2* (Sept. 1966), 103–119.

[34]George B. Pidot, Jr., "The Public Finances of Local Government in the Metropolitan United States," unpublished doctoral dissertation, Har-

vard University, 1965, 55–83, 244–246; Campbell and Sacks, *Metropolitan America.*

[35]Coleman *et al., Equality of Educational Opportunity,* Appendixes, Table 106.

[36]Miner, *Social and Economic Factors in Spending for Public Education,* explains 54 percent of the variance with communities as observations; Campbell and Sacks, *Metropolitan America,* explain 53 and 56 percent of average central city and average suburban ring variations, respectively; Benson, *Economics of Public Education,* (rev. ed., Boston: Houghton Mifflin, 1968). 400–401.

[37]Benson, *Economics of Public Education,* and *id. et al., State and Local Fiscal Relationships in Public Education in California* (Sacramento: Senate of the State of California, 1965), 57.

[38]Floyd Hunter, *Community Power Structure* (Chapel Hill: University of North Carolina Press, 1953), generalized this model from observations of Atlanta.

[39]Robert A. Dahl, *Who Governs?* (New Haven, Conn.: Yale University Press, 1961), and Edward C. Banfield, *Political Influence* (New York: Free Press, 1961), for applications of this model.

[40]See Richard Hofstadter, *The Paranoid Style in American Politics, and Other Essays* (New York: Alfred A. Knopf, 1965).

[41]See the model of the "satisficing" as opposed to maximizing administrator, in Herbert A. Simon, "Thories of Decision-making in Economics," *American Economic Review,* 49 (May 1959), 253–283; cf. Armen Alchian, "Uncertainty, Evolution, and Economic Theory," *Journal of Political Economy,* 58 (June 1950), 211–221, for a model in which the survival of the efficient in an uncertain world is largely a matter of luck. School systems, of course, survive whether or not they are efficient, although particular administrators may not.

[42]Lawrence W. O'Connell, "The Citizen Reform Group in Central City School Politics: The Boston Experience, 1960–1965," unpublished doctoral dissertation, Syracuse University, 1968, 53–77, presents some data on the proportion of school committeemen, superintendents, and teachers who are Irish. See Nathan Glazer and Daniel P. Moynihan, *Beyond the Melting Pot* (Cambridge, Mass.: MIT Press, 1963), 217–287; William Shannon, *The American Irish* (New York: Macmillan, 1963); and Oscar Handlin, *Boston's Immigrants* (New York: Atheneum Publishers, 1968) suggest these reasons for the peculiar political behavior of the Boston Irish. Glazer and Moynihan note that it was characteristic of Irish politicians of the local Boston genre that they never did much with their power except to provide their friends with jobs and favors.

[43]Walter B. Miller, in a personal communication, says that his studies of delinquency in Boston identify the Irish rather than Negro neighborhoods as having greater delinquency. School vandalism is especially high

in the Irish neighborhood of South Boston where several schools were recently destroyed by arsonists, O'Connell, "Citizen Reform Group," 169–171.

[44]O'Connell, "Citizen Reform Group," 118, on the Boston parent-teacher association and on the overwhelming proportion of their time which the school committee devotes to problems of particular concern, e.g., stretching sick leave regulations for a faithful custodian. This is not an unusual preoccupation for a system run by working-class "ethnics"; see Edward C. Banfield, "Political Implications of Metropolitan Growth," *Dædalus, 90* (Winter 1961), 61–78.

[45]Peter H. Rossi and Alice S. Rossi, "Parochial School Education in America," *Dædalus, 90* (Spring 1961), 300–328, tender this hypothesis.

[46]Oldman and Aaron, "Assessment-Sales Ratios under the Boston Property Tax"; cf. Musgrave and Daicoff, "Who Pays Michigan Taxes?"; Groves and Knight, *Wisconsin's State and Local Tax Burden;* and Brownlee, *Estimated Distribution of Minnesota Taxes.*

[47]Sexton, *Education and Income;* Jesse Burkhead, Thomas G. Fox, and John W. Holland, *Input and Output in Large-City High Schools.*

[48]Edward C. Banfield, *Big City Politics* (New York: Random House, 1965) compares the political systems and school politics in nine cities, including Boston, Detroit (studied by Sexton), and Chicago and Atlanta (studied by Burkhead).

[49]John K. Folger and Charles B. Nam, *Education of the American People,* US Bureau of the Census Monograph, (Washington, D.C.: Government Printing Office, 1967).

[50]John F. Kain and Eric A. Hanushek, "On the Value of 'Equality of Educational Opportunity' as a Guide to Public Policy," Harvard University, Program on Regional and Urban Economics, Discussion Paper No. 36, 1968.

[51]Otis Dudley Duncan, "Ability and Achievement," *Eugenics Quarterly, 15* (Mar. 1968), 1–11.

6. RESTRUCTURING BIG CITY SCHOOL SYSTEMS

[1]Mark Blaug, "Economic Aspects of Vouchers for Education," in *Education: A Framework for Choice* (London: Institute for Economic Affairs, 1967), 33.

[2]See Alan B. Wilson, "Educational Consequences of Segregation in a California Community," in US Commission on Civil Rights, *Racial Isolation in the Public Schools* (2 vols., Washington, D.C.: Government Printing Office, 1967) II, Appendix C 3; Nancy H. St. John, "Minority Group Performance under Various Conditions of School Ethnic and Economic Integration: A Review of Research," unpublished manuscript, US Office of Education, summarized in *Information Retrieval Center on the Disadvantaged, Bulletin, 4* (May 1968).

[3] Eric A. Hanushek, "The Education of Negroes and Whites," unpublished doctoral dissertation, Massachusetts Institute of Technology, 1968, Tables 3.1 and 4.1.

[4] Dick Netzer, *Economics of the Property Tax* (Washington, D.C.: Brookings Institution, 1966), 164.

[5] Oliver Oldman and Henry Aaron, "Assessment-Sales Ratio under the Boston Property Tax," *National Tax Journal*, 18 (Mar. 1965), 36–49.

[6] See Richard A. Musgrave, *The Theory of Public Finance* (New York: McGraw-Hill, 1959), chaps. iv and v, for a careful review of the benefit and ability-to-pay principles of taxation.

[7] See Netzer, *Economics of the Property Tax*, 45, 79, *et passim*.

[8] Mayor's Advisory Panel on Decentralization of the New York City Schools, *Reconnection for Learning: A Community School System for New York City, New York, 1967 passim.*, commonly known as the Bundy Report, does not recommend fiscal autonomy, a function preserved by the central administration, presumably to provide a broader fiscal base for the poor districts. Such support, however, could be granted by state or federal funds as suggested above.

[9] Edward C. Banfield, "The Political Implications of Metropolitan Growth," *Dædalus*, 90 (Winter 1961), 61–79.

[10] On a purely judicial basis, the Bundy Report, pages 16–17, recommends district sizes of twelve thousand to forty thousand students in New York City.

[11] Richard F. Carter and William G. Savard, *Influence on Voter Turnout on School Bond and Tax Elections*, US Office of Education, Cooperative Research Monograph, No. 5, 1960.

[12] In *Hobson v. Hansen*, 269 F. Supp. 401 (D.C.D.C. 1967), Judge Wright remarked on the inadequacy of this principle for the integration of Washington, D.C., a reasonable judgment whether or not decentralization be adopted.

[13] See, for example, the argument of Mancur Olson, "The Principle of 'Fiscal Equivalence,'" *American Economic Review Papers and Proceedings*, 59 (May 1969), 479–487.

[14] Herbert Gans, *The Urban Villagers: Group and Class in the Life of Italian-Americans* (New York: Free Press, 1961), chap. i, and *The Levittowners* (New York: Random House, 1967), chap. iv; William Dobriner, *Class in Suburbia* (Englewood Cliffs, N.J.: Prentice-Hall, 1963).

[15] See Robert J. Havighurst, *Education in Metropolitan Areas* (Boston: Allyn and Bacon, 1966), chap. v.

[16] John H. Fischer, "The School Park," in US Commission on Civil Rights, *Racial Isolation in the Public Schools*, II, Appendix D 2.1; Francis Keppel, "Educational Technology and the Educational Park," in *ibid.*, Appendix D 2.3; and Dan C. Lortie, "Towards Educational Equality: The Teacher and the Educational Park," in *ibid.*, Appendix D 2.4.

[17]See Edward C. Banfield and James Q. Wilson, "Public-Regardingness as a Value Premise in Voting Behavior," *American Political Science Review,* 58 (Dec. 1964), 876–887.

[18]Lawrence A. Cremin, *The American Common School: An Historical Conception* (New York: Teachers College Press, 1951).

[19]Milton Friedman, "The Role of Government in Education," in *Capitalism and Freedom* (Chicago: University of Chicago Press, 1962), 85–107. Cf. Theodore R. Sizer, "The Case for a Free Market," *Saturday Review* (Jan. 11, 1969), 34ff.; Kenneth Clark, "Alternative Public School Systems," *Harvard Educational Review,* 38 (Winter 1968), 100–113; E. G. West, *Education and the State* (London: Institute for Economic Affairs, 1965); A. C. G. Beales *et al., Education: A Framework for Choice* (London: Institute for Economic Affairs, 1967).

[20]See Lawrence W. O'Connell, "The Citizen Reform Group in Central City School Politics: The Boston Experience, 1960–1965," unpublished doctoral dissertation, Syracuse University, 1968, chap. v, for example, on the creation and exploitation of the "Negro problem" in Boston school politics.

[21]Victor Fuchs, *The Service Economy* (New York: National Bureau of Economic Research, 1969).

[22]Martin T. Katzman and Ronald Rosen, "The Science and Politics of National Educational Assessment," *Teacher's College Record,* 71 (May 1970), 571–587.

[23]Eugene J. Devine and Morton J. Marcus, "Monopsony, Recruitment Costs, and Job Vacancies," *Western Economic Journal,* 5 (Sept. 1967), 352–359, a consideration of the monopsony power of local governments to affect the wage rates of their employees and the effects of unionization.

[24]John F. Kain, "Housing Segregation, Negro Employment, and Metropolitan Decentralization," *Quarterly Journal of Economics,* 82 (May 1968), 175–197, on the costs of housing segregation to Negroes in terms of employment.

[25]Milton M. Gordon, *Assimilation in American Life* (New York: Oxford Press, 1964); Rossi and Rossi, "Parochial School Education in America"; John Higham, *Strangers in the Land: Patterns of American Nativism, 1860–1925* (New York: Atheneum Publishers, 1967).

[26]Andrew M. Greeley and Peter H. Rossi, *The Education of Catholic Americans* (Chicago: Aldine Publishing Co., 1966).

7. THE BURDENS ON BIG CITY SCHOOLS

[1]Charles Hamilton, "Race and Education: A Search for Legitimacy," *Harvard Educational Review,* 38 (Fall 1968), 671.

[2]*Ibid.*; John H. Fischer, "Race and Reconciliation: The Role of the School," *Dædalus,* 95 (Winter 1966), 24–44.

[3]Herbert A. Simon, "Theories of Decision-Making in Economics," *Papers and Proceedings of the American Economic Association, 49* (May 1959), 253–283.

[4]Edward C. Banfield, "The Political Implications of Metropolitan Growth," *Dædalus, 90* (Winter 1961), 61–79; William Dobriner, *Class in Suburbia* (Englewood Cliffs, N.J.: Prentice-Hall, 1963); Peter H. Rossi and Alice S. Rossi, "Parochial School Education in America," *Dædalus, 90* (Spring 1961), 300–328; Lawrence W. O'Connell, "The Citizen Reform Group in Central City School Politics: The Boston Experience, 1960-1965," unpublished doctoral dissertation, Syracuse University, 1968.

[5]The Boston *Herald-Traveler* series on the Boston Schools (Mar.-Apr. 1966) compares the recruitment pattern of city and suburban schools. The authors of the series argue that the inbred bureaucracy makes no serious effort to recruit quality teachers comparable to other big cities; cf. O'Connell, "Citizen Reform Group," *passim.*

[6]O'Connell, "Citizen Reform Group," *passim.*

[7]For a discussion of the Assessment program, see Martin Katzman and Ronald S. Rosen, "The Science and Politics of National Educational Assessment," *Teacher's College Record, 71* (May 1970), 571–587.

[8]Fritz Machlup, *The Production and Distribution of Knowledge in the United States* (Princeton, N.J.: Princeton University Press, 1962).

[9]Public goods cannot be sold on the market because those unwilling to pay cannot be excluded from consumption. See Paul A. Samuelson, "The Pure Theory of Public Expenditures," *Review of Economics and Statistics, 36* (Nov. 1954), 387–389.

[10]Psychologist David Krech predicted before a Senate committee that chemical control of intelligence and memory would be feasible within the next five or ten years, reported in *The New York Times,* Apr. 3, 1968.

APPENDIX A.   MISCELLANEOUS DATA PROBLEMS

[1]US Census of Population, 1960, *Boston Standard Metropolitan Statistical Area, Final Report PC (3)–1D* (Washington, D.C.: Government Printing Office, 1963), Table 1–3.

[2]Research Unit, Boston Redevelopment Authority, "Population Summary—City of Boston by Ward and Precinct, 1965," Nov. 1965 (mimeo.), and "Report on Distribution of Negro Population, 1950-1960, Projected 1970," no date (mimeo.).

[3]US Commission on Civil Rights, Massachusetts Advisory Committee, *Hearings,* 1964.

[4]US Census of Population, 1960, *Boston.*

APPENDIX B. THE USE OF MENTAL TEST SCORES IN
REGRESSION ANALYSIS

[1]An argument of this sort is made by Frederic M. Lord and Melvin R. Novick, *Statistical Theories of Mental Test Scores* (Reading, Mass.: Addison-Wesley, 1968), 20–22.

[2]Randall Weiss, "The Effects of Scholastic Achievement Upon the Earnings of Whites and Negroes: Experiments with Single Equation and Recursive Models," unpublished bachelor's thesis, Harvard College, 1968, finds that linear relationships between achievement and income are as good as polynomial or higher order relationships.

[3]*Ibid.*; Otis Dudley Duncan, "Ability and Achievement," *Eugenics Quarterly, 13* (Mar. 1968), 1–11.

[4]Benjamin S. Bloom, *Stability and Change in Human Characteristics* (New York: John Wiley & Sons, 1964), chaps. i and ii.

[5]These data were kindly shown me by my colleague, Nancy St. John.

APPENDIX C. SPECIFYING AN EDUCATIONAL PRODUCTION
FUNCTION

[1]H. D. Vinod, "Econometrics of Joint Production," *Econometrica, 36* (Apr. 1968), 332–336.

[2]See William W. Cooley and Paul R. Lohnes, *Multivariate Procedures for the Behavioral Sciences,* (New York: John Wiley & Sons, 1962), chap. ii, for a description of canonical correlation.

[3]After Vinod.

[4]Arnold Zellner and Henri Theil, "Three-stage Least Squares: Simultaneous Estimation of Simultaneous Relations," *Econometrica, 30* (Jan. 1962), 72–81.

[5]See Oskar Morgenstern, *On the Accuracy of Economic Observations* (Princeton, N.J.: Princeton University Press, 1965), 17–26; Cf. Herbert Feigl, "Notes on Causality"; and Ernest Nagel, "The Causal Character of Physical Theory," in *Readings in the Philosophy of Science,* ed. Herbert Feigl and May Brodbeck (New York: Appleton-Century-Crofts, 1953), 408–418, 419–427.

[6]See Jacob Marschak and William H. Andrews, Jr., "Random Simultaneous Equations and the Theory of Production," *Econometrica, 12* (July-Oct. 1944), 143–205.

INDEX

Administrators, educational, vulnerability of, 103
Andrews, William, 202
Apartheid model, of resource allocation, 146, 148
Astin, Alexander, 41, 43
Asymmetric model, of resource allocation, 146, 148
Atlanta, schools compared to Boston's and Chicago's, 135–136, 173
Attendance, average daily, 46, 48, 171
Attractiveness of schooling, measure of, 171

Banfield, Edward C., 2, 12, 121, 177; quoted, 77
Benson, Charles, 37, 38, 42, 68, 89, 124
Bias: factors contributing to, 119–123; in expenditures, 120–123; in physical resources, 123; degree of, 123–124; beneficiaries of, 127–129; in big city distribution, 136–137
Big city rich, 141, 144, 148–150, 166, 167
Big city school systems: equating of supply and demand in, 115–116; distribution within, 124–137, 173; distribution in Boston, 129–135; in other cities, 135–137; restructuring

of, 140–168. *See also* Boston; Current organization of big city schools; Repair of current system
Blaug, Marck, 41; quoted, 140
Bloom, Benjamin, 25, 191
Boston, elementary schools in: case study of, 45–76; production model for, 45–53, 171; working hypotheses, 53–57; best linear production functions, 57–66; contribution of resources to performance in, 66–73; hypotheses suggested by, 73–76; as employer, 83–84; costs of education within, 85–88; comparison of districts within, 101, 145; lack of community control in, 108; process of distribution in, 126–127; beneficiaries of bias in, 127–135; distribution of resources in, 129–135; and socioeconomic characteristics, 176
Bowles, Samuel S., 40, 99
Boys' Latin High School, 47, 171
Burdens, of big city school systems: ineffectiveness, 173–175; lack of responsiveness, 175–176; inequalities, 176–179
Burkhead, Jesse, 38–39, 43, 60–61, 88, 121; study of Chicago and Atlanta by, 135–136

Callahan, Raymond, 79
Campbell, Alan K., 122; quoted, 105
Canonical correlation (CC), 197
Catholics, effect of parochial
  education on, 164. *See also*
  Irish; Parochial schools
Caucasians, average expenditures
  on, 122
Chicago: schools compared to
  Atlanta's and Boston's,
  135–136, 173; possible
  bussing in, 158
Chinese: performance of, in
  Boston schools, 62, 64; spatial
  conceptualization of, 110
City versus suburbs, socioeconomic
  characteristics, 176
Class size, decrease in, related
  to performance, 73. *See also*
  Scale
Cobb-Douglas function, 194
Cognitive development: measured
  in Boston schools, 46–48;
  measures of, 171
Cognitive scales, ordinal, interval,
  and ratio properties of, 30
Cognitive skills, school as
  transmitter of, 29
Coleman, James S., 39, 42
Coleman Report. *See* Equal Edu-
  cational Opportunity Survey
College attendance, 60
Community income, allocation
  of, to schooling, 114–115.
  See also Resources
"Compensatory education," as
  alternative to racial integra-
  tion, 74–75, 100–103
Consumption efficiency: defined,
  141; in current organization
  of big city schools, 143–144;
  and structural reform, 165
Continuation, of students in
  school, 60
Cost-benefit analysis, possibility
  of, for social systems, 8
Cost curves, 85, 92–93, 95
Costs: reduction of, in scientific
  management, 81; input,

85–88, 90–91
Criterion validity, 32
Critical period, concept of, 26
Crowding of classrooms, 171
Current organization of big city
  schools, 142–151, 165;
  consumption efficiency in,
  143–144; equality of
  opportunity in, 144–145;
  integration in, 146–148;
  distributional consequences
  of, 148–151. *See also* Big City
  school systems; Repair of
  current system

Data problems, Boston: calculating school variables, 185–186;
  calculating socioeconomic
  variables, 186–188
Davis, Otto, 121
Decentralization: as means of
  restructuring, 154–158, 165;
  technological efficiency of,
  156; and parental participation, 156; and integration,
  156–158; and interest
  groups, 166, 167
De facto segregation, consequences of, 129
Desocialization of education, by
  tuition vouchers, 161
Detroit, study of educational
  resources in, 135
Development, equal opportunity
  for, 109
Distribution, defining objects of,
  107–113; absence of racial
  segregation, 107–108, 110;
  equal control over resources,
  108, 110; equal resources,
  108–109, 110; equally effective resources, 109, 111;
  equal academic performance,
  109, 111; equal opportunity
  for maximum development,
  109–110, 111; as social indicators, 110–112; equality for
  whom, 112–113; within
  big cities, 124–137

Dobriner, William, 11
Downs, Anthony, 7n
Dropout, lack of, 171
Dubos, René, 4, 7

Early experience, importance
    of, 25
Economic enterprises, schools as,
    14; outline of present work
    concerning, 14–18
Educational efficiency, 75–85;
    middle-class orientation, 79–
    82; working-class orientation,
    82–85
Educational establishment, 141,
    166, 167, 177
Educational objectives: socializa-
    tion, 29; cognitive skills,
    29–30; indicators of, 30–33;
    multiple, 33–34
Educational park, concept of,
    158–159
Educational production function,
    specification of, 194–203;
    functional forms, 194–196;
    statistical techniques, 196–
    200; error terms, 200–201;
    behavioral assumptions,
    202–203
Edwards, Allen L., 49, 62
Efficiency: technological, 77–78;
    educational, 78–85; and
    costs of educational quality,
    85–103
Elasticity of performance, related
    to changes in school re-
    sources, 67–68, 69, 172
Elementary schools: production
    process of, 15; case study
    of, 16. *See also* Boston
Empathy, measure of, 20
Employee orientation, in working-
    class attitude toward
    schools, 82–83
Enrollment: size of, 37; related
    to performance, 58–59,
    related to cost, 88–89
Equality of educational oppor-
    tunity, 13, 106; confusion of

sameness with, 109; ambiv-
    alence of public policy on,
    112–113; problems connected
    with criteria for, 138–139;
    problems of, in big city
    systems, 176–179
Equality of Educational Opportu-
    nity (EEO) Survey (Coleman
    Report), 39–40, 70, 108,
    119, 122, 123, 137, 180
Ethnic minorities, 141, 150, 166,
    167; under current organi-
    zation of resources, 150
Ethnic patterns, differences in, 110
Ethnicity: classification of stu-
    dents by, 39–40; related to
    bias in expenditures, 122
Evaluation of educational quality,
    19–44; traditional modes
    of, 19–23; production model
    of school systems, 23–29;
    measuring objectives of
    schooling, 29–34; review of
    studies on, 34–44; under sys-
    tem of tuition vouchers, 162
"Expansive" subcultures, 12
Expenditures: evaluation based
    on, 21–22; as indicator of
    school resources, 49; lack of
    impact on performance,
    54–55, 73; specific kinds of,
    73–74; per student, in Boston
    schools, 86–87; inequalities
    in, 118 119
Experiments, natural vs. con-
    trolled, 34–35

"Fate control," 108
Finance Commission of the
    Commonwealth of Massa-
    chusetts, 84
Financial aid, as means of repair-
    ing current system, 153–154
Firms, nonprofit versus profit, 15
Fiscal federalism, institutions of,
    and distribution of educa-
    tional resources, 113, 114
Fiscal issues, social class attitudes
    on, 12

Fourteenth Amendment, 113
Fox, Thomas, 135
Friedman, Milton, 160, 161

Gans, Herbert, 12
German-Americans, and Lutheran
    school system, 164
Girls' Latin High School, 47, 171
Goodman, Samuel, 37, 42

Hamilton, Charles, quoted, 169
Hanushek, Eric, 40, 42, 60–61; on
    integration, 62, 64, 147; on
    elasticity, 68
Heterogeneity, benefit or harm,
    146
Hirsch, Werner, 121
Hobson v. *Hansen*, 111, 135, 136
Holding power, measures of, 46–47
Holland, John, 135
Housing market, and distribution
    of educational resources,
    113, 117
"Human capital," 81
Human development, character-
    istics of, 25–27; early
    experience, 25; stages of
    development, 26; learning
    theory, 26–27

Immigration, and quality of
    schooling, 79
Income elasticity, 121–122
Income-expenditure curves, 116
Indicators: of educational objec-
    tives, 30–33; of educational
    progress, 179
Ineffectiveness as problem of big
    city school systems, 173–175
Inequalities in educational oppor-
    tunity: measurement of, 118;
    in expenditures, 118–119; in
    physical resources, 119; in big
    city school systems, 135–136,
    173
Input costs, 85–88; linear approxi-
    mation of, 90–91
Inputs: weakness of "physically
    defined," 22–23; related to
    outputs, 24

Institutional change, criteria for
    evaluation of: technological
    efficiency, 141; technological
    progress, 141; consumption
    efficiency, 141, 143–144;
    equality of opportunity, 141,
    144–145; integration, 141,
    146–148
Institutions subject to change in
    structural reorganization:
    financing, 142; administrative
    decision making, 142; student
    placement, 142
Integration: defined, 141; asym-
    metric model for, 146;
    apartheid model for, 146, 148;
    in current organization of
    big city schools, 146–148;
    possibility of complete, 152–
    153; under decentralization,
    156–158; under metropoli-
    tanism, 158, 165; under
    tuition vouchers, 163–165;
    under status quo, 166, 167
Intellectuals, lack of interest in
    social technologies, 6
Interest groups of metropolitan
    community: educational
    establishment, 141; suburban
    rich, 141, 144; big city rich,
    141, 144, 148–150; urban
    poor, 141, 144, 151; ethnic
    minorities, 141, 150; choices
    of types of structural reform
    by, 167
Interval scales, in measurement
    of cognitive properties, 30, 31
Irish-Americans, as "private-
    regarding," 12, 177
Irish Catholics: restrictive orienta-
    tion of, 12; in Boston school
    system, 127; and parochial
    school system, 164
Italian-Americans, as "private-
    regarding," 12, 177
Italian Catholics, expansive orien-
    tation of, 12

James, H. Thomas, 119

Jews: expansive orientation of, 12; numerical ability of, 110; as "public-regarding," 177

Katzman, Martin T., 89
Kiesling, Herbert, 38, 42, 68, 89; on expenditures and outputs, 98
Kreinen, Mordecai, 33

Latin High Schools. *See* Boys' Latin High School; Girls' Latin High School
Learning theory, 26–27
Lesser, Gerald, 109
Level of performance, school resources and, 67, 68
Levin, Henry M., 40, 43, 99
Liberalism, measurement of, 30
Linear models, 194–196
Lower middle class, modal attitudes of toward schools, 11–12. *See also* Social classes

Maintenance, costs of, 86, 88
Marschak, Jacob, 202
Massachusetts Racial Imbalance Act, 113
Mathematics scores: related to teacher experience, 61; as measure of cognitive development, 171
McGinnis v. *Ogilvie*, 113
Melville, S. Donald, 37, 43
Mental test scores, in regression analysis, 189–193
Methodological problems, in specifying educational production functions: choosing mathematical form, 45; arriving at statistical design, 45; measuring relevant variables, 45, 46–49
Metropolitan Council for Educational Opportunity (METCO), 117n
Metropolitanism: as means of restructuring, 158–160, 165; and interest groups, 166–167

Mexican-Americans, expenditures per student, 122
Middle class: orientation of, toward efficiency in schooling, 79–82; and distribution of school resources, 148–150. *See also* Social classes
Miner, Jerry, 119, 121
Mollenkopf, William G., 37, 43
More Effective Schools program, N.Y.C., 100
Moynihan, Daniel P., quoted, 45
Multicollinearity, defined, 55
Multiple objectives, problems of, 33–34
Multiplicative models, 194–196

National Educational Assessment Program, 162, 179–180
Negroes: performance of, in Boston schools, 61–64; average expenditures on, 122; under metropolitanism, 159. *See also* Integration
Nonprofit enterprises: schools as, 14; theory of, 15. *See also* Social service enterprises
Nonprofit firm: schools as, 14; need for systematic study of, 15; production process in, 15–16; distribution in, 16–17; structural reorganization in, 17

Objectives of schooling, measurement of, 29–34; what is learned, 29–30; indicators of, 30–33; problem of multiple objectives, 33–34
O'Connell, Lawrence W., 82, 135
Open enrollment, 117, 149, 158
Opportunity, educational, 105–139; defining objects of distribution, 107–113; patterns of distribution, 113–124; distribution within big cities, 124–137; inequalities of, 137–139; equality of, defined, 141; in current organization

of big city schools, 144–145; measurement of, 172

Ordinal properties, of cognitive scales, 30

Ordinary least squares (OLS), 196–197

Output cost function, or supply curve, 85, 88

Overcrowding, 50; effect on performance, 60; reduction of, 74

Parental participation, under decentralization, 156

Parochial schools: effect of, on public schools, 127, 128, 151; under tuition voucher system, 164

Patterns of distribution, 113–124; inequalities in, 118–119; factors contributing to bias, 119–123; degree of bias, 123–124

Peer effects, in allocation of resources, 148

Performance: measurement of, in Boston schools, 46–49, 172; as function of school expenditures, 54, 73–74; as function of physical resources, 56, 66–73, 74; level of, 67; variations in, 67, 68, 70–72; elasticity of, 67–68, 69; and race, 74

Perlman, Selig, 82

Pidot, George, 122

Plessy v. *Ferguson,* 109

Plowden Report, 40, 42

Pluralism, cultural, ideal of, 110

Poles, as "private-regarding," 12, 177

Political conflicts, in solutions of social service enterprises, 8–14

Poor, urban, 151. *See also* Interest groups

Predictive validity, 32

Private school system: and public school expenditures, 122, 149, 150, 151; use of, by Boston

residents, 177

Private-regarding voter preferences, 12, 177

Privatization of education: by tuition vouchers, 161; and interest groups, 166, 167

Production, educational: review of studies of, 34–44; table of, 42–43; in Boston elementary schools, 45–76; possibilities, 97–98, 99

Production function: characteristics of, 27–29; and validity of measures of educational opportunity, 172

Production model of school systems, 23–29; characteristics of human development, 25–27; characteristics of the production function, 27–29; operationalizing of, 45–53

Productivity, and amount of education, 32–33

"Program" for eliciting responses, as attribute of schooling, 27

Protestants: orientation of rural, 12; perception of public interest by, 12, 177

Public-regarding voter preferences, 12, 177

Puerto Ricans, average expenditures for, 123

Pupil to teacher ratio, 50, 171

Quality, educational costs of, 85–103; input costs, 85–88; economies of scale, 88–89; linear approximation of input costs, 90–91; derivation of supply curve, 91–94; production possibilities, 97–98; supply price vs. actual expenditures, 98–100; compensatory education, 100–103

Race, effect of, on performance, 61–64, 74, 172

Racial integration, 13; alternatives

to, 74–75. *See also* Integration
Racial segregation: and
    performance, 61–64; vs.
    socioeconomic segregation,
    107–108; absence of, 110
Ratio scales, in measurement of
    cognitive development, 30, 31
Reading gains: supply curves, 96;
    as measure of cognitive
    development, 171; related
    to resources, 172
Reading scores, related to teacher
    quality, 60–61
Regional factors, and bias in
    expenditures, 122–123
Reliability in measurement of
    educational objectives, 30
Repair of current system of big
    city schools, 151–154;
    altering placement policies,
    152; complete integration,
    152–153; federal and state
    financial aid, 153–154
Representation, or fractional
    measurement, 34
Research, educational, lack of
    interest in, 80, 180–181
Residence, choice of, and choice
    of school, 163
Resources: reallocation of, 3, 13;
    indicators of, measured in
    Boston, 49–52; contribution
    of, to performance, 66–73,
    74, 172; equal control over,
    108, 110; equal, 108–109,
    141; equally effective, 109;
    and academic performance,
    109; inequality of physical,
    119, 123; distribution within
    big cities, 124; distribution
    in Boston, 129–135; distribu-
    tion as function of social
    factors, 131; preferred allo-
    cation of, 143; peer effects
    in allocation of, 148;
    equalization of, by federal
    grants, 154; under metro-
    politanism, 165
Responsiveness, lack of, in big

city school systems, 175–176
"Restrictive" subcultures, 12
Restructuring. *See* Structural
    reform
Rich, the. *See* Big city rich;
    Suburban rich; Upper
    middle class
Riew, John, 89

Sacks, Seymour, 122
Salaries, consequences of single
    salary schedule, 84, 125
Salsburg v. *Maryland,* 113
Scale, and distribution of edu-
    cational resources, 113–114
School buildings, age of, 51,
    58–59, 171
School Committee, Boston, 126,
    128, 174
School quality, evaluation of, 64–66
Schools, attitude toward, by
    social class, 10–11. *See
    also* Social classes
Scientific management: applied
    to schools, 79; and middle-
    class orientation, 79–82; and
    working-class orientation,
    82–85
Segregation, and privatization
    of schools, 165. *See also*
    Integration
Sexton, Patricia, 121, 135
Shaycroft, Marion, 36, 43
Single salary schedules, 84, 125
Skinner, B. F., 24
Social accounting, possibility of, 8
Social classes: differences in
    modal attitudes of, 10–11,
    76; attitudes of, toward fiscal
    policy, 12; measures of, in
    Boston study, 52–53; effect
    of, on performance, 54–55,
    57–59, 64; and level of ability,
    109. *See also* Interest groups;
    Lower middle class; Middle
    class; Upper middle class
Social factors: dispersion of, and
    distribution of resources,
    130; correlations among, in-

Index

fluencing distribution, 130;
distribution of school quality
as a function of, 134
Social sciences, clientele for
discoveries in, 6–7
Social service enterprises: normative conflicts in development
of, 9–13; political problems
related to, 9, 13–14
Social technologies: underdevelopment of, 4; multiple
influences on, 4–5; outcomes
as long-term, 5; lack of
interest in, 6–7. *See also*
Technological efficiency;
Technologies
Socialization, school as agent of,
29–30
Socioeconomic characteristics:
city vs. suburbs, 176; calculation of, 186–188
Stages of human development, 26
States, inequalities of educational
opportunity between and
within, 119–120
Status quo, and interest groups,
166, 167. *See also* Current organization of big city schools
Stodolsky, Susan, 109
Structural reform, of big city
school systems, 140–168;
current organization, 142–
151; repairing the current
system, 151–154;
decentralization, 154–158;
metropolitanism, 158–160;
tuition vouchers, 160–165;
summarized, 165–168
Subcultures: defined, 9; differences in, related to normative
conflicts, 9; differences along
class dimensions, 10–12;
differences along ethnic
dimensions, 12–13
Subgoals, measurement of, 34
Suburban rich, 141, 144, 166, 167
Successive approximation, 26
Summary, of arguments developed
herein, 170–173

Supply curves: derivation of,
91–94; reading gains, 96; vs.
actual expenditures, 98–100;
short-term vs. long-term, 104
Supreme Court, rulings of, 113
Systems analysis, for social
policy, 8

TALENT Project, 36, 180
Taste, changes of, with education,
33
Taylorism. *See* Scientific management
Teacher resources: measurement
of, 49–52; accreditation, 57–
59; experience, 57–59, 74;
additional training, 57–59, 74
Teachers: and single salary
schedule, 84, 125; turnover
of, 93, 102, 111, 125, 171;
transfer privileges of, 125;
altering placement of, 152;
preference of, for suburbs, 175
Technological efficiency: of
school systems, 16; defined,
141; under tuition voucher
system, 161–163
Technological progress, defined,
141
Technologies: underdevelopment
of social, 4; need for invention of new, 179, 180–181
Thomas, J. Allen, 36, 43
Three-stage least squares (TSLS),
197, 200
Tracking, 111
Traditional modes of evaluation,
19–23; Verstehen, 20–21;
expenditure per student,
21–22; measurement of
physically defined inputs,
22–23; student performance
in standardized tests, 23
Tuition vouchers, 160–165; nature
of the market, 161; and technological efficiency, 161–163;
and integration, 163–165
Turnover, teacher, 50, 171; negative effect of, on performance,

234

55, 57; control of, 111; inequality in, 119; related to parental interest, 132

Unions, effect of teachers', 84–85

Upper middle class: modal attitudes toward schools, 11; on fiscal issues, 12; and distribution of school resources, 148–150; under metropolitanism, 160, 167; under privatization, 167. *See also* Social classes

Urban poor, and current allocation of resources, 151, 166, 167

Urbanization, early, and quality of schooling, 79

Validity of educational objective, 31–32; criterion validity, 32; predictive validity, 32

Variations in performance, related to bias in school resources, 67, 68, 70–72

Verstehen, as traditional mode of evaluation, 20–21

Voting participation: and teacher quality, 132; and distribution of resources, 135

Washington, D.C., distribution of educational resources, 135

Whites, performance of, in Boston schools, 61–64

Wilson, James Q., 12, 121, 177; quoted, 1

Woodhall, Maureen, 41

Working class: modal attitudes toward schools, 10–11; on fiscal issues, 12; orientation toward efficiency in education, 82–85

Wright, Judge Skelly, 111

Zero point, absolute, on ratio scales, 30, 31

Zymelman, Manuel, 33

The Joint Center for Urban Studies, a cooperative venture of the Massachusetts Institute of Technology and Harvard University, was founded in 1959 to organize and encourage research on urban and regional problems. Participants have included scholars from the fields of anthropology, architecture, business, city planning, economics, education, engineering, history, law, philosophy, political science, and sociology.

The findings and conclusions of this book are, as with all Joint Center publications, solely the responsibility of the author.

Published by Harvard University Press

The Intellectual versus the City: From Thomas Jefferson to Frank Lloyd Wright, by Morton and Lucia White, 1962

Streetcar Suburbs: The Process of Growth in Boston, 1870–1900, by Sam B. Warner, Jr., 1962

City Politics, by Edward C. Banfield and James Q. Wilson, 1963

Law and Land: Anglo-American Planning Practice, edited by Charles M. Haar, 1964

Location and Land Use: Toward a General Theory of Land Rent, by William Alonso, 1964

Poverty and Progress: Social Mobility in a Nineteenth Century City, by Stephan Thernstrom, 1964

Boston: The Job Ahead, by Martin Meyerson and Edward C. Banfield, 1966

The Myth and Reality of Our Urban Problems, by Raymond Vernon, 1966

Muslim Cities in the Later Middle Ages, by Ira Marvin Lapidus, 1967

The Fragmented Metropolis: Los Angeles, 1850–1930, by Robert M. Fogelson, 1967

Law and Equal Opportunity: A Study of the Massachusetts Commission against Discrimination, by Leon H. Mayhew, 1968

Varieties of Police Behavior: The Management of Law and Order in Eight Communities, by James Q. Wilson, 1968

The Metropolitan Enigma: Inquiries into the Nature and Dimensions of America's "Urban Crisis," edited by James Q. Wilson, revised edition, 1968

Traffic and the Police: Variations in Law Enforcement Policy, by John A. Gardiner, 1969

The Influence of Federal Grants: Public Assistance in Massachusetts, by Martha Derthick, 1970

The Arts in Boston, by Bernard Taper, 1970

Families against the City: Middle Class Homes of Industrial Chicago, 1872–1890, by Richard Sennett, 1970

The Political Economy of Urban Schools, by Martin T. Katzman, 1971

Published by The M.I.T. Press

The Image of the City, by Kevin Lynch, 1960

Housing and Economic Progress: A Study of the Housing Experiences of Boston's Middle-Income Families, by Lloyd Rodwin, 1961

The Historian and the City, edited by Oscar Handlin and John Burchard, 1963

The Federal Bulldozer: A Critical Analysis of Urban Renewal, 1949–1962, by Martin Anderson, 1964

The Future of Old Neighborhoods: Rebuilding for a Changing Population, by Bernard J. Frieden, 1964

Man's Struggle for Shelter in an Urbanizing World, by Charles Abrams, 1964

The View from the Road, by Donald Appleyard, Kevin Lynch, and John R. Myer, 1964

The Public Library and the City, edited by Ralph W. Conant, 1965

Regional Development Policy: A Case Study of Venezuela, by John Friedmann, 1966

Urban Renewal: The Record and the Controversy, edited by James Q. Wilson, 1966

Transport Technology for Developing Regions, by Richard M. Soberman, 1966

Computer Methods in the Analysis of Large-Scale Social Systems, edited by James M. Beshers, 1968

Planning Urban Growth and Regional Development: The Experience of the Guayana Program of Venezuela, by Lloyd Rodwin and Associates, 1969

Build a Mill, Build a City, Build a School: Industrialization, Urbanization, and Education in Ciudad Guayana, by Noel F. McGinn and Russell G. Davis, 1969

Land-Use Controls in the United States, by John Delafons, second edition, 1969

Beyond the Melting Pot: The Negroes, Puerto Ricans, Jews, Italians, and Irish of New York City, by Nathan Glazer and Daniel Patrick Moynihan, second edition, 1970

The Joint Center also publishes monographs and reports.